Praise for The Growth Equation

"This book is the perfect encapsulation (about early stage startup growth. Sure, different newsletters, listen to a bunch (growth. Or you could buy this book."

Jake Knapp, Author of Sprint

"Andy has a perfect mix of product, design, and founder thinking, at both startup and scale stages, so when he writes about growth and how design can enable it, you'd better take some notes."

Des Traynor, Co-Founder of Intercom

"Andy has written the essential guide to every major decision you'll need to make as an early stage founder. How are you going to attract your first customers? How are you going to differentiate yourself in the market? How are you going to figure out pricing? And most importantly, how are you going to reach Product-Market Fit?"

Kate Aronowitz, Google Ventures

"Andy offers a wealth of practical, actionable insights for anyone trying to build and grow a product or company. Filled with great examples that illustrate his points, this book is an entertaining and easy read that all founders and team members should have."

Irene Au, Partner at Khosla Ventures

"This book offers new founders valuable recommendations to help them grow their business, from acquisition to long-term monetization. A solid read that should be on the shelf of everyone starting a new company."

Krystal Higgins, Author of Better Onboarding

"Early stage startups often overlook growth strategies because they're typically tailored for larger organizations. However, The Growth Equation provides a thorough guide to fueling startup growth, drawn from Andy's own experiences as a product advisor, investor, and coach."

Chetana Deorah, Ex-Design Director for Global Growth & Acquisition at Netflix

"Andy's done a masterful job distilling a ton of industry knowledge into clear, practical, actionable steps to get your startup off the ground and to its first $1MM. A must-read for all founders."

Jeff Gothelf, author of Lean UX, Sense & Respond, and Who Does What by How Much?

"The Growth Equation is like having a startup coach in your pocket. It fills all the knowledge gaps a founder might have, helping you see around the next bend and sets expectations for how you should be performing at every stage."

Philip Fierlinger, Co-Founder Xero and Upstock

"Andy has a clear understanding of what makes a successful product and where founders often go wrong. While the equation itself provides a 1,000-foot view, it's the individual details I loved. Practical advice on how to find your first customers, how to successfully onboard people, how to get them experiencing value as soon as possible, and how to keep them coming back for more. This is as close a step-by-step guide to startup success as I have seen. Great work."

Shreyas Doshi, Product Leader (ex-Stripe, Twitter, Google)

THE GROWTH EQUATION

How Early Stage Startups
Can Build a Powerful
Engine for Growth

ANDY BUDD

The Growth Equation: How Early Stage Startups Can Build a Powerful Engine for Growth

Edited by Dana Publicover and Jo Ann Liguori.
Designed by James Gilyead.

First Edition: November 2024

ISBN: 978-1-0687461-2-3 (hardback)
       978-1-0687461-0-9 (paperback)
       978-1-0687461-1-6 (eBook)

Published by The Design Coach Ltd, The Old Casino, 28 Fourth Avenue, Hove, East Sussex, United Kingdom, BN3 2PJ

Foreword

The Internet is full of talks, articles, newsletters and podcasts offering up the secrets of startup growth. While the content they provide is super interesting, the majority of this advice comes from people working at much larger companies; companies which have raised multiple rounds of funding, have good traction, and their own dedicated growth teams.

Most of these companies have already found Product-Market Fit — a term used to describe a product which does a sufficiently good job of meeting a set of user needs that it generates at least some level of organic growth. Once you have Product-Market Fit—or PMF as it's often called—driving growth becomes easier. However this advice often misses out a hugely crucial component; how do you get to Product-Market Fit in the first place?

As both a startup advisor and Venture Partner at an early stage Seed fund, this is a problem I see founders running up against time and again. A lot of the advice out there is tailored towards these later stage companies with larger teams, longer runways and an initial base of customers that can build from. However the bulk of startups fail to get to this stage. They've managed to deliver a working product, but have yet to secure enough users, or demonstrate enough of a repeatable and scalable growth engine to convince growth stage funds to invest. This is why I felt compelled to write a book on early startup growth.

This book is squarely aimed at startup founders who have yet to reach Product-Market Fit. Folks with relatively small teams who will need to take on a lot of the growth work themselves. The goal of this book is to help those founders find early adopters to help them test and perfect their product; figure out a right Go-To-Market Strategy (or GTM for short) to match their product, market and team; and then build out a sustainable growth engine to deliver Product-Market Fit.

The ultimate goal of all this book is to help founders deliver their first $1million in Annual Recurring Revenue (ARR) by the time you need to raise your Series A Investment—which is typically the investment you raise after Pre-seed and Seed.

With most investment rounds giving you around 18 months worth of working capital, this means coming up with a plan to deliver $1m in ARR in roughly 3 years time. This might seem like a long time, but it comes round super quickly. As such you can't simply build a product and hope users will show up, only to panic a few months before your next raise when the numbers don't stack up. As somebody far wiser than me once said "hope is not a winning strategy." Instead it's important for founders to understand the levers they have at their disposal from the outset, in order to develop a solid Go-To-Market Strategy and Growth Plan.

How you get there is likely to depend heavily on the market you're working in. If you're running an enterprise level SaaS business charging $10-15k a month, this might mean closing as little as 5-8 sales. However if you're running a freemium selfserve company charging $5 a month, you'll need a whopping 300k users (assuming a 6% conversion to paid rate). As such this book looks at a variety of different approaches including founder-led sales, founder-led marketing and the increasingly popular product-led growth (or PLG for short). Once you have a steady flow of customers using your product, this book looks at how to optimize your customer acquisition funnel, and build in scalable growth loops.

But before all that, let's take a deeper look at why founders need to focus on growth in the first place.

Introduction

I n my early 20s, I worked as a dive instructor in South East Asia. People sometimes laugh when I say this, but I believe helping people learn to dive shaped the way I work as a venture capitalist. Taking someone who wants to embark on a potentially risky adventure and teaching them how to get comfortable, gain confidence, and ultimately reduce as many risks as possible—doesn't that sound like early stage startup life to you?

Life without some level of risk is really boring, and while diving does carry a small amount of danger, those risks are mitigated by your own behavior. That personal responsibility and decision-making—what keeps you alive during a cave dive, for example—is also what determines a founder's success.

The founders I see succeed are deeply, personally motivated and will lean into a level of risk that others find uncomfortable. They experiment, they're willing to try things out, and they're not afraid of failing—because risk is necessary for success. You can't get very far doing the same things everyone else has already done.

Through watching these founders succeed and fail over many years, a pattern has emerged. Just as in diving, where there are common practices to ensure a safe and fun dive, in a startup's growth, I've noticed seven factors that play an outsize role in success.

This is not one of those "forget everything else you know about startups" books, because there are hundreds if not thousands of factors that can affect a startup's fortunes. But with my experience, and looking back on nearly every company I've ever advised, when a company is struggling, the most likely cause lies with one of these seven:

1. Audience: the number of people you're able to connect with who have the problem your product solves.
2. Motivation: the level of motivation your audience has to get over the inherent switching costs involved in giving your product a try.
3. Value: your ability to deliver on this promised value as quickly and consistently as possible.
4. Stickiness: your ability to embed your product into your users' daily workflow to maximize value creation and minimize churn.
5. Virality: your product's natural ability to attract additional customers through use.
6. Friction: the inherent friction in your product, causing people to grow frustrated and eventually churn.
7. Competitive Pressure: the effectiveness of your competition at doing all of the above in order to tempt your users away.

These seven factors combine into a simple formula I'm calling The Growth Equation. It looks like this:

$$\text{Growth} = f[(A, M, \Delta V/t, S, K) / (\mu, C)]$$

Figure 0.1: Introducing The Growth Equation.

Cool, huh? If you're a non-math person and feeling intimidated, stick with me through this section, as I'll be delving into what each of these factors (in mathematical notation, we call them "arguments") mean and why I think they matter.

At this point, you're probably thinking, "That's great, Andy, but what are the other chapters for and couldn't this have been a blog post rather than a book?" I get that frustration. There are far too many books on the market that should have stayed a blog post. I promise you; this isn't one of them. Here's why:

Understanding Growth Is Simple, but Delivering Growth Is Hard

While you were reading the above list, you might have found yourself thinking, "Well, this is all pretty obvious stuff." You'd be right. You might have even been thinking, "We're a much more complicated business, so we need more nuanced solutions." I get this. As the saying goes, "Every ~~family~~ startup is dysfunctional in its own way." However, these dysfunctions fall into common patterns. The thing that's unique isn't the problem itself but what *you're* going to do about it. Like someone learning to dive, it will be your personal decision-making that mitigates the risk.

That's the real value of this book.

Over the course of this book, I'm going to take a deep dive (sorry) into everything you need to know as an early stage founder to drive growth. From building an amazing product, finding your first few users, and figuring out a sustainable Growth Engine to nailing Onboarding, Activation, and Retention. We'll look at topics like Founder-Led Sales and Founder-Led Marketing versus Product-Led Growth. Along the way, we'll explore early Pricing and Monetization, the use of Behavioral Psychology, and when, how, and who to hire.

Though my concept of the equation and these seven specific factors is a fresh take, the information on how to execute each of these areas well is not groundbreaking or unique. This information is already out there in hundreds of podcasts, newsletters, and blogs. There are industry best practices and proven advice for most of these topics, but because it's so scattered, it's difficult to see how it all fits into the bigger picture. My goal is to bring this information together in one place. If I'm successful, this is the only book you'll need to read about Growth (at least until you reach a few million dollars in revenue).

As you read, I'd like you to think about your own challenges and goals for growth and assess them through the lens of the seven factors that make up The Growth Equation. Which element(s) have you not considered? Which factor is currently holding you back? Which factor can you tweak to have the biggest impact? But first, let's dive into each of these seven factors in slightly more detail.

Breaking Down the Equation: Market

$$\text{Growth} = f[(\mathbf{A}, \mathbf{M}, \Delta V/t, S, K) / (\mu, C)]$$

Figure 0.2: The market elements of The Growth Equation.

The first argument in the equation is A for Audience Size. Though not all startups raise funding, there's a good chance that you'll have a pitch deck somewhere showing an outrageously high Total Addressable Market (TAM). This is the total amount of money that everyone in the world with the problem you solve spends on solving that problem. TAM is the total opportunity of your product. This is *not* the Audience Size I'm referring to.

In this equation, Audience Size is the number of people you're currently able to connect with who have the problem you solve. Many founders take this work for granted. "We have the best product, so people will just find us." However, finding and connecting with people who care is surprisingly difficult. It requires effort and strategy. If you're unable to build up a sufficient audience you can convert, you'll run out of money before even scratching the surface of your TAM.

This is where your Go-to-Market (GTM) strategy comes in—something that takes up the first few chapters of this book. How are you going to find your early adopters? What acquisition channels are you going to test? Are you going to take a Founder-Led approach to sales and marketing? Will you need to hire? Or are you going to lean into Product-Led Growth? And, perhaps most importantly: Can you build a big enough audience and convert enough of them to paying customers before the cash runs out?

Many founders quickly realize that size isn't everything. I've seen plenty of startups with huge waitlists and large social media followings struggle to close deals. This is because their audience isn't composed of potential buyers. They might not even be people with the power to influence buying decisions. They might just be there because of the founder's charm or the marketing team's ability to hit the cultural zeitgeist and throw out the right dank memes.

Total audience size doesn't actually matter, but relevant audience size does. Have you been able to identify the right Ideal Customer Profile? Have you been able to connect with the right Buyer Personas in a channel that makes sense? Do your audience even realize they have the problem your product aims to solve, or will you need to invest in audience education? When I look at many struggling startups, their relevant audience size is just too damned small to sustain them. This brings us nicely to the topic of Motivation: the M in our list of arguments.

Even if you've managed to cultivate a large audience of potential buyers, how motivated are they to check out your offering and switch? Have you managed to get your positioning right? Do they understand who you are, what you do, and, crucially, why you're better than the other solutions out there?

As a culture, we learn to satisfice—to put up with substandard solutions. So what can you do to increase Audience Motivation to the point that it gets them over their natural inertia? What would make the costs of switching to your product worthwhile?

Ultimately, it doesn't matter a jot if you think the product is amazing. What matters is what your audience thinks.

Breaking Down the Equation: Product

$$Growth = f[(A, M, \Delta V/t, S, K) / (\mu, C)]$$

Figure 0.3: The product elements of The Growth Equation.

One way to get your audience over these switching costs is to promise outsize value. But often, once users sign up, that value is hard for them to find. Sometimes it's there, it's just well hidden—often as a result of bad design and usability. I'll cover this in great length in the chapters on onboarding and activation. I'll also go into the importance of Time to Value (TTV): the speed at which you deliver value to new customers.

For products to really catch on, they need to deliver a high amount of value constantly. I describe this as your product's ability to deliver sustainable Value Over Time. In The Growth Equation, I've listed this as $\Delta V/t$ where V is Value, t is Time, and Δ is the Greek letter delta, which is often used to describe the change in some value. I'll admit it. This is totally indulgent. I could have just called it V. I just thought this looked cooler.

For your users to experience this value on a regular basis, your product needs to easily embed into their daily workflows. This is sometimes described as product Stickiness (the S in the equation). Stickiness is an awkward term that often conjures up images of manipulation and, in the worst instances, addiction (something I tackle in Chapter 12). I think there's something about the sound of that word that just feels wrong in a business context. I debated using "adoptability" or "engagement" instead, but they didn't quite have the same breadth of meaning; so in lieu of a better, less tacky term, I guess it'll have to do.

If users are continually experiencing high levels of value from your product in a way that lives up to (or ideally exceeds) their expectations, there's a good chance they will attract new customers to your platform. Sometimes, this will be through direct recommendations and referrals. Other times, it will be through the existence of viral growth loops. These are both topics that deserve their own chapters, so we'll go into them in more detail in the second half of the book. Every product decision you make will affect the Viral Coefficient of your product: its innate ability to attract new customers through use. Sometimes called the K factor, this is the last major factor that has a positive impact on growth.

There are two other factors that I find affect growth in a major way, though their effects are usually negative. First, there's Friction: essentially how hard, annoying, and frustrating your product is to use. Most founders believe their products are an absolute delight to use—so much so that they're basically frictionless. This is very rarely the case.

Founders are often so good at deluding themselves about how easy the product is to use that they only realize the truth once it's too late. Don't be that person. Instead, listen to (or better yet watch) how users interact with your product and do everything in your power to remove unnecessary obstacles.

In the world of applied physics, the Greek letter μ (mu) is generally used to denote friction, so I've used the same naming convention here.

This leaves us with our final factor—Competitive Pressure. In The Growth Equation, I'm using a C to denote this. As the name suggests, Competitive Pressure is essentially all the things your competitors are doing to attract your customers away from you. Just as you managed to draw your customers away from their old product or workflow, every other solution provider in the market is trying to do the same to you. Charge too much, deliver too little value, get complacent when it comes to adding features or removing friction? Someone in the market will try and use their growing audience, superior positioning, and value delivery to tempt your customers away.

These are just your direct competitors: companies that sell a product or service that does something similar to yours. Founders often forget about their indirect competitors—like the free spreadsheet your prospects are using instead of the $100 per month SaaS product you've built to replace it. The competitive landscape is a big reason for people to stick with their current way of doing things and an equally big reason why people might switch away from you at some later date. So don't get complacent and watch out.

Summary

Now you've been introduced to the seven factors that make up The Growth Equation: Relevant Audience Size, Audience Motivation, Value Delivery Over Time, product Stickiness, product Virality, product Friction, and Competitive Pressure.

$$\text{Growth} = f[(A, M, \Delta V/t, S, K) / (\mu, C)]$$

Figure 0.4: The Growth Equation.

Before we jump into the details of how to drive growth, let's take a quick look at why growth is so important.

CHAPTER 1

Why Growth Matters

"A startup is a company designed to grow fast," explains Paul Graham, the well-known investor and co-founder of Y Combinator. In his essay "Startup = Growth,"[1] Graham states that simply being "newly founded does not in itself make a company a startup." He also claims it's not necessary for a startup to be a tech company, to be venture-funded, or to be looking for an exit.

"The only essential thing is growth. Everything else we associate with startups follows from growth."

While this might feel like a contentious statement for some, if you buy into the core premise that Startups = Growth, then it's a short hop to the realization that your primary responsibility as a founder is to deliver said growth. And for founders who don't come from a growth background, the learning curve can be surprisingly hard.

Of course founders are also expected to do a dozen other things, from raising funds and setting company strategy to managing day-to-day operations. New needs, capabilities, and competitors continue to emerge, causing you to constantly reassess the backlog; while internal challenges with process and team dynamics can lead to constant organizational change. These are all challenges that can be solved with adequate time, money, and expertise. Sadly these are all things typical early stage startups lack.

As such, founders find their attention divided between focusing on business growth (growth that could fund the support they need) and

[1] https://www.paulgraham.com/growth.html

business management (tasks they could hand over once growth is achieved).

If your company is growing fast enough, the resulting revenue can be invested into hiring your way out of these issues and acquiring more customers in the process, creating a powerful flywheel effect—the ultimate, self-feeding machine (more on this later). Too many new customers signing up to your service? Time to hire a customer success manager to help with onboarding. Too many inbound leads for you to handle yourself? Time to hire a sales director to take over. Too many customers churning because they can't figure out how to use the product? Time to invest in your user experience team.

Growth can also create a defensive moat. For example, if two companies offer a similar product, but one is growing much faster and generating more hype than the other, people will naturally (although potentially erroneously) assume that one product is better than the other. As such, growth acts as a form of Social Proof, which can help attract even more customers.

"The good news," says Paul Graham, "is, if you get growth, everything else tends to fall into place. Which means you can use growth like a compass to make almost every decision you face." While I wouldn't go as far as claiming that growth will solve all your problems, it can help you power over potholes and the occasional chasm that might slow down (or swallow up) a slower-moving company.

Growth is, without a doubt, a necessary and challenging endeavor for any founder and something that requires serious dedication to achieve. But by the mere fact that you are here, reading this book, you are already taking the right steps to build the company you envision.

Introducing the S-Curve

We can't talk about strategies for growth without talking about the S-curve. Nearly all companies experience some variation of this classic model. Take note of the following diagram. Rather than a visually pleasing, up-and-to-the-right diagonal line (or the famed hockey stick we've all dreamed about), most growth actually looks like this: a slowly increasing but relatively flat line at the start, a period of drastic change in the middle, followed by a gradual tapering-out toward the end.

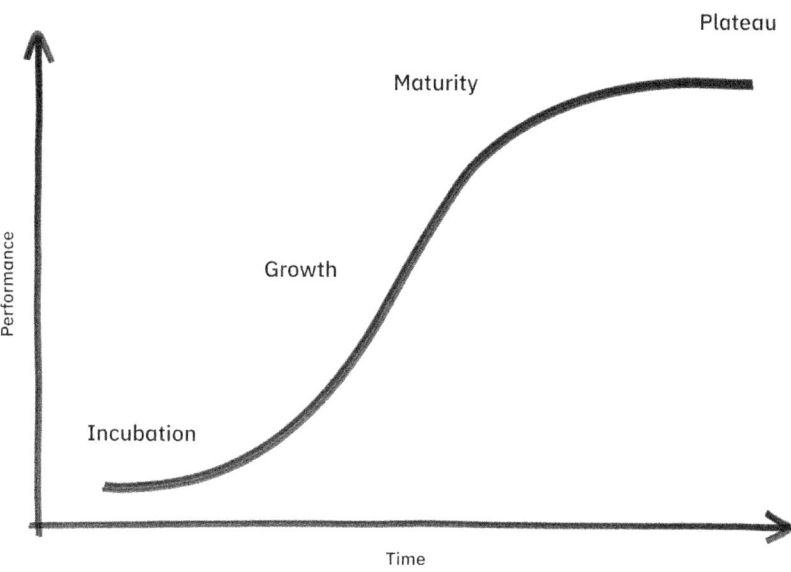

Figure 1.1: The classic startup S-curve.

Growth is always slow at the beginning because starting anything new is hard and requires extra effort to break through the inertia. If you are starting a traditional business you might need capital to hire staff, buy equipment or stock, find office space, and connect with suppliers or clients—capital that may take a while to come through or require certain success metrics to unlock.

If this is your first business (or even your second or third), you're also going to spend time evaluating the right software to use, setting up new processes, and figuring out how the business works. There are likely financial and regulatory hurdles you need to clear: registering your company, getting your accounts in order, and complying with local employment laws. This is even more true with tech startups, which often need to devote months (or sometimes years) building out their core technology before they can start charging a penny. This requires time and talent, which often means raising money from external investors (angels and venture capitalists) to get you over that initial hump.

As companies build out their product or service, hone their value proposition, and connect that value with more and more customers, they are able to pay down that initial time and capital investment. At the same time, they also learn to become more efficient and effective as a team, and growth starts to take off.

This all means one thing: Growth in the early years can feel slow. Sometimes painfully so.

Startups Naturally Orient Toward Growth

Different companies grow at different speeds. A small shop serving a local audience might reach its maximum growth potential pretty quickly, while an international brand might keep plodding along for years. This isn't necessarily true for tech startups. Thinking back to the Paul Graham quote at the beginning of this chapter: "A startup is a company designed to grow fast." And tech startups have the potential to grow even faster.

That's because tech startups have two things in their favor. First, tech startups typically use software to build highly efficient systems that can service many more customers than a traditional human-powered business can. While this software obviously requires design and engineering talent to create, the degree of scale is limited only by platform efficiency, as opposed to people power. A tech startup can run a lean team while supporting many users—if the product is good.

Secondly, tech companies typically rely more on digital distribution channels than their traditional counterparts do. This allows them to connect with customers much quicker than those relying on traditional means. You can literally serve customers and make money while your traditional competitors are asleep—or launch in new countries before you have a single person on the ground.

In short, certain constraints that typically slow growth for more traditional companies are reduced (or removed completely) for tech startups. As a result, this lack of constraint arguably orients startups toward faster growth—and it's this orientation that allows them to raise capital far easier than other businesses can.

Speed vs. Momentum

While many startups are obsessed with how fast they are going, investors are typically trying to gauge a company's momentum: something you might remember from your physics classes as being a combination of mass, speed and direction. Momentum is important to investors as it hints at a company's potential.

The best way to describe momentum is by looking at a flywheel—a concept we'll reference heavily throughout this book. In mechanical engineering, a flywheel is a heavy circular weight that can be used to store energy. Apply energy to the wheel and it begins to spin. It starts slowly due to its natural inertia, however, the more energy you apply to the wheel the more momentum you build up and the faster it spins. At some point, you can stop applying energy and the flywheel will keep spinning on its own—for a while at least.

Startup growth is very much like a flywheel. In the early stages, you must constantly apply energy to get things moving. Nearly everything begins at zero. When you have no customers, it's hard to get your first few customers, so more energy is required. The more customers you have, the easier it is to gain more customers (to a point). The momentum builds, partly because you learn where to find, approach, and close new customers (and get better at doing those things). You're gaining impressive customer logos you can use as proof points, which will help convince even more impressive buyers.

Your early product will also be relatively feature-light and missing things your later, larger, and more sophisticated customers will need. This means your early customers will be super dedicated people who will need much less convincing and onboarding (and from whom you'll learn how to build the product your future customer needs). As your feature set becomes more competitive, you continue to build social proof, and improve your acquisition skills, all of this becomes easier.

It'll be hard at first, but as you get over the initial inertia, momentum will build. This is when the S-curve starts to tick up from that initial slow phase.

Founders often want to know the exact speed at which their flywheel must be turning in order to raise their next round of funding. For instance, how many customers should I have, or how much revenue do I need to unlock the next round of funding?

I wish the answer were more straightforward, but the reality is that every product, company, and sector is different so there's no definitive checklist. This is why investors are more interested in momentum: At what rate are your metrics growing? And is that rate increasing or starting to taper off? How much of this growth is a direct result of your input and whether you've figured out a sustainable approach for acquiring new users yet, or has it just been a mix of charisma and luck? This all helps inform investors whether their investment is going to help you "make the ship go faster," rather than just keeping you afloat for a little bit longer.

Growth Is a Series of S-Curves

In a world of finite people and resources, there is always a limit to how big and fast a company can grow. In the environmental sector, this is known as a system's Carrying Capacity. In the startup world, we often describe this as your Serviceable Obtainable Market (SOM), which is effectively the percentage of the Total Addressable Market (TAM) you can realistically capture.

I have spoken with many (many, many) early stage founders who insist their customer truly is "everyone." As an investor, I can tell you that—even if your product is something every human on the planet both needs and could obtain—investors want you to be realistic about the market opportunity. I have witnessed many pitches where founders project $100M ARR within a couple of years. While I understand the desire to be impressive, most investors know that figures like this are highly unlikely. Even with investment, you'll be lucky to hit $1M ARR in your first year. We are far more impressed by specific, realistic estimates than by unlimited potential.

Within that serviceable market, you'll always start by attracting the early adopters. These are people who are desperate to use your product or service because of the problem it solves—often regardless of how well it's designed. These are folks who are often frustrated with the status quo, feel like their current solution has been letting them down, and have been waiting for a product like yours to emerge. As such, these people will jump at the chance to use your product, warts and all. Early adopters are your beta users. They tend to have a generous tolerance for small issues (UX and UI idiosyncrasies and bugs in software), as they understand they are getting in at the ground floor of something potentially ideal for their need (typically at a more than reasonable discount). These users want you to succeed so they're generally super active at giving feedback and sharing your product with their community.

Following the early adopters are the early majority users, who are generally a little harder to acquire. They require more information before making purchase decisions, need more certainty around the suitability of your solution before they are happy to commit, and are therefore much harder to convert. As such, you'll generally need a more formalized sales and marketing process to close these accounts.

Early majority users will also have higher expectations when it comes to the user experience of the product and be less tolerant of annoying bugs and usability issues, making them more likely to churn. So while you might have been able to get away with a developer-heavy product team in the early days, you'll find yourself quickly needing to boost out your design, product management, quality assurance, and customer success functions to meet their increasing demands. What worked before might not be working now, and this is something founders can really struggle to wrap their heads around.

This phenomenon, known as "crossing the chasm" (from the book of the same name) is the make-or-break point of many startups. Can your company survive the shift from early adopters to early majority customers? If so, you'll continue to ride that S-curve until you reach that final plateau: the late majority users, who are even harder and more expensive to acquire, at which point growth slows and eventually levels off.

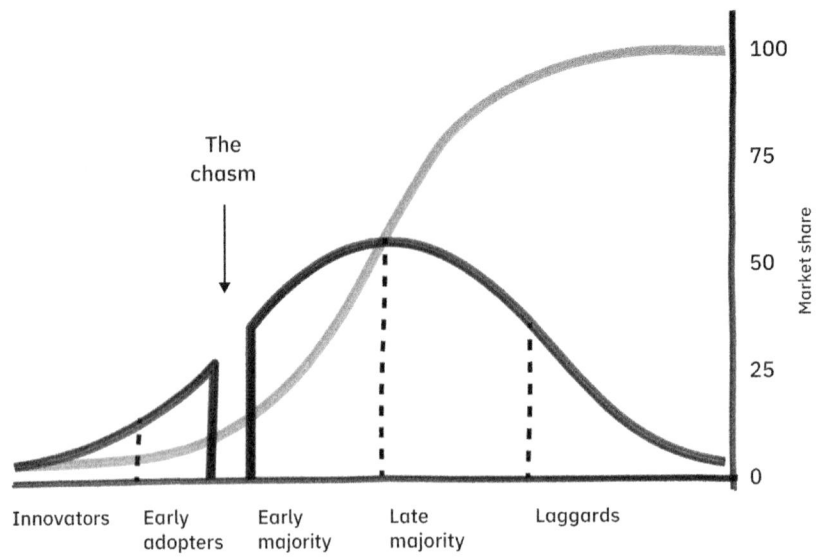

Figure 1.2: A graph of the famous startup growth chasm.

Some businesses hit their natural limit pretty quickly. The most successful companies, however, will go through a series of growth spurts, one after another, perhaps as a result of releasing new products or services, growing into different markets or geographies, or leveraging new acquisition channels once the older ones start to dry up. It's possible to sustain growth for quite some time this way, and most fast growing companies would agree that growth is a series of initiatives rather than a single thing.

If you look at growth this way, it's generally the case of chaining together a series of smaller S-curves; starting your next initiative before the last one starts delivering diminishing returns. In this way, companies are able to keep growing for extended periods. As such, founders should be constantly on the lookout for their next growth initiative before their current one plateaus. That being said, growth can't go on forever and even the fastest-growing companies eventually slow down.

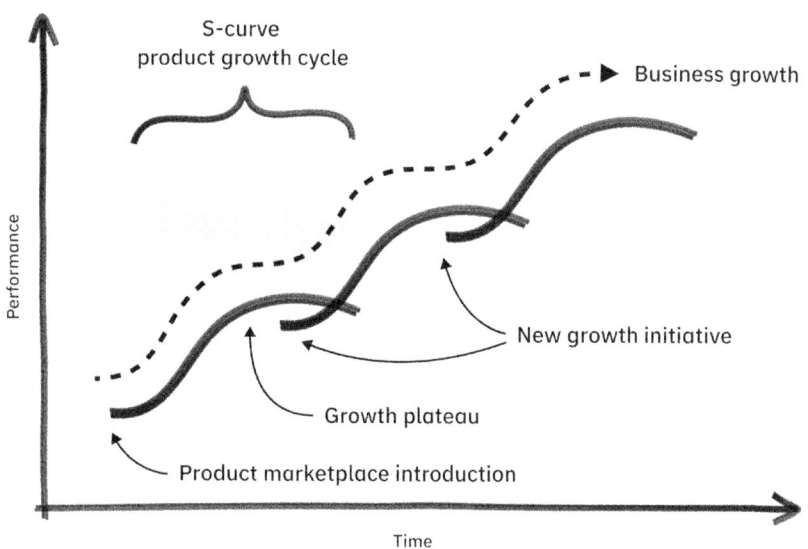

Figure 1.3: Growth is a series of S-curves.

What Early Growth Looks Like

Every company and every market is different, so it's hard to say definitively what constitutes good growth. In the early stages of the product, before you've reached Product-Market Fit (PMF), growth will understandably be slower—especially as you try to figure out which acquisition channels work best for you. Once you've hit PMF, however, growth ramps up.

Rather than one singular target, early stage companies will have a number of micro goals during their first few years of business. It usually starts with acquiring their first handful of beta testers and design partners (companies who have agreed to use the product in return for giving you a ton of feedback) to help you iron out the kinks. Once you're ready to launch, you're focused on landing your first 100 and then your first 1,000 active users (we'll go into this further in Chapter 4).

On a revenue front, securing $1K MRR (Monthly Recurring Revenue) is a great early milestone, followed by $10K and then $100K MRR. Revenue amounts will vary greatly depending on the sector you're working within, but reaching $1M ARR (Annual Recurring Revenue) in the first 18 months will set you in good stead for raising your Series A investment.

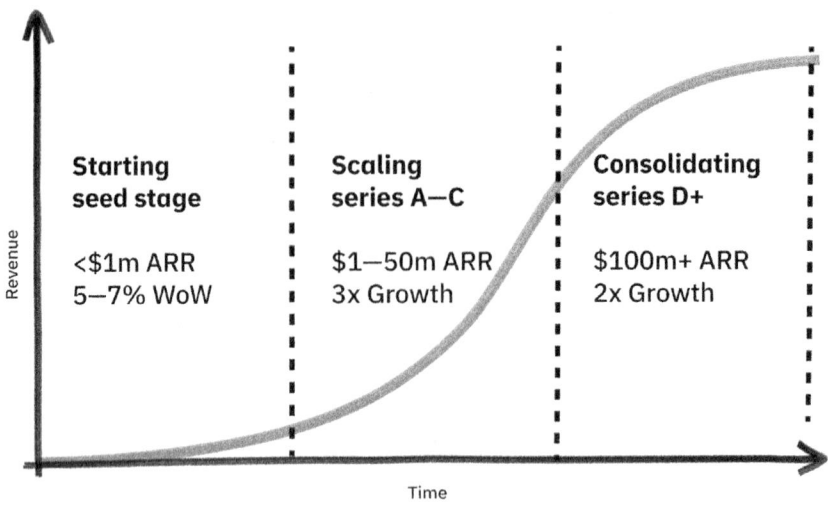

Figure 1.4: Startup stages and their associated growth targets.

Whether you are focusing on user growth, customer growth, activity, or revenue, we go back to Paul Graham, who generally considers 5–7% Week-on-Week (WoW) growth to be a good indicator of progress, and 10% to be exceptional. This might seem like a lot, but in the early days, if you were to go from 10 to 11 customers in a week, that's 10% growth. Just remember that if you get an additional customer next week your WoW growth is now 9.1%—the goalpost has now moved. If you add another new customer the following week, it's 8.3% and by the end of the month with that additional customer, your WoW growth is 7.7%. So while it's tempting to focus on absolute numbers, tracking growth as a percentage is usually smarter (and what investors are looking for). As a result, if your first month's target is to land four new enterprise customers, the following month you'll probably want to target five or six.

Later Stage Growth

Once you've reached Product-Market Fit—something that can take several years, if you get there at all—growth should become more predictable. One popular growth model in the SaaS world is known as T2D3 (please hold your Star Wars jokes), which means once you've reached Product-Market Fit you should aim to triple your growth over the next two years, and then double your growth the following three.

This idealized model is based on the idea that tech companies should aim to IPO (the initial public offering of the company's stock) in around eight years. And to IPO, you probably need to be hitting at least $100M in ARR. It's worth mentioning that though an IPO after eight years might have been common back in the day, it's taking longer and longer for startups to IPO, so this T2D3 model might be more aspirational than realistic. However, it still hints at how important growth is, and what sort of growth rate you might be looking for in a best case scenario.

People also like to talk about the Rule of 40, which says that the combination of your growth rate and your profit margin should be at or above 40%. So for a later stage company, you might have a) a 40% profit margin but negligible growth; b) 30% Year-on-Year (YoY) growth with a 10% profit margin; or c) 100% YoY growth with a 60% loss.

$$\text{Rule of 40} = \text{Y/Y revenue growth} + \text{EBITADA margin}$$

Figure 1.5: The Rule of 40.

A recent research project[2] looking at 70 public companies suggested that in their core growth phase, they were all growing at around 113% per annum or more. As such, if you've reached Product-Market Fit, doubling in size each year (or more) seems like a sensible growth target.

This is the point where we must do a bit of level-setting. Benchmarks like T2D3 and the Rule of 40 aren't much help to early stage startups. It's important to understand where you are headed and what the goals

---

[2] https://techcrunch.com/2013/08/24/how-fast-should-you-be-growing/

will become, but in your first few years, the best advice is to pick one or two North Star metrics (that is, metrics to prioritize rather than trying to achieve everything) and dedicate most of your energy to growing those by 5–10% WoW. With growth like this, you'll have investors knocking down your door in no time.

Building Your Growth Engine

If you buy into the idea that growth is a startup's defining quality (and if you're still with me, that probably means you do), then your primary job as a founder is to deliver said growth. This may sound obvious, but I see far too many founders fixating on product (the fun bit) and delegating growth to somebody else on the team. This regularly leads to poor results, with the founding team only realizing their mistake when it's too late to fix.

Growth is difficult to achieve without all facets of a company working together with a common goal in mind. As such, not only the founder but every member of the team needs to understand the answer to this question: Where does the growth for our product come from and how am I contributing to that growth?

Every startup will end up with a slightly different approach to growth (sometimes called their Growth Engine) depending on the market they're in, the customers they want to attract, and the unique set of skills they have at their disposal. Some startups will build a strong enterprise sales motion that drives 90% of their growth. Other companies will create amazing content, which helps new customers find their product. Some companies will invest heavily in paid acquisition—ads to you and me—while others will embed powerful viral usage loops or flywheels inside their product that draw in new users.

I like to visualize a company's Growth Engine as the engine powering a light aircraft. The more powerful the engine, the quicker you can take off and the faster you can climb. All engines need some sort of fuel. In our case, this is likely to be a combination of money (especially for paid advertising) and talent. Engines also need constant tweaking to improve performance and lubricants to keep them running smoothly.

To get your Growth Engine started, you'll need to first prime the pumps with an initial injection of users (your early adopters). And to get things moving faster, you might need the occasional turbo-boost, which I see as short-term growth initiatives (riskier initiatives with short-term shelf life like discounts, promotions, and other activities that won't necessarily scale). If you get all these working at the right time and in the right combination, you'll generate enough lift to counter the natural effects of gravity and take off before you hit the end of the runway.

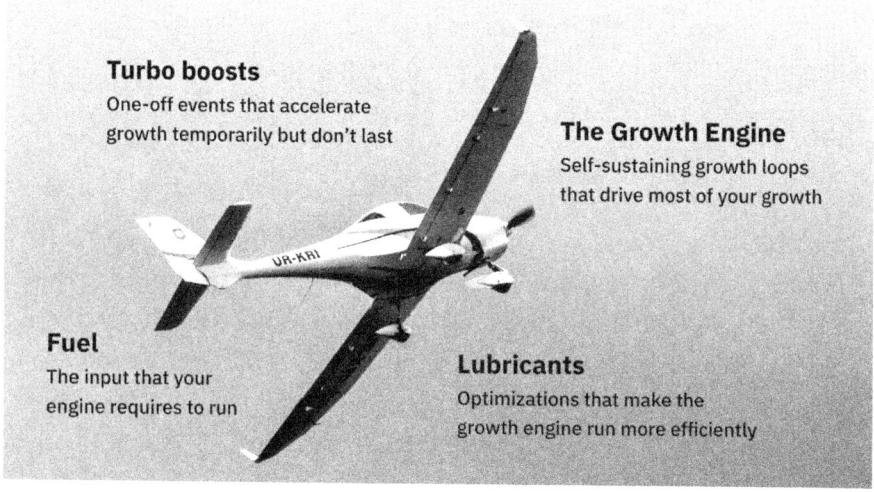

Turbo boosts
One-off events that accelerate growth temporarily but don't last

The Growth Engine
Self-sustaining growth loops that drive most of your growth

Fuel
The input that your engine requires to run

Lubricants
Optimizations that make the growth engine run more efficiently

Figure 1.6: The different elements which affect your Growth Engine.

Finding Product-Market Fit

Most founders have a strong opinion on how they will achieve their early growth. Some believe that growth will happen naturally. However, founders are often surprised by how hard it actually is to build a consistent Growth Engine. You'll probably need to experiment with a range of different approaches before one takes hold, and this process might conceivably take several years.

This is essentially the market side of Product-Market Fit: the art of figuring out how to connect the value your product offers with the right group of people in a consistent and cost-effective way. This obviously goes hand in hand with having a product that delivers that value in the first place—the subject of our next chapter. If you look at The Growth Equation, you'll see a natural balance between product-related arguments and market-related arguments. To achieve PMF, you'll need a balance of both.

$$Growth = f[(\mathbf{A}, \mathbf{M}, \Delta V/t, S, K) / (\mu, \mathbf{C})]$$

Figure 1.7: The **Market** elements of The Growth Equation.

$$Growth = f[(A, \mathbf{M}, \mathbf{\Delta V/t}, \mathbf{S}, \mathbf{K}) / (\mathbf{\mu}, C)]$$

Figure 1.8: The **Product** elements of The Growth Equation.

You'll know you've reached Product-Market Fit when you have a product that delivers enough value to enough people in a sustained way, while still leaving some money left over for profit. Until you get there, each new user and each new customer will be hard-won. You'll likely have to do things during this period that don't scale. Plus there's a good chance that your first few customers will cost you more to acquire than you'll make in revenue. Growth at this stage typically comes from a series of short-term initiatives—something we'll be looking at in more depth in Chapter 4.

Sadly, many startups fail because they're unable to develop a Growth Engine powerful enough to achieve Product-Market Fit, so don't underestimate the importance of this step, or outsource this crucial work to somebody else.

Summary
Growth is fundamental to a startup's success. Good growth allows you to overcome challenges that might take down slower-moving companies. It also gives a clear signal to potential investors that you're

on the right path, making fundraising easier. As such, founders need to become laser-focused on growth. This requires a good understanding of the various growth levers at your disposal, in order to build a solid Growth Engine that will power you through the bumpy road ahead. Having a great product that solves a meaningful problem for a specific set of customers is a great place to start. As you'll see in the next chapter, however, a good product is the raw material for growth, rather than the solution itself.

CHAPTER 2

Build a Genuinely Useful Product

Most founders start their entrepreneurial journey because they believe they've found a gap in the market: some problem or opportunity they've seen (and ideally experienced) that lacks a simple yet elegant solution. They believe the world will be better if somebody can solve this problem, and they believe that they are uniquely placed to be that person—by their understanding and background in the market, their track record of building successful products and growing teams, or their ability to sell that vision to others. So they set about raising money, assembling a team, and building a product to fill that gap. This sounds pretty straightforward. So why do so many products fail to take off?

Why Startups Fail

In my experience working with founders, accelerators, and businesses at many stages, I have seen five main reasons why early startups fail:

1. The problem the product aims to solve exists, but it isn't big or painful enough for people to care (or pay to solve it).
2. There are already pretty good solutions on the market, which the founder has missed (bad research) or discounted (hubris).
3. The product doesn't deliver enough value for customers to justify the hassle of changing their workflow to adopt a new product.

4. The product is actually pretty good, but the founders can't connect the value the product delivers with enough potential customers (merchandising and positioning).
5. The market for this new product turns out to be much smaller than they'd anticipated.

Let's break down these problems one by one and analyze exactly how they contribute to failure (and what you can learn or change to avoid falling into these patterns).

The first three problems all concern the real value that your product delivers.

1. The problem the product aims to solve exists, but it isn't big or painful enough for people to care (or pay to solve it).

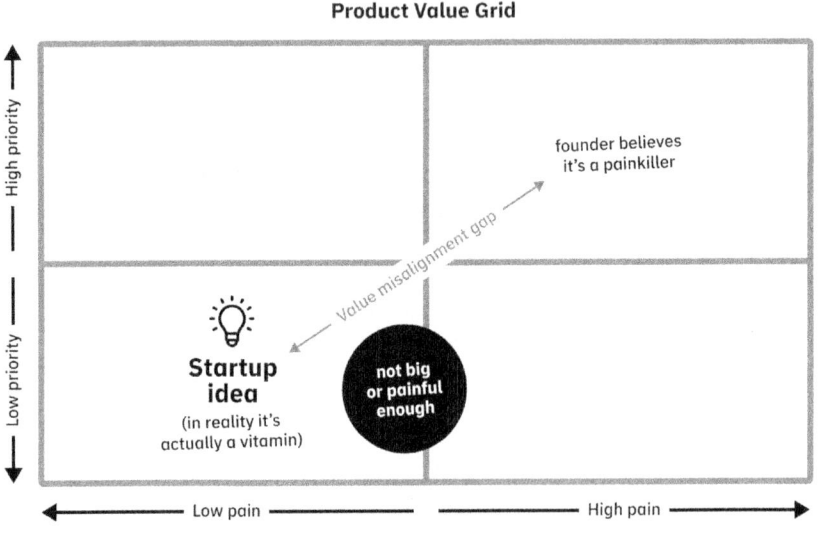

Figure 2.1: A 2x2 showing pain intensity and pain importance. In this instance, you've picked a product that has low pain intensity or priority.

While your product might solve a particular problem, it's not a particularly immediate or painful problem. Your product does potentially solve this problem well, it's just not a priority for people at the moment. This is often described in startup circles as having created a vitamin rather than a painkiller. Now, it's fair to say that the vitamin market (the actual sale of supplements) is huge, and there are plenty of successful vitamin (low-priority pain point) products out there. Just be aware that vitamins are a discretionary spend, which means they're harder to sell and tend to be affected more by economic downturns. So if you can, it's better to have a painkiller product that people rely on to make money and get their work done.

2. There are already pretty good solutions on the market, which the founder has missed (bad research) or discounted (hubris).

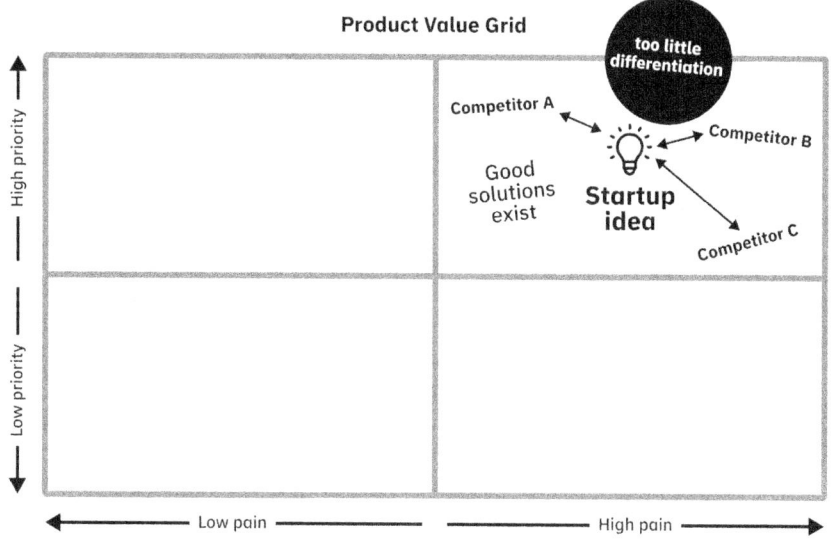

Figure 2.2: A 2x2 showing pain intensity vs. priority. You've picked a painful problem but have too many competitors.

You've created a product that delivers a reasonable amount of value, only to discover that there are existing products that do pretty much the same thing. They might not be identical, but it turns out that the features you thought separated you from your competition just aren't compelling enough. You've misunderstood the market and have ended up with an undifferentiated me-too product. In these situations, early products, well-funded products, and products with a strong brand and good marketing are likely to win. Having too many undifferentiated competitors is often described as a Red Ocean problem (due to the sheer number of companies in the water being nibbled on by sharks).

3. The product doesn't deliver enough value for customers to justify the hassle of changing their workflow to adopt a new product.

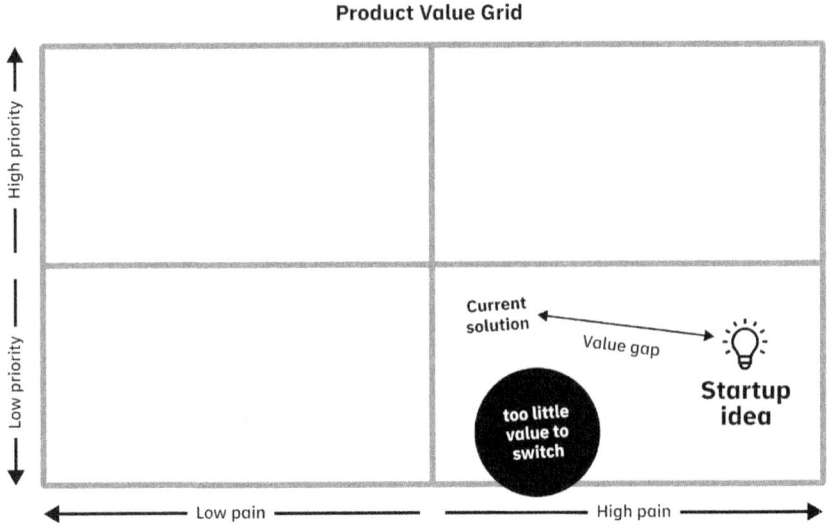

Figure 2.3: A 2x2 showing pain intensity vs. priority. In this instance, you've got a product that has high pain intensity but low importance.

Even if you create a product that solves a meaningful problem, the solution needs to deliver so much value to the user that it compensates for the hassle of switching from their existing solution. Essentially, the delta between the value the current solution delivers and the value the new solution delivers needs to be significantly more than the cost of switching, so that even when they do switch, users are still left with some value (we'll talk about 10X products shortly).

Many founders are so in love with their own solution that they struggle to understand why anybody would stick with the old way of doing things. However, don't underestimate the role of inertia and how comfortable people are with the status quo—sometimes described as satisficing.

4. The product is actually pretty good, but the founders can't connect the value the product delivers with enough potential customers (merchandising and positioning).

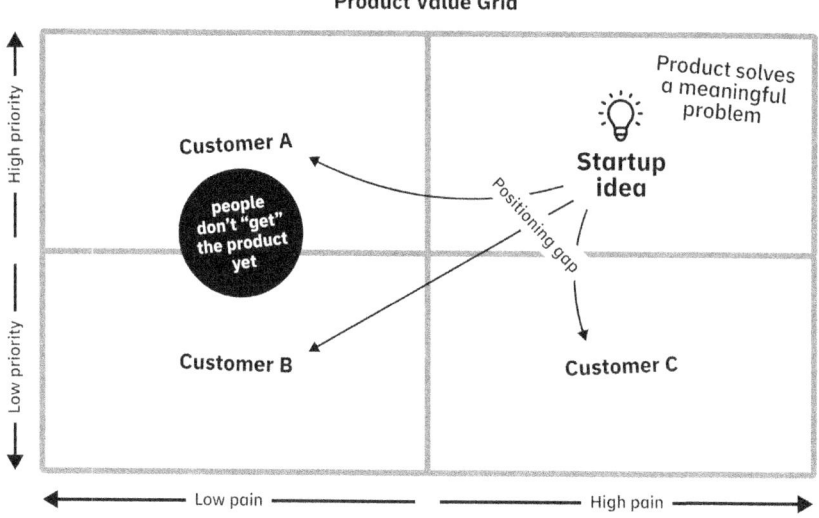

Figure 2.4: A 2x2 showing pain intensity vs. priority. In this instance, you solve a meaningful problem but users don't realize this yet.

I see the value your product claims to deliver as a magnet that draws customers through your acquisition/activation (getting new customers) and retention funnels (keeping them). If you communicate that value in a way that lands, people will be motivated to sign up and give your product a go. If you do a good enough job of delivering that value as quickly as possible, folks will stick around long enough to pay.

The challenge here is that sometimes what customers expect (the value they're sold up front) is not actually delivered to them. This dissonance between expectations and reality is typically the culprit for extremely high churn rates (more on this in Chapter 9). By managing expectations up front—or by properly positioning the product in the right way, to the right audience—you'll improve attraction and retention.

5. The market for this new product turns out to be much smaller than they'd anticipated.

Product Value Grid

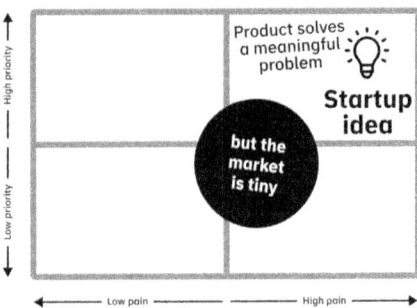

Figure 2.5: A 2x2 showing pain intensity vs. priority. In this instance, the problem is big and meaningful, but the market is too small.

In order to be a venture-investable company, you need to have a large serviceable market—ideally one that can propel you to at least $100M in annual revenue. Many startups believe that they have huge potential, but the market often has other ideas. For many founders, building a $10M or $50M business is a huge, potentially life-changing outcome. For the investors, however, this might not even return them their initial stake. So if you find yourself getting to the top of the S-curve too quickly, you might require a pivot.

Sometimes this is as simple as finding a different audience for the same product, or subtly tweaking the product to make it more attractive to a wider market. Often, however, this requires going back to the drawing board and coming up with a completely new idea. The quicker you come to this realization, the more time and money you'll have left to switch paths. Just remember that some of the most successful products came as the result of a pivot: products like Slack, which emerged from a browser game called Glitch, and Twitter (I refuse to call it X), which emerged from the podcasting app Odeo.

The (Almost) Mythical 10X Product

In the previous section, I touched on the conditions by which a customer with an existing solution would be willing to adopt a new solution. We're essentially creatures of habit so are happy to stick with familiar tools and processes, even if they're suboptimal. Some of this relates to our appetite for risk. It just feels safer to stick with what we have than to try something that could be 10% better but might also be 10% worse—especially if our standing in the organization relies on us not getting this wrong.

To counter this, we need to present people with a product that's so overwhelmingly better that they'd be foolish not to switch. This is often described as a 10X product because it needs to be 10X better than the existing solution. While I think it's almost impossible to create a product that's genuinely 10X better, it's often possible to create something that's 2X better—especially if you're focusing on a particular customer segment that has been largely ignored.

In the same way that most people believe their children are smarter and more talented than those of their neighbors and friends, I meet many founders who are convinced that their product is 10X better than their competition. This often comes as a result of talking to early customers and taking everything they say at face value. However, people are generally bad judges of future behavior and are often just saying encouraging things to be nice. Take all early feedback with a huge grain of salt and don't let it cloud your judgment.

Founders are often too close to the problem to see things clearly. Because they know their own product inside out, they're able to point to a host of small features that their competitor doesn't have as proof of superiority (sometimes called Motivated Reasoning). The challenge is that many of these features are nice-to-haves: great if you're already on the platform but not enough to pull people over. In fact, many of these features are ultimately taken out when it's eventually proven that they are not adding value or driving growth. (Perhaps that's why the competitors didn't have them?)

Like proud parents, founders can also have selective awareness when it comes to the shortcomings of their own product, often ignoring or downplaying certain gaps and problems. As such, founders need to have a highly critical viewpoint and be intellectually honest about the true value their product delivers. The best way to do this is to build empathy for your users and see things from their perspective—something described as approaching things with a "beginner's mind." This usually comes from doing good competitive research and immersing yourself in the lives of your users (rather than filtering out what you don't want to hear). This doesn't come naturally to many founders, who understandably act as their product's biggest fan. Designers can be a great asset here, as they don't have a horse in the race and are trained to think from the perspective of the user.

Ultimately, if you believe your Minimum Viable Product (MVP) is already 10X better than your better-funded competitor, you're going to be clouded by hubris and much less likely to exert the effort needed to build a truly 10X experience. Watch out for phrases like "The users just don't get it," because (at least 95% of the time) it's not the users' fault. Instead, you've either misunderstood how good your product actually is or have done a poor job of communicating it (more on this later).

The Feature Parity Trap

Feature Parity is the belief that in order to beat the competition, you must first deliver the same set of features they currently offer. When entering into an already crowded Red Ocean marketplace, it's tempting for founders to believe that they need to reach Feature Parity quickly. This is especially true if they talk to sophisticated customers who are already happy with their existing solutions. They'll tell you that in order to move they'll need all the things their existing provider delivers (a provider that's probably been around for years, has raised a ton of money, and has a fairly big team), plus several additional features. Founders are told to listen to their customers, so they set off trying to deliver everything the existing solutions provide and more.

Sadly, Feature Parity is a constantly shifting target. By the time your small team has reached parity, the competition has released a dozen new features.

Chasing features is rarely the way to go. Some estimates[3] suggest that around 80% of product features are rarely if ever used and have negligible impact on growth. That's a lot of wasted time and effort working on things that fail to shift the dial—not to mention the opportunity cost (i.e., the more impactful things you could have been building otherwise). Even if the new feature gives you a short spike in growth, it's likely to dip back down shortly after. Founder and former HubSpot Director Joshua Porter described this mindset as the Next Feature Fallacy: the belief that "the next feature you add will suddenly make people want to use the entire product."

Companies that constantly chase new features in the hope they'll deliver growth are often described as Feature Factories and the resulting loop is known as the Product Death Cycle. The name itself is a good indicator that this isn't a path you want to follow.

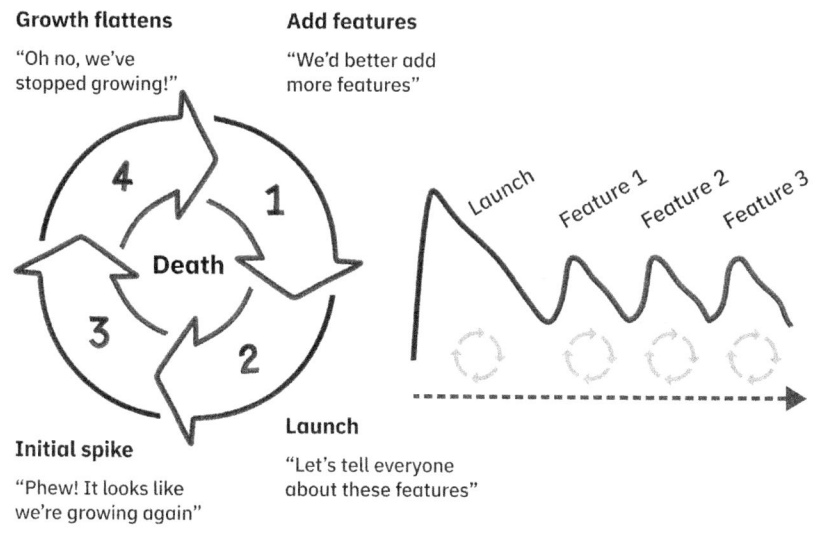

Figure 2.6: The Product Death Cycle.

If we can agree that not all features are created equally, it's super useful for early stage founders to understand how your features rank

[3] https://go.pendo.io/rs/185-LQW-370/images/
2019%20feature%20Adoption%20Report%20Digital.pdf

in the minds of your users. One way to do this is by mapping your core features onto this 4x4 chart. If your product feature set mostly sits in the top-right quadrant, you have features that most users get value from most of the time. If most of your features are in the top-left quadrant, this means that you have several useful features, but they aren't evenly distributed across your customer base. Some users like feature A, some like feature B, but not enough people like both A and B. This is often an indication that you haven't really tied down who your target users are yet.

Lastly, if you find yourself in the bottom-left quadrant, as many founders do, your product just isn't delivering enough value to enough people on a regular enough basis, and you're likely stuck in the Product Death Cycle. As such, you're going to need to take stock, figure out the two or three core features that deliver the most value to your users most of the time, and focus your attention there.

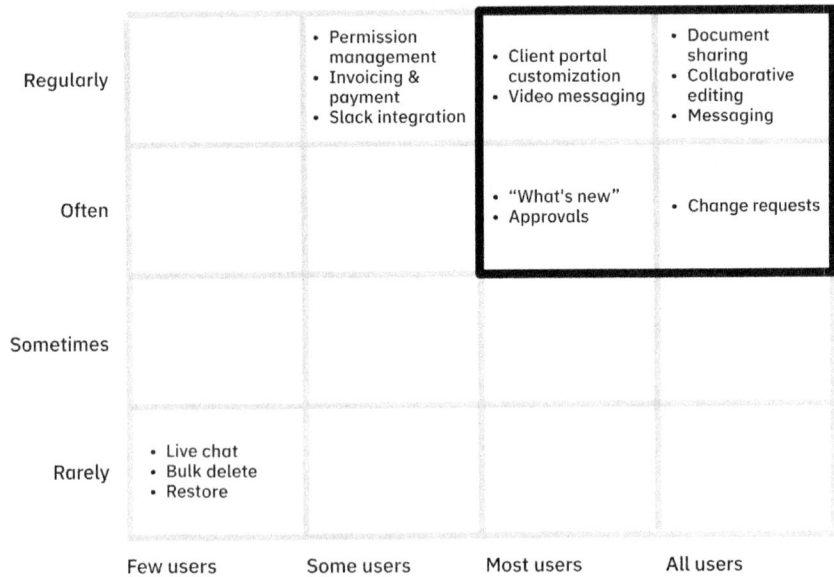

Figure 2.7: A 4x4 table showing the usage of different feature sets by different user types across a product.

Get to Know Your Users

When starting a new project, it generally makes sense to start with a problem you want to solve, and then talk to people who might have experienced that problem to understand how they currently go about solving it, and how impactful a better solution might be to them (this process is known as product discovery). Because this is the first thing you should do, this section should logically be at the start of this chapter. Unfortunately, most first-time founders seem to skip this step and jump straight to the solution, coming up with a possible product idea, assembling a deck, raising money, building a beta version, and *then* start talking to potential users to validate their idea.

You can see why this is problematic. They've already spent time building a solution and raised money on the basis that this is the right solution, and thus they have a vested interest in the outcome. As such, a lot of early product discovery tends to be clouded by Confirmation Bias: founders looking for confirmation that their idea is correct and ignoring any inconvenient signals that they might be going down the wrong path.

As a result, plenty of first-time founders end up spending way too long following dead ends and often run out of money before they've had time to get back on track. This is one of the reasons why I suggest that founders fall in love with the problem rather than the solution and talk to potential users before they are too settled on a particular idea.

The process of trying to find the right solution for the problem you're trying to solve is sometimes called Problem-Solution Fit, and it is something you need to achieve before you can obtain Product-Market Fit. This phase of the journey is typified by trying out a range of possible solutions to find the one that's most effective.

This is also the reason why it's a good idea to create an MVP.

The Minimum Viable Product: Don't Skip This Section!

I believe the MVP is one of the best-known yet least-understood concepts in startup land. It's why I specifically flagged down the skimmers in the subhead. The concept is pretty self-explanatory: Build the smallest thing you possibly can in order to get meaningful feedback on your idea. When you read up on MVPs, the advice is often to create something truly small: a landing page to test the proposition and see if people sign up or a super simple page with a couple of forms, where everything is done manually in the background, à la the Wizard of Oz.

Unfortunately I see plenty of founders spending six or more months building the first version of their product, sure that they're on the right track, only to be surprised when uptake is low and traction minimal. One founder I know spent three years building and testing a product that they thought was minimal. Nearing the end of their runway and out of desperation, they scrapped their old product and spent three weeks building a lite version. To their amazement, this lite version took off. A few weeks later, their product manager told me, "It's crazy. At the time we really thought we were building an MVP. It was only when we pared the product back to its absolute minimum that we realized what an MVP truly was."

To be completely honest, I don't expect any of my readers to heed this advice: Do good customer discovery and build a truly minimal MVP in order to test their ideas. As a designer, I understand human nature and am aware of how invested we get in our own ideas. So, I mention this in the hope that if you find yourself going down the wrong path, you will remember this conversation and consider backtracking to the previous turning—before you get too lost in the woods.

The Minimum Lovable Product

Thanks to the rise of smartphones, we've all been spoiled by consumer-quality digital experiences: products that not only solve our problems and are easy to use but are also fun and delightful to use. As such, people are often willing to switch to a new product if the experience is a lot better, even if it lacks some core features. This is especially true if it's a highly commoditized tool they use every day, which is where the idea of a Minimum Lovable Product (MLP) comes in.

MLPs are still minimal in the sense that they still have limited functionality and aren't striving for Feature Parity with their competition. Instead they're focused on building a core set of features that deliver outsize value. People who build MLPs realize the importance of a great experience, so they're focused on building the smallest possible product their users can fall in love with and then expanding out from there.

Organizations like Superhuman, Cron, Linear, and The Browser Company have done a great job building lovable products in heavily saturated markets like email, calendars, project management, and browsers by focusing heavily on User Experience (UX). These companies have all proved that early adopters, and superusers are willing to switch from well-established (and free) products because of a superior experience alone.

While this approach seems sensible, I see many startups with engineering and feature-driven mindsets (as we mentioned earlier) focused on creating new features over making existing features more delightful to use. This is especially true in companies that lack significant design capabilities. I believe much of this comes down to modern engineering practices like Agile, which focuses on breaking things down into smaller, shippable user stories.

If you are in a fairly new market, with very little competition, the value you're delivering is usually tied to the capabilities the features enable. However, in more established markets (the more likely scenario), where Feature Parity takes longer to deliver, focusing on experience over feature set is ideally the way to go.

The Kano Model: Must-Haves and Have-Nots

The Kano Model is a popular product framework that divides product improvements into different camps. The first type of features are the must-haves. In the context of a hotel room, a bed would be considered a must-have. These aren't the things your customers will get excited about when you have them, but they'll definitely notice if you don't.

The next group of improvements are things that have a linear impact on customer satisfaction. Using the hotel analogy, a better entertainment system with a bigger screen, more channels, and more free movies will be better than a small TV with the default cable package. I think most product teams fixate on these sorts of features in the hope that they'll move the dial. However, how often do you book a hotel based on the size of the TV?

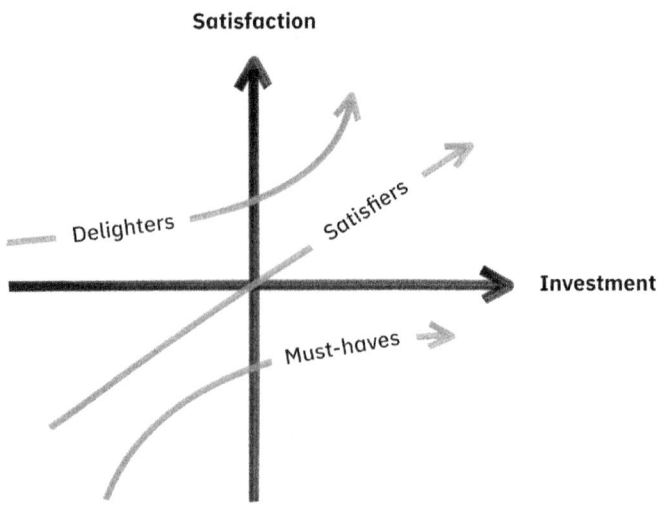

Figure 2.8: The Kano Model.

This brings us to the final group of features, which are known as delighters. These are often small and relatively cheap things that can make an outsize difference to users. One good example is the U.S. hotel chain that gives everybody a warm chocolate chip cookie upon check-in. It's a tiny thing, but I've met several corporate travelers who are loyal to that brand for the cookie alone. This might seem trivial, but these are the sort of touches that people remember beyond the size of the bed or whether you had HBO.

Early stage startups struggle to compete on the must-haves and performance improvements, as they generally require a lot of engineering resources. Delighters, on the other hand, are something smaller companies do well. As such, it's often better to focus on new or emerging markets with slightly lower needs and then excel at the details.

This approach is how Airbnb navigated its early years. The company found a group of people who were willing to give up some of the things more sophisticated travelers expected, like a proper mattress, a dedicated bathroom, room service—or basic fire safety—in return for a more personal experience.

Of course, Airbnb quickly grew out of customers willing to sleep on an inflatable mattress in somebody's spare room. But by that time they had proved the model and raised more capital, so they were able to backfill all the cleanliness, safety, and security issues that regular hotel users demanded. In fact, this is one of the reasons incumbents often discount up-and-coming competitors. They often don't see them as credible competitors until it's too late.

A Good Product Is Just the Start

Jeff Bezos claims that "advertising is the price you pay for having an unremarkable product or service," while product consultant and futurist John Willshire talks about the importance of "making things people want" rather than "making people want things." I think there's truth in both these statements, so it makes sense to put effort into early product development—not least because truly useful products are often easier to market and therefore multiply your marketing effort.

However, herein lies a Heffalump trap, leading founders and product teams to believe that this is all they need to do—that if they create a great product, users will come flooding in.

While it's true that getting the product right is a big part of achieving Product-Market Fit, it's generally the part founders feel most comfortable with. Sadly, I've seen too many superior products wither on the vine, while mediocre ones thrive, because the founders neglected the market part of the equation. Having a great product is therefore just one part of reaching PMF, and you can't let yourself be seduced by the idea that the best products automatically win.

Summary

Successful products solve meaningful problems for a specific set of users. The value they claim to deliver creates a powerful magnet that draws people to your product, while the value they actually deliver hopefully keeps them there. Founders often have strong views on what they want to build. While this is great, these views need to be tested with real users.

When the funding environment is buoyant, you might be able to raise your next round of investment on a well-delivered product alone. However, in more challenging economic climates, investors will be looking for indications of early traction: something that can demonstrate you have a product people care about and that you're starting to figure out how to connect the value your product delivers with the market.

Even if you're not thinking about the next round just yet, early usage is going to be vital to your product development efforts because it's hard to know what's properly working and what isn't with a handful of customers. In the next chapter, we're going to look at how to stimulate that early growth in order to land your first users.

Next Steps

Take this opportunity to review your product with a beginner's mind. Is your product genuinely 2x better than your competition? If so, why? What's the one big, painkiller problem this product solves better than any other? Who does it solve it for and how? Maybe more importantly, how does your user's life change as a result?

Try writing this down on a single sheet of paper. If you come up with dozens of different user types, your target market is probably too broad. Similarly, if you come up with a dozen different reasons why your product is better, you're probably falling into the trap of Motivated Reasoning. At the very least, it's going to be difficult to accurately position your product based on a dozen small things rather than one or two big differentiators.

Consider splitting all your major features out into the 4x4 matrix we saw earlier. Which features will be used by all your users all the time, which will be used by all of your users some of the time, and which will be used only by a handful of people very occasionally? Make sure that you're building a truly minimal MVP/MLP for a well-defined user, rather than wasting engineering cycles creating a me-too product.

Try stress-testing an early prototype with prospective customers. Rather than trying to convince them that the product is great, really listen to what they have to say, and take their feedback on board. Ask your investors and advisors what they truly think. How about your designers and developers? It's often hard for people around you to share their true feelings for fear of hurting yours. I meet a surprising number of product teams who have low conviction about what they're building but won't tell the founder for fear of upsetting them. Your job is to approach every conversation with curiosity, in order to expand your own understanding, rather than to convince others of yours.

CHAPTER 3

Finding Those First Precious Users

T he concept of the Cold Start Problem comes from the world of social media, where the value of the network rises in relation to the *size* of the network. The most often cited example is that of the fax machine. The first fax machine ever was basically useless. Connect that to a second fax machine, and you now have the ability to send documents to a single location—say from your head office to your factory. Send a few more fax machines to your bank, lawyer, distribution centers, and key clients, and you now have a small but useful local network. If more banks, lawyers, and clients start buying fax machines, those networks can interact; and every additional node that gets added to the network makes the network stronger and more valuable.

The Cold Start Problem is how to get those first users to install a fax machine when the value of the network is still small (or nonexistent). The example above demonstrates one approach: finding a customer who will get value from the product without a large network effect and help you build the network out. This is sometimes described as having a single-player mode, meaning the product is useful, even if no one else is there. Other ways include starting with one community or geographic location, as Facebook and Uber did. This allows you to create local network density from which you can build.

While the Cold Start Problem might be most noticeable in social networks and marketplace products, it's not limited there. Getting your first 10, 100, or 1,000 users is really difficult, and the conventional wisdom is generally to start by finding a niche: people for whom your solution is so valuable (or the switching costs are so low) that they don't mind taking a risk on an unproven solution. In other words, your typical early adopter.

Finding Your Early Adopters

For some early stage startups, their early adopters are quite obvious. There's a good chance they'll be founders like yourself, who don't currently have an incumbent solution (because they've just started) and are comfortable trying out new technology. For others, you might have a hunch who your early adopters will be, but I'll warn you here that hunches get startups killed unless they're validated quickly.

To validate these hunches, you can prime the pumps with an initial burst of traffic and then see which of the various segments you've attracted start showing signs of interest. The more variety you have on your waitlist, the more types of people you can talk to in your product discovery calls. That means you can onboard more people and have them kick the tires in your beta, and you'll quickly learn who your product is and isn't currently working for.

This seems like a sensible (and relatively low-risk) approach, so I'm often surprised at how many startups do things the other way around. They start with a super specific niche in mind, bring in five early users from that niche, make a bunch of (often fairly major) product decisions based solely on what those five users say, then launch a now heavily tailored product to a niche that—ultimately—turns out to be too small or have little or no interest in the product. The founders then try another niche and the cycle continues until they either find one that works or they run out of money.

This obviously all depends on the type of business you're building, but I'm a big advocate for getting an early injection of nonspecific users in order to see what segments find the most value. You might be surprised by who your early users actually are. For instance, you might imagine that the first 1,000 Calendly users would have been early adopters at Bay Area tech companies, when in fact they were Korean parents and teachers. It turns out that the developers who built Calendly also built a data and analytics company in the education space. Their sales agents started using it to set up meetings with parents, those parents then started using it to set up parent-teacher meetings, and things basically exploded from there.

Similarly, the founders of online collaboration tool Butter assumed that their early users would be workshop facilitators at agencies; so they were equally surprised to see a big spike in users coming from—you guessed it—Korean teachers again. It turns out that an influential YouTuber in the education space posted a video that went viral and led to a massive uptake of use in a surprising segment.

The moral of this story is twofold. First, you often can't always predict where early growth will come from; and second, the Korean education system is clearly full of early adopters.

Leveraging Your Own Network

One of the reasons investors like to support founders with an existing network is that a lot of early growth will come from your community. As Y Combinator co-founder Paul Graham puts it: "You don't need to get the word out, you need to get the word *in*. What you need is to find an initial group of early adopters, which you can probably find among your peers."

This sentiment is backed up in an excellent article[4] by growth supremo Lenny Rachitsky, where he surveyed 100 well-known companies to understand where their early adoption came from. It should come as no surprise that the most effective method was leaning heavily on the founding team's network.

A great example of this is Karri Saarinen, the former head of design at Coinbase and principal designer at Airbnb. Saarinen already had a sizable following on Twitter when he announced his new venture: a beautifully designed product to manage the software development process called Linear. This allowed him to hook into a dense and well-

---

[4] https://www.lennysnewsletter.com/p/consumer-business-find-first-users

connected network of potential users who were keen to see what this already successful designer was going to do next.

> **Paul Graham** ✓
> @paulg
>
> When you first start a startup, you don't need to get the word out. You need to get the word *in*. You do not, in the very beginning, need the whole world to know about it. What you need is to find the initial group of early adopters, which you can probably find among your peers.
>
> 12:33 PM · Aug 27, 2021
>
> 💬 49   ↻ 440   ♡ 2.9K   🔖 393

Figure 3.1: Tweet from Paul Graham on the importance of "getting the word *in*."

How to get your first 1,000 users

Strategy	Companies
1. Reach out to friends and colleagues	yelp ⬛substack reddit 📌 lyft STRAVA Linked🅸🅽 Quora 🅵
2. Reach out to targeted strangers	cameo 🎵 YouTube nextdoor DOORDASH Bēhance airbnb ⬛substack Uber caviar Product Hunt Udemy
3. Go where they already hang out, online/offline	NETFLIX 🎵 📌 lyft 🅵 Robinhood Etsy MORNING BREW tinder Tik Tok Dropbox Product Hunt PATREON airbnb Uber Glossier. PayPal HIPCAMP
4. Enlist influencers, paid or organically	Spotify tinder reddit Quora cameo Product Hunt
5. Get press	instacart Zillow Robinhood SUPERHUMAN airbnb Udemy Product Hunt Spotify
6. Create viral content	Calm PATREON ⬛substack duolingo SUPERHUMAN
7. Get physical placement	DOORDASH tinder instacart yelp GRUBHUB NETFLIX

Figure 3.2: Image from Lenny Rachitsky showing how different startups landed their first customers.

I discovered Twitter in a similar way, when a friend of mine from an audio startup called Odeo sent a message to our friend group using an experimental tool called Twttr that one of his colleagues had created. This was probably one of the first 100 or so tweets ever sent but quickly propagated around my whole network until everybody I knew had signed up for an account.

While having a strong social media following can help, you can also build businesses off your existing professional connections. For instance, the founders of Intercom ran a previous company targeting a similar market. This meant they already had a rich address book of prospective contacts who knew and trusted them. In the early weeks of business, Intercom's co-founder, Des Traynor, sent around 100 personally written emails a day to this list, introducing their new product and fishing for interest.

Sadly, not everybody has an existing network they can leverage. So it comes as no surprise that the next most effective strategy is cold outreach—something many founders feel super squeamish about. As technical people, we generally hate getting unsolicited emails ourselves so we can't imagine ever responding to a cold contact through LinkedIn. However, if the message is written in a natural voice, is sent by the founder of the company, and is targeted toward the person receiving it, you'll be surprised how high the open rate can be.

Go Where Your Customers Hang Out

Another approach that involves a lot of work but can be surprisingly effective is going where your customers already hang out. College campuses have turned out to be a fertile proving ground over the years. As we all know, Facebook created artificial scarcity in the early days by launching at Ivy League colleges and requiring a university email address to join. More recently, the founder of Bumble, Whitney Wolfe Herd, toured universities showcasing the product and enlisting a network of campus ambassadors to organize promotional events. Bumble was super effective at getting students to join its ambassador program, partly for the experience it promised to add to their resume:

"The Honey Ambassador Program gives you the unique opportunity to expand your network and gain real-world marketing and project management experience. You'll bring Bumble into your community by planning events, creating content, distributing branded merch, partnering with local businesses, executing engaging stunts, and working with different student organizations. You'll also work with Bumble HQ employees on local and national campaigns to bring awareness to the Bumble brand and mission."

Bumble investor Jacob Westphal from a16z sees huge value in this approach: "Ambassador programs are an excellent way to use a college campus to kickstart network effects within a group of like-minded target users with potentially lower costs than other strategies like digital advertising. Indeed, college campuses are natural environments for developing, testing, and growing consumer products."

While campuses might work for some startups, the key is going where your potential customers hang out. For instance, the founders of Etsy spent their early months attending local craft fairs and telling people about their platform. If you know anything about marketplaces, you'll know that they have the added problem of needing both sellers and customers. Fortunately, the team at Etsy was able to onboard sellers at craft fairs who used the tool as their primary shop window, bringing their own customers onto the marketplace with them. Many sellers also acted as buyers themselves, using the marketplace to source raw materials for their creations.

Conferences can be another useful hunting ground. I remember speaking at The Next Web when Uber had just launched in Amsterdam. The event was awash with free ride tokens, presumably left lying around by Uber team members who were also attending (but notably not sponsoring) the event. Handing out discount coupons is one of those approaches that feels decidedly old-school but can be surprisingly effective in the early days.

Airbnb is another company that used conferences as an early growth channel. They realized that attendees to a popular tech conference were struggling to find places to stay as all the hotels in town were booked; so they promoted their service to attendees looking for a cheap room.

One clever way they did this was by automatically cross-posting all their listings to Craigslist, effectively taking advantage of somebody else's distribution channel. Craigslist locked this down pretty quickly, but not before Airbnb built a reputation among design and tech conference goers. In fact, during the company's first few years of operation, every Airbnb I stayed at was owned by somebody I was just two degrees of separation from. ("Oh, so you work as a designer at The New York Times with my friend Khoi? Cool.") This network density had the added benefit of making staying in a stranger's spare room much less scary.

Viral Videos and Influencer Marketing

Using existing digital platforms to get the word out is an understandably popular approach. Dropbox famously got its first users through a video it posted to Hacker News entitled "My YC app: Dropbox—Throw away your USB drive." This also got the attention of Y Combinator co-founder Paul Graham, helping Dropbox join the now-popular accelerator. The following year when they were ready to publicly launch, Dropbox posted a similar video to Digg and Reddit titled "Google Drive killer coming from MIT startup." This time they included a bunch of niche references in the video that only Digg and Reddit users would get, leading the Dropbox waitlist to jump from 5,000 to 75,000 overnight.

If you don't have your own network, enlisting the help of influencers can also be a surprisingly cost-effective approach in the early days— especially if you target influencers in the process of building up their own following. Unlike people with millions of followers who are very good at monetizing their content, people with 5-10K followers (aka micro-influencers) are much more likely to share what you're doing for free or in return for free samples. When compared by sponsorship costs, micro-influencers significantly outperform those who have already achieved influencer status, with up to 151% higher engagement rates.[5] With regard to social platforms, YouTube, Instagram, and TikTok videos can work especially well for direct-to-consumer brands, while getting

---

[5] https://www.smartinsights.com/social-media-marketing/instagram-marketing/average-engagement-rates-of-instagram-influencer-marketing/

on the right podcast can provide a nice boost for Software as a Service (SaaS) businesses.

A good example of this is Gymshark, a direct-to-consumer fitness brand founded—in classic startup style—out of the founder's mother's garage. The brand got an early break by attending the BodyPower fitness expo and raking in $42K in orders on a single day. Back in 2013, they realized that YouTube was a huge and growing channel for fitness influencers like Lex Griffin and Chris Lavado, so they sent out free apparel samples. This proved to be a highly cost-effective way to get the brand out and sales took off as a result. "They absolutely loved it," Ben Francis, the co-founder of Gymshark explains, "and they're still with us today. That started, I guess, what you'd now call an influencer market for us."

There are other approaches you can take, like launching PR campaigns or creating viral videos. TLDV is a great example of a Seedcamp portfolio company for which viral videos were effective. They created a super cool mash-up that spliced a scene from The Shining with the company's founder talking about the product.[6] If they work, stunts like this can lead to viral interest and help a new brand get noticed.

Just beware: I've seen many companies waste quite large amounts of money on PR campaigns, launch parties, and viral videos without moving the dial, so it's worth noting that campaigns like the TLDV one tend to be the exception rather than the rule. It's also important to remember that viral videos and the like will be effective in attracting customers only if they reach the right audience.

The Big Launch

Founders will often put a lot of effort into their launch. They have this idea that excitement for their products will have been building up over time and once they fling the doors open, people will naturally come rushing in. If you're a fan of the TV show *Silicon Valley*, you'll no doubt remember the episode where they rented out Alcatraz for a media launch, to hilarious (and painful) consequences.

---

[6] https://www.youtube.com/watch?v=etLHPhLy8Q0&t=8s

Sometimes the timing of your launch can be more important than the location. The founder of Superhuman, Rahul Vohra, explains how a competitor closing down gave them the perfect launch platform:

> "The best way to do it is to pick one or two events a year where you can insert yourself into the cultural zeitgeist. For us, one such event was when Mailbox was being shut down. I currently have one of the most widely read articles on how to survive an acquisition. It was written in response to the Mailbox shutdown. That article probably took me three days of doing nothing else, and another day of shopping it around. So four days all in. But those four days bought north of 5,000 sign-ups."

While most product launches aren't quite as bad as the one on Silicon Valley, I've seen many founders spend a ton of time and money on big launch campaigns with disappointing results. Of course, it's nice to be listed on Sifted or TechCrunch after beavering away in stealth mode for the past 12 months. However, it's rare that the resulting traffic leads to a big spike in customers. This is because the people consuming fundraising and launch announcements often aren't the same people who are looking for a solution to the problem your product offers. They aren't your customer, and so their spike in your landing page traffic is most likely low-converting. So maybe see launch parties more as an internal celebration than as a key plank in your Go-to-Market Strategy (GTM).

These days launches aren't really a one-time thing, so don't get too bogged down on a particular date. The best launches are a series of activities that might take place over 12–18 months. You might find other events like coming out of beta, landing your 100th customer, announcing a successful fundraise, or celebrating a year in business as more impactful—especially if you can rope existing customers into the story. This is where Product Hunt can be particularly useful.

Launching on Product Hunt

Though founders have increasingly moved away from the traditional PR launch, Product Hunt launches still seem super popular. For those of you who haven't come across Product Hunt, it's a community website that lists new and interesting products. Some notable Product Hunt launches have included Notion, Zapier, and Loom.

Loom co-founder Shahed Khan shares why they decided to launch on Product Hunt rather than another channel. "You might launch on Twitter and if you have a really good following, you might get a good reaction," he explained in an article on the Product Hunt blog. "But the Product Hunt community is also just a very positive community. Product Hunt lifts these products up and gives feedback so you can build a better company."

Because of the number of well-known startups that have launched on Product Hunt, gaining number one status is seen as a badge of honor among some founders. As such, I see an increasing number of companies who view a successful Product Hunt launch as an integral part of their Go-to-Market Strategy.

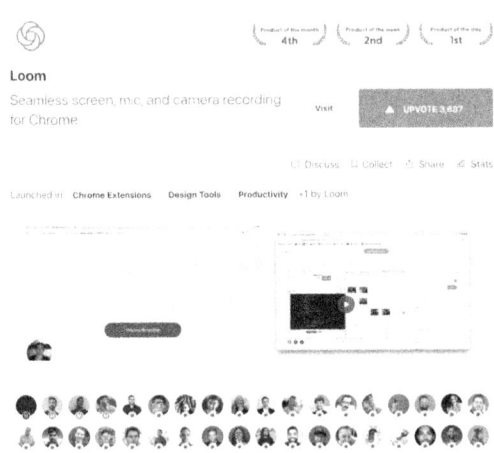

Figure 3.3: The Loom listing on Product Hunt.

Managing Your Product Hunt Launch

The mechanics of Product Hunt are super simple: Every 24 hours Product Hunt nominates one product to be the "Product of the Day." This was originally calculated just from the number of upvotes the product received. These days, however, it's calculated in part by how many votes the product gets per hour, in order to avoid big early spikes (and people gaming the system). This means scheduling your promotional messaging around different time zones in order to keep momentum going throughout the day.

As with fundraising platforms like Kickstarter, it used to be the case with Product Hunt that you could simply list your products and gain immediate interest. But now Product Hunt launches can take weeks (or even months) to put together. This includes activities like warming up your network; creating social media assets, website banners, an impressive launch video, and an upcoming page;[7] scheduling announcements; and generally building up buzz. Consider joining online communities of potential users, other founders, and potential hunters and anywhere else you can go to help promote your launch. You might also want to enlist the help of a Product Hunt expert hunter like Chris Messina[8] or even a professional marketing team experienced in running such launches.

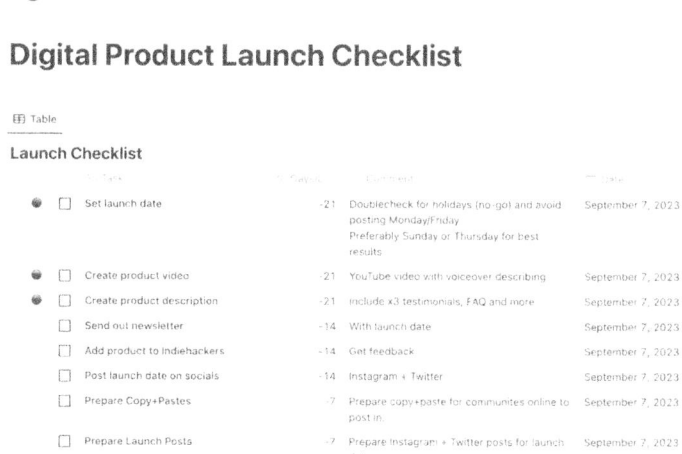

Digital Product Launch Checklist

⊞ Table

Launch Checklist

●	☐	Set launch date	-21	Doublecheck for holidays (no-go) and avoid posting Monday/Friday Preferably Sunday or Thursday for best results	September 7, 2023
●	☐	Create product video	-21	YouTube video with voiceover describing	September 7, 2023
●	☐	Create product description	-21	Include x3 testimonials, FAQ and more	September 7, 2023
	☐	Send out newsletter	-14	With launch date	September 7, 2023
	☐	Add product to Indiehackers	-14	Get feedback	September 7, 2023
	☐	Post launch date on socials	-14	Instagram + Twitter	September 7, 2023
	☐	Prepare Copy+Pastes	-7	Prepare copy+paste for communities online to post in	September 7, 2023
	☐	Prepare Launch Posts	-7	Prepare Instagram + Twitter posts for launch date	September 7, 2023

Figure 3.4: A free Product Hunt launch checklist by Pascio.[9]

Picking the right time to launch is a bit of an art. Launching mid-week can give you a lot of traffic. However, it might also give you a lot more competition. As such, for a first-time product, a weekend launch

---

[7] https://www.producthunt.com/coming-soon
[8] https://chrismessina.me/hunt-me
[9] https://pascio.gumroad.com/l/launchchecklist

might be less competitive—and give you a greater chance of hitting the number one spot. Generally you want to launch early in the month to give yourself time to earn a "Product of the Month" badge and increase your chances of also being nominated for a Product Hunt annual "Golden Kitty" award.

It's worth mentioning that Product Hunt frowns on founders actively asking for upvotes, so doing so might get you banned. Instead, your goal should be to drive folks to your launch and have people vote because they love what you're doing. It's also worth noting that Product Hunt doesn't like brand-new accounts, so it would be sensible to encourage your team (as well as your wider community) to sign up a few months in advance of your launch. Even better if you can convince them to be active on the platform: hunting products, upvoting, and commenting on other launches. Doing this raises your credibility (and karma points) making your upvotes count for more. As your launch gets closer, you might want to contact other founders you and your team supported to see if they'd be willing to support you in return. Maybe even send folks a calendar invite for the day of the launch so they don't forget.

As with an effective promotional site, you need to put a reasonable amount of effort into your Product Hunt listing, particularly the first comment. This is especially true, as around 70% of number one listings have a strong first comment from the maker.[10] As the co-founder of Loom explains: "I think people tend to just put up an essay in their first post on Product Hunt, rather than giving just enough information to where they want to visit the homepage. Having a very clear first launch page helped us a lot in getting the skeptics to click into the post. They read the first comment; they even look at a YouTube video or some screenshots that we uploaded."

So use your first comment to introduce yourself, the product, and who it's for. Call out important features, highlight any launch deals you're offering, connect with the community, and remember to ask for feedback rather than votes.

---

[10] https://www.producthunt.com/launch/preparing-for-launch

Make sure that you're super active on launch day. That means posting promotional messages, responding to comments, and thanking people for their support. Don't do what one of my founders did and post an initial message at 9 a.m. and then nothing for the next seven hours. Instead, consider sharing regular updates letting folks know your ranking and how they can help push things forward. As the Product Hunt launch spans Europe, the Americas, Africa, and Asia, you'll probably need to get some help covering the full 24-hour cycle. The last thing you want to happen is to go to bed at number one and wake up the next day to find you've been pushed down to third or fourth place, as another one of the founders I advise recently experienced.

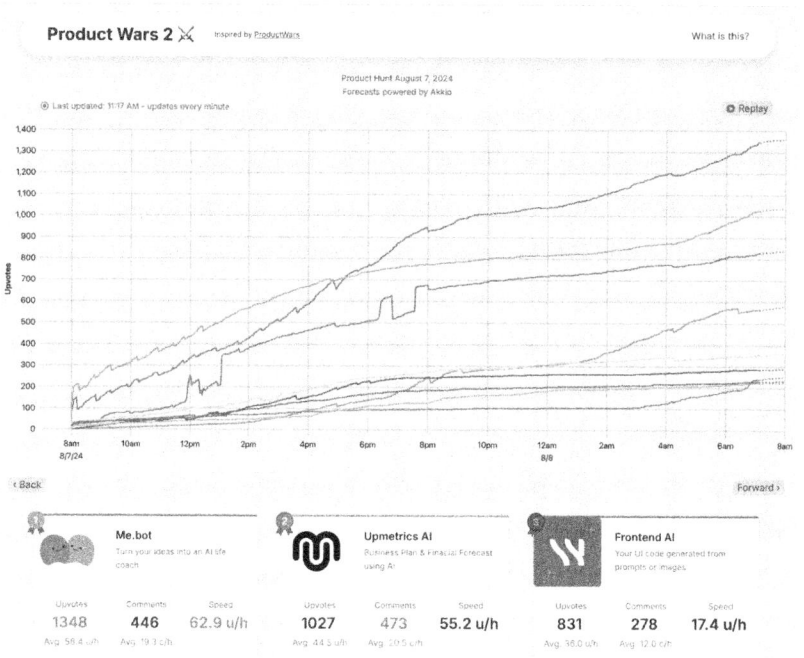

Figure 3.5: Product Wars 2 helps track your launch.

One potentially useful tool to help with your Product Hunt campaign is Product Wars 2,[11] a predictive analytics tool that reviews the current Product Hunt launches and attempts to estimate what ranking they'll

---

[11] https://pw2.akkio.com/

get. This can help founders explore historic launches, as well as make sure they've got enough momentum happening on the day.

While Product Hunt launches are becoming increasingly popular, I think they have some of the same problems as more traditional PR launches—namely that the people who spend their time upvoting companies on Product Hunt are more likely to be bored tech workers than prospective users. So the bounce you get from a number one listing on Product Hunt can be short-lived. However it is a nice piece of social proof you can add to your next newsletter or investor update. As such, I see the main benefit of a Product Hunt launch as a way of galvanizing your existing community, while having a number one ranking gives you a good excuse to contact people you've spoken with in the past.

The Importance of Doing Things That Don't Scale

As entrepreneurs and engineers, we're hardwired to focus on growth techniques that scale, which is why there's a natural tendency to explore things like pay-per-click advertising and Product-Led Growth. However, these sorts of approaches tend to work better once you've nailed your proposition and found Product-Market Fit. As such, early stage founders need to get comfortable doing things that don't scale. This might mean doing things that don't feel especially sophisticated or startuppy—like handing out flyers on the street or traveling across the country to close a $1,000 deal. Figma co-founder Dylan Field was famous for doing just this; touring round Bay Area design teams to demo the product in the hope of landing a sale.

A while back, I advised the founder of a "field to fork" marketplace on their growth strategy. Their early approach was to create campaign content on Instagram about the plight of farmers. It was gaining a bit of interest, but it was mostly background noise that wasn't converting into sales. I helped them reposition themselves as "The Online Farmers Market" and encouraged them to hang out at local farmers markets and hand out discount codes. The founders didn't buy into this as they felt it was too analog and old-school for them. Instead, they doubled down on paid advertising and sadly went out of business shortly after.

A slightly more successful example of an early (non-scalable) marketing initiative was the competition Shopify's co-founder Tobi Lütke ran, in partnership with author Tim Ferris. The competition offered a $100K prize for the fastest-growing company on the platform, pulling in 1,000 new customers and netting them an additional $3M in revenue. A $100k prize pot is likely to be out of most early stage startups' grasp, but a $20k prize might work: Especially if it delivers a similar 30 times return.

In addition to running in-person demos, handing out discount coupons, and running competitions, there are many other non-scalable approaches that have worked well. Here are a few more to get you thinking:

- Get interviewed on a popular newsletter or podcast
- Convince an influencer to mention you
- Create a free tool, report, template, or white paper
- Pick a fight with a big competitor (tread carefully with this approach)
- Speak at a conference
- Publish a viral piece of content
- Do a publicity stunt that lands
- Create a time-limited offer, deal, or collaboration (e.g., AppSumo)
- Run a competition or giveaway
- Partner with a bigger platform
- Have guest bloggers write content on your site
- Do something controversial to get people talking about you (again, be careful here)
- Piggyback on somebody else's network (like Airbnb did with Craigslist)
- Launch in a new language or location
- Do a live video with a well-known influencer
- Sponsor an event or podcast
- Buy cheap (and possibly temporary) outdoor advertising in an area where your customers hang out
- Bundle your offering with complimentary products
- Run your own conference or event

You can see these sorts of activities as short-term turbo boosts. They allow you to get a bit of momentum into your acquisition flywheel. Once that's going, you can start exploring more sustainable and scalable approaches.

Summary

In order to get your first 10, 100, or 1,000 users, you're going to need to try a lot of things that won't scale. A big part of that will involve leaning on your existing network, going to where your customers already hang out, and experimenting with ways to connect the value your product claims to deliver with communities who need that value. This might also involve activities you're not entirely comfortable with, like sending cold emails or handing out fliers. Just remember that growth is your primary goal at this stage, so if you're not leading the charge, nobody else will. While things might feel a little inefficient at the start, once you've managed to prime the pumps with an initial burst of users, you can start building a more scalable and sustainable GTM strategy—the subject of our next chapter.

Next Steps

Start by creating a list of all the people you're connected with on various social media platforms who you think might be interested in your product, or who might know somebody who would. Close friends are great but don't limit yourself. That person you went to school with 10 years ago who's now working at one of your Ideal Customer Profile companies. That slightly spiky engineer you worked with two jobs back who's now at Facebook. That manager you met at your friend's wedding but haven't spoken to since. A good start is 100 names; 200 is even better. Now get your co-founders and senior team to do the same. With some work, you should be able to pull together a list of 500 or 1,000 people.

Think about the most influential people in your network. A former boss? An investor? That friend who has 20K followers on Twitter. Can you reach out to them for a coffee? Make a helpful intro? Offer a demo? Ask if they'd introduce you to the most connected person in their network? If they know somebody who would definitely find your product valuable? If every person you speak to can introduce you to one other person, you'll never run out of potential leads.

Now start thinking about the communities you're currently a member of. Are there folks in your industry Slack group, that Reddit channel you hang out in, or that Discord you recently joined who might find what you're working on interesting? Where do the folks who might buy your products hang out online? Try creating a list of the top 20 or 50 communities you should join and start contributing, too. How about physical spaces? Are there conferences or events coming up where you can chat with potential users? Are there co-working spaces you can visit, and do they have a notice board you could post something to? For non-tech products, are there other places your audience hangs out?

Your goal here is to create a list of all the people you know, all the communities you can join, all the influencers you can connect with, and all the locations you can find where your users might spend time, and then use this and the basis of connecting with and landing your first 100 users. And once you've done that, you need to do it again to get your next 100. This is what early stage growth looks like. It's a lot of work, a lot of leveraging your existing network, a lot of manual outreach, and a lot of things that don't scale. All that, and a lot of rejections. The more of this you can do, the more you'll figure out what works and the quicker you'll be able to formalize your Go-to-Market Strategy.

CHAPTER 4

Create Your Go-To-Market Strategy

Your Go-to-Market Strategy (GTM) is the approach you plan to take in order to launch your product and start acquiring customers. As we saw in the previous chapter, this usually starts by acquiring early adopters, design partners, and fans: a small cohort of users willing to give your incomplete product a try. This allows you to start learning what works, what doesn't, and how to best communicate the value of your product to more people. Once you've managed to acquire all the early adopters from your existing and adjacent networks, however, you're going to need a more structured approach.

Arguably, your GTM strategy finishes at the point you reach Product-Market Fit since by then you've created a product people want and have figured out how to get it to them in a replicable and cost-effective way. By that time, you're in the market (and doing great).

Most founders, however, massively underestimate how long it takes to validate their product in the market. In fact, Startup Genome estimates that it takes two or three times longer[12] than the 12 months founders typically expect. As such, it can come as a shock when you're three years in and still haven't cracked it yet. A CB Insights survey cited

---

[12] https://startupgenome.com/articles/discover-the-patterns-of-successful-internet-startups-in-the-startup-genome-report

this as the main reason why startups fail[13]—because they were unable to find a clear market need for their product before running out of cash. As such, cracking your GTM strategy is critical for the life of a new startup.

The Field of Dreams Approach

As we've alluded to already, many founders believe that their product is so good that all they need to do is launch and users will come flooding in. This is sometimes described as the Field of Dreams approach, from the film of the same name.

In the movie, the lead character, played by Kevin Costner, is visited by an apparition (played by James Earl Jones) who encourages him to build a baseball diamond in the middle of his farm with the prophetic words "If you build it they will come." To be honest—if James Earl Jones showed up with his deep voice and told me to do something, I'd probably do it, too.

Though founders are rarely visited by apparitions, we're generally visited by some vision of a better future. We discover a problem that we care about. We see the current solutions are suboptimal. We invest a ton of time, money, and sleepless nights into imagining a better future, and we hope that enough people will be inspired by our vision that they'll give our product a try.

Over the years, I have witnessed many superior products struggle, while clearly substandard products blossomed. This left many talented founders questioning the received wisdom and scratching their heads. What the hell was going on here?

Why the Field of Dreams Approach Rarely Works

I see this pattern play out all too often: Founders invest all their energy into building what they believe to be a superior product, only to be surprised—and often disheartened—by the lack of early uptake.

Some of this can be ascribed to a concept known as the Endowment Effect. It's the idea that we value the things we create and own much

---

[13] https://www.cbinsights.com/research/report/startup-failure-reasons-top/

more than other people do—arguably up to three times more than anyone else, if the psychological studies are to be believed. "If only they'd give it a try," we reason, "they'd see how much better our product is than everything else on the market."

When you combine this sentiment with the Inertia Effect (our natural resistance to change), you suddenly realize that having the best product doesn't really matter—if you can't get enough people to discover your product, get over the psychological barriers to giving it a try, and stick around long enough to extract the value you believe it holds (essentially the first four arguments in our beloved Growth Equation).

$$Growth = f[(A, M, \Delta V/t, S, K) / (\mu, C)]$$

Figure 4.1: The first four arguments of The Growth Equation.

This is why I believe the following post from Twitch co-founder Justin Kan holds so much truth: the idea that first-time founders are obsessed with product, while second-time founders are obsessed with distribution.

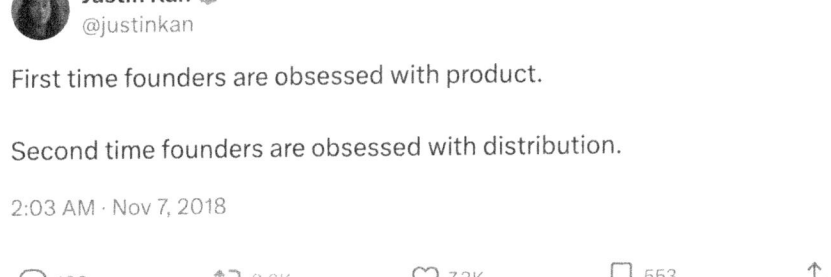

Justin Kan ✔
@justinkan

First time founders are obsessed with product.

Second time founders are obsessed with distribution.

2:03 AM · Nov 7, 2018

160   2.2K   7.3K   553

Figure 4.2: Tweet outlining the importance of distribution.[14]

You can create the best product in the world, but if you don't effectively connect the value your product delivers to a large enough audience as quickly as possible, you'll run out of runway before the

---

[14] https://twitter.com/justinkan/status/1059989657218248704

viral word-of-mouth effect has a chance to kick in. So how do you effectively take a new product to market?

You've Built a Cool Product. Now What?

In order to launch and market your product, you need to be able to answer the following questions:

- Where do I find innovators, early adopters, and potential design partners willing to give us a try?
- What are the major problems my product solves, and how important are these problems to my potential customers?
- Is this the right problem, and is ours the right solution?
- What part of the user's workflow is my product disrupting, and how can I insert myself into their existing workflow?
- Who are my main competitors, and how are we markedly different?
- Have we identified the right buyers?
- Do we have the right pricing and business model?
- Are we doing an effective job at positioning our product and explaining its value?
- What success metric does our product help customers improve, and by how much?
- How can we make a strong business case for users switching?
- What features are our users currently getting the most value from?
- How can we get people to experience the value our product delivers faster?
- How can we keep users coming back and, even better, telling their friends?
- If we're still not growing, what do we need to change and when might we need to consider a change in strategy (aka pivot)?

These are all questions The Growth Equation aims to help you consider.

Unsurprisingly many of these questions are the sorts of things that come up when using tools like the Business Model Canvas and Lean Canvas. I believe that the period between launching your product and finding Product-Market Fit is about iterating your product, business model, and acquisition strategy in order to find the answers to these questions that work best for you. This also means that if things aren't going to plan, you can use tools like the Lean Canvas to understand which parts of your business model aren't working and might need to change.

Problem	Solution	Unique value proposition	Unfair advantage	Customer segments
List your customers' top 3 problems. **2**	Outline possible solution for each problem. **4**	Single, clear, compelling. Turns unaware visitor into interested prospect. **3**	Something that can't be easily copied or bought. **9**	List your target customers and users. **1**
Existing alternatives List how these problems are solved today.	**Key metrics** List key numbers telling how your business is doing today. **8**	**High-level concept** List your X for Y analogy. eg YouTube = Flickr for videos.	**Channels** List your path to customers. **5**	**Early adopters** List characteristics of your ideal customer.
Cost structure List your fixed and variable costs **7**			**Revenue streams** List your sources of revenue **6**	

Figure 4.3: The Lean Product Canvas.

Let's start this exploration of Go-to-Market Strategy by making sure you're targeting the right customers.

Ideal Customer vs. Beachhead Customers

Many early stage startups will devise what's called an Ideal Customer Profile (ICP), which is essentially a snapshot of the type of customer you think will get the most value out of your product. For B2C (Business-to-Consumer) products, your ICP is going to be an individual, so the profile will likely contain personal information like their job title, income bracket, and where they work. As such, for B2C customers your ICP is essentially the same as your Buyer Persona. However, for B2B

(Business-to-Business) companies, your ICP is likely to be a type of company (as distinct from your Buyer Persona). This profile will include things like the sector the customer works in, the number of employees, turnover, and geographic location.

While it's important for founders to think big, I often see early stage startups target overly sophisticated ICPs straight out of the gate. These are often the late majority customers who would be a great fit in two years once the company has reached Feature Parity and/or Product-Market Fit. These late majority customers tend to be fairly discerning, however, and come with a big list of asks and expectations. For instance, rather than targeting a scrappy startup, founders might try to target an enterprise customer that will require reporting functions, complex custom workflows, dedicated customer support, and SOC2 or ISO 27001 compliance. While it's tempting to try and land the occasional whale, it's often easier to start with a less-demanding (and more forgiving) customer.

I generally look for customers who've been overlooked by the current incumbents: people whose needs aren't being precisely met and who would be easily tempted away by a highly targeted experience. This would mean that, rather than trying to create a 10X product for everyone, you would find an underserved niche and create a 2X product just for them.

This approach requires finding one or two things that this audience really cares about and delivering them well. For example, rather than starting life as a fully featured design app, Canva initially launched as a tool for making high school yearbooks. Once they'd served this limited niche market well, they were able to expand into other areas like making flyers, posters, and social media assets. It was only later that Canva started targeting more sophisticated marketing teams.

I generally call these segments Beachhead Customers, after the military concept of the same name. In military circles, a beachhead is the place where you land your forces, muster resources, and use as a staging post to expand. By focusing on a small number of beachheads, military leaders can concentrate their efforts in a few strategically important places, rather than spreading themselves too thin.

While I avoid using too many military metaphors—we're building companies rather than occupying a territory after all—I do believe identifying a Beachhead Customer is a good strategy. These are customers you believe you have a higher than average chance of securing with the product and resources you currently have. Once you've secured these easier-to-acquire customers, you can then land and expand to adjacent areas.

Finding Your Beachhead Customers

Most likely, you already have a working hypothesis on who your Beachhead Customers are. This is a result of your early discovery calls and of identifying which customers from your alpha and beta derive the most value from the product. It's quite common at this point to prove that hypothesis wrong, by the way—hence the hypothesis rather than an absolute. Perhaps your hypothesis was that product managers would get the most value out of your business dashboard app, when it turns out that freelancers and small business owners seem to be using it more frequently.

Most startup advice suggests that founders should build their early product with a highly targeted set of customers in mind and then build out from there. While this is true, if you end up picking the wrong users, you might spend six months and several development cycles building custom features for that user type, only to realize that you've built for the wrong audience and need to pivot. As we saw in the previous chapter, it's often helpful to build a slightly more general MVP (Minimum Viable Product), obtain many different types of customers, and see which of them gain the most value. Once you've tested a few different potential landing spots—to extend the beachhead metaphor— you'll have a much better understanding of where to marshal your resources to meet the least resistance.

Taking a Sales-or Marketing-Led Approach

Most of the early stage acquisition techniques we discussed in the previous chapter fall into either the sales or marketing camp. While I'm a huge fan of Product-Led Growth—a technique that leverages existing usage to generate new usage—you're still going to need early users for your Product-Led activities to work. As a result, Product-Led companies tend to grow surprisingly slowly before reaching Product-Market Fit. As such, it's much more likely that your early growth will come from traditional sales or marketing strategy in order to start your growth flywheel spinning. So which approach do you pick?

Whether you decide to take a Sales-or Marketing-Led approach will depend on a number of factors, including the strength and appropriateness of your existing network, the maturity of the market, the price and complexity of the sale, how easy it is to reach your target audience, and the makeup of your team.

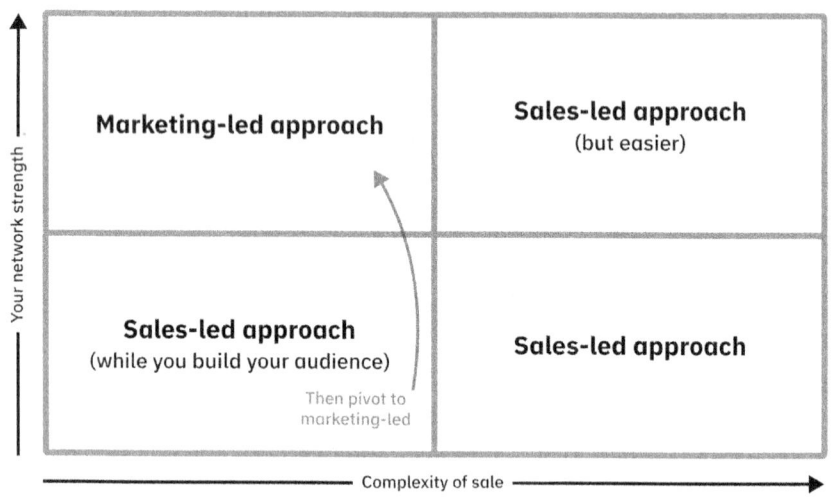

Figure 4.4: A 4x4 demonstrating how the strength of your network and the complexity of the sale might influence your GTM.

If you already have a large following among your target audience, the value of your product is clear, and it's a relatively affordable self-serve offering, a Marketing-Led approach is likely to generate a good amount of early interest. You can effectively piggyback on the founder's existing network, capture interest, and use that to grow an audience interested in receiving your marketing communications.

If you have a good network but the value of your product isn't immediately clear, the cost of sale is high, or the buying and integration cycle is long, you might find that a Sales-Led approach will be more effective. This consists of targeting people directly rather than taking a broadcast approach (an outbound versus inbound approach). It's likely your actual strategy will combine both of these approaches, but it makes sense to focus slightly more of your time (70/30) on the sales side of things.

If you don't have a strong network, you can still take a Marketing-Led approach. Just be aware that you'll first have to find, buy, or build your audience before you can start marketing to them. This typically takes time and money, which means more time before you start seeing the results. This is one of the reasons why founders who lack a strong network typically opt for the direct approach: contacting people through LinkedIn to introduce them to their product. You have much more control over who and how many people you can reach this way.

It's worth bearing in mind that if you have a relatively cheap product with a low Lifetime Customer Value (LCV), the direct approach usually isn't sustainable, as you'll end up spending more to acquire customers than you'll be able to capture. Don't worry too much about this at the start. As we saw in the previous chapter, you might need to do things that don't scale in the early stages of your business. This approach might work for the first few dozen customers—especially if you're using it to gain some impressive logos or useful customer intelligence—but you'll probably want to switch to a more scalable GTM strategy later on. If your product delivers a high LCV, an enterprise sales approach is likely to form a big part of your acquisition strategy moving forward.

Whatever your approach, be aware that acquiring customers for a new and untested product is often hard, slow going, and expensive. Once you've proved to your investors that you can build a product, the next thing they're going to want to see is whether you can build an effective and ultimately affordable Growth Engine. This usually comes down on the founder's shoulders, so nailing acquisition is key.

The Customer Acquisition Funnel

Whether you choose a Sales-or Marketing-Led approach, most of your early customers can be viewed through the lens of your Customer Acquisition Funnel.

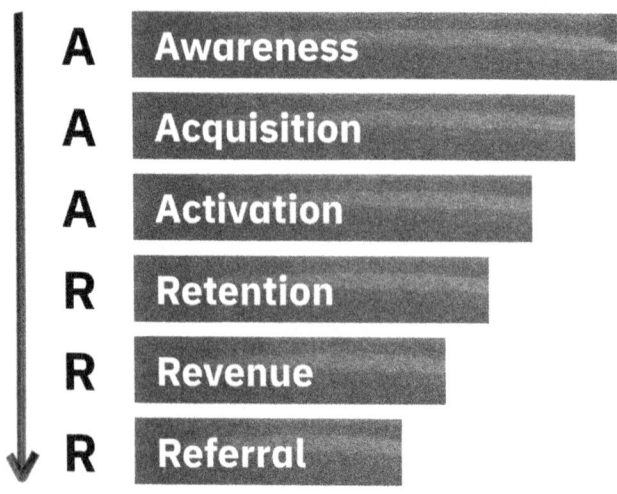

Figure 4.5: The Customer Acquisition Funnel.

The Customer Acquisition Funnel (sometimes called the sales funnel) is a view of how potential users flow through your system, dropping out at various points along the way. You start by driving customers into the top of funnel by generating awareness. Top-of-funnel activities include writing content aimed at people searching for the sorts of issues your product solves, or by identifying people who might have these issues and reaching out to them directly.

Once you've captured people's attention, you need to encourage them to sign up. This could be signing up for a trial or ideally paying for the full product. Many first-time founders believe that the work generally stops here. However, it's amazing how few people who sign up actually start using the product—a process known as Activation.

Once people are using your product, you need to do everything in your power to keep them engaged and receiving value, or they might churn (and leave your product prematurely). Your ability to keep users engaged and actively using your product is described as Retention. Your retained customers will generate revenue, both by paying for the existing service and potentially buying new services (this is known as Expansion Revenue). If your customers like the product, they might even help you gain new customers through Referrals.

At each step along the way, users will drop out. This is sometimes described as having a leaky funnel. In future chapters, we will look at each of these stages in more detail and explore ways of plugging the gaps to ensure that as much of that valuable traffic turns into active, happy, and profitable customers.

Setting Targets and Having a Plan

As I've mentioned previously, it's super common for founders to build a product they have high conviction around, under the belief that users will discover their product, realize instantly how great it is, and sign up on the spot. So these founders will set high-level aspirational targets, have a big launch, and hope that the users start to flow in. Time and time again, I've seen founders fling open the doors expecting a deluge of users, only to be surprised by a relatively modest trickle.

One of the problems with this approach is that these aspirational targets are usually uncoupled from anything practical the founders can do to affect them. So they become a wish-list item rather than something that can be monitored and changed. This is where a bit of sensible business planning comes in.

As a founder, you probably know what sort of target you're going to need to reach in order to secure your next raise. If you don't, you really should. Let's say, for instance, that you've got a handful of early users, have proved to your investors that some of them are willing to pay, and have raised a seed round as a result. You know that you're going to want to be doing at least $1M in ARR (Annual Recurring Revenue) in 12 months to secure the next round, which means ideally you'll be adding $250K in ARR each quarter, or just over $80K a month.

If you're following a Sales-Led approach and are charging each customer $10K a month, you know that you're going to need to land two customers each quarter to deliver $250K ARR. By knowing or estimating the various conversion rates in your sales funnel (i.e., how many emails generate how many demos, which generate how many trial customers, which convert into how many paying customers), you can work out the sales efforts required to hit your goals.

Monthly revenue per customer	10K
Number of customers	2
Time to deal close	1 month
Close rate	50%
SQL/MQL	4
ARR	250K

Figure 4.6: Growth activity plan.

Similarly, if you're following a Freemium model pushing free users to a $5 per month contract, you can work out that you're going to need around 80K users a quarter or 25K users a month in order to deliver $1M in ARR at a Freemium-to-Paid conversion rate of 6%. If you know that your conversion from a website visitor to a Freemium user is 5%, that means your marketing team is going to need to drive around 500K visitors to your site a month.

To be able to put together a logical plan, you're going to need to ask yourself the following questions:

- How many website visitors do I need to have each month?
- How many outbound emails do I need to send each month?
- How many customer calls or demos do I need to be doing each week?
- How much of my revenue should be coming from inbound versus outbound and from sales versus marketing?
- How much time and money do I need to spend on acquisition activities to comfortably meet my next fundraising target?

Answering these questions will help you accurately predict the volume of sales and/or amount of marketing effort you need to undertake and what resources you need in place. It will also hint at what activities you might need to try if you aren't hitting your desired targets. This might mean increasing the number of outbound emails your sales team sends or increasing their open rate; it might mean raising the free-to-paid conversion rate and/or the average contract value.

The result of this work is typically described as a Financial Model. It sounds quite sophisticated, but it's really just a bunch of assumptions you're making about the efficiency of your acquisition funnel, costs, and revenue, which you're capturing in some sort of spreadsheet. This allows you to test your assumptions, track your progress, and change your approach when necessary.

Summary

While it's tempting to launch your product in the hope that people will turn up, hope is never an especially effective strategy. Instead, you need to develop a Go-to-Market Strategy outlining how you are going to launch your product, acquire customers, and grow. Most GTM strategies fall either into the sales or marketing camps, so we're going to look at each of these in detail in the next two chapters. Whichever approach you take, it's best not to rely on luck, so set clear and achievable targets—ideally on a weekly basis—and then closely monitor your progress. It generally takes longer than most founders expect to get things working. As such, you need to have an iterative mindset and constantly be assessing the various elements of your GTM strategy: Do we have the right target market? Is the product delivering enough value? Is the revenue model correct? Are we targeting the right channels? Does our proposition land? These are all questions we're going to help you answer over the rest of this book.

Next Steps

I'm constantly amazed by the number of founders I meet who are unable to articulate a meaningful ICP clearly. Instead, they'll share some vague slide explaining that their target market is "any company between 10 and 10,000 people who think IT security is important."

If you don't have a clear picture of your ICP, you're going to struggle with knowing who to approach, how to approach them, and what to say when you do. You'll also struggle to prioritize your roadmap, often leading to an overly generic me-too product that doesn't really work for anybody. As such, if you have an existing ICP written down somewhere I'd review that document now to make sure you have a clearly articulated Beachhead Customer. And if you haven't written something down yet, do so now.

However, don't just stop at one beachhead. Try coming up with a selection of different potential customers. What is it about your product that is particularly suited to that customer type? What does that customer look like? What do they care about? Where do they hang out and how are you going to find them? It sounds simple but your Go-to-Market Strategy is all about identifying a gap in the market where your product can excel—and then figuring out how you're going to approach said market. This is just a hypothesis at the moment, so having a few different Beachhead Customers to try, and a few different ways to approach them, creates some resilience. It allows you to look at each prospective Beachhead Customer and the strategy you're going to use to acquire them and pick the approach you think is most likely to succeed. If it doesn't succeed, however, you have a number of alternate landing sites in your back pocket to try next, rather than having to go back to the drawing board.

The other benefit of writing down your customer segment and acquisition strategy hypothesis (beyond making it easy for you to think through your approach) is that it allows you to realize that you might very well need to pivot your approach later on. While you might need to make certain product decisions to effectively target different segments, this awareness can prevent you from creating a product that is so specific to one type of customer before you've had a chance to validate their needs, that you end up painting yourself into a corner.

CHAPTER 5

Founder-Led Sales

I n the early stages of your business, the founder is hands down the best person to do sales, as they have the best understanding of the problem, the market, and the product vision. This allows them to connect with prospects over the pain they are feeling, address most of their sales objections, and get them excited about the way things are developing. They also have the most skin in the game, allowing them to go the extra mile necessary to close each and every sale. From the buyer's perspective, it's actually quite an ego boost to have a conversation with the founder themselves rather than a member of their team. There's something about experiencing a founder's passion that leads to a much higher close rate.

Sadly I meet many early stage founders who claim they're not very good at sales. This often revolves around the myth that you're either a born salesperson or not, so they'd prefer to pass this off to a pro. In truth—and like most things in life—sales is a learned skill. And the reason you think you're no good is because you've made a conscious decision not to lean in. Ironically I'd argue that most founders are a lot better at sales than they think. After all, they've been able to sell the company to early employees who could almost certainly get a better-paid job elsewhere. They've also been able to sell the company to investors who could have given their money to any number of other founders. This is borne out by the fact that I regularly see startups needing to hire two or three salespeople to have the same impact as one highly motivated founder. So what's going on here?

Why Some Founders Avoid Sales

I think one of the reasons founders avoid doing sales is that it isn't always a bundle of laughs. There's usually a lot of admin work involved with sales—assembling lists of prospects, writing cold emails, sending calendar invites, organizing demos, and then following up afterward—all things your average founder might not have the patience for. Sales usually involves talking to people, which can be super hard for the more introverted among us. Sales often feels squishy, imprecise, and hard to scale, which engineers can find particularly frustrating. Sales also has a bit of a cultural stigma, especially among design- and engineering-focused founders. It also means having to deal with quite a lot of rejection, which is never comfortable. As such, you can understand why founders often want to avoid doing the hard and unglamorous work and delegate it to somebody else.

Many founders believe that good products simply sell themselves and will point to companies like Slack and Zoom or trends like Product-Led Growth as proof. As such, there's a general feeling that the highest-leverage use of their time is coming up with new feature ideas and deciding what to ship next. And let's be honest here: Product is just a lot more fun, so it's easy for founders to convince themselves that this is where they should be spending their time.

If you dig into the success stories of those companies, however, you'll learn that a whopping 40% of the revenue Slack made in 2019 came from just 575 enterprise customers.[15] Zoom went further, explaining how "our sales model allows us to efficiently turn a single nonpaying user into a full enterprise deployment" and that just "344 customers contributed 30% of revenue in the fiscal year ended January 31, 2019." This goes to show that even the most Product-Led companies rely heavily on sales.

The truth is that Founder-Led Sales is often the best way to get early customers onto your platform. It's cost-effective as it does not require a ton of money to grow an audience, pay for ads, or produce a ton of content. It's also fairly immediate. You can create a list of prospects

---

[15] https://www.investopedia.com/articles/investing/012616/how-does-slack-work-and-make-money.asp

tomorrow, send some emails, and start having conversations by the end of the week. No more writing content or producing ads and then hoping somebody shows up. As such, it's something you have quite a bit of agency over. Need to double the number of demo calls you do? Simply double the number of outreach emails you send.

Lastly, taking a Sales-Led approach puts you right in the middle of a conversation with your target customers, providing a super valuable source of insight and product feedback. Do they understand your positioning and does it resonate with them? Does your product solve a meaningful problem for them? Meaningful enough for them to pay for? What objections do they give you and how might these affect your product, marketing, and GTM strategy?

A well-honed sales approach allows a founder to drive the first $1M ARR (Annual Recurring Revenue) all on their own—something your team will appreciate and your investors will love. So, how can founders overcome their psychological barriers and operationalize their approach?

Using Discovery as an Early Sales Approach

Though founders often feel shy when it comes to sales, they usually have no problem reaching out to people for a customer discovery call. As such, I generally recommend founders build their early sales motion off the back of these conversations.

In a typical customer discovery call, you aim to understand your prospective customer's problems in order to create a meaningful solution. So you ask people about their role, what a typical day looks like, what they find challenging about their work, what tools or processes they currently use to solve these issues, what features of capabilities might make their lives easier, and what their lives would be like if their key problems could be solved. You note the answers, thank them for their help, and let them know that you'll be in touch when the product is ready.

A sales discovery call is very similar in structure. You might start by asking prospective customers to describe their current situation: what have they been brought in to achieve, what's not working about the current process, and what are the negative consequences as a result. You might then ask your prospective customers to describe their ideal future state: If they were able to solve these problems, what would it mean to them and their business? How might they use the extra time or money they save to further advance their goals? Now it's time to explore what features they need to achieve these goals. Ideally, you'll already have many of these features in your product, allowing you to position your product as a step toward its ideal future state. It's also a good idea to find out what success looks like for your prospective customers, so you can align your product with their success.

If folks seem interested, you might be able to close a sale then and there. However, if you're shy about asking for money—something you really need to get over—you could try to land them as a design partner or beta user or get them started on a proof of concept or pilot project (all euphemisms for a product trial). Knowing what a successful outcome looks like for the customer will allow you to set some criteria for the trial. Once the trial has ended, you can reach back out to see whether the product did everything you said it would and delivered the agreed-upon goals. Of course you hope the answer is yes, in which case it should be relatively easy to close the sale. However, if they've not received enough value to commit, that's useful information as well.

Current State	Future State
• What are they trying to achieve? • How's it currently going? • What's getting in the way? • What are the risks of not achieving their goals?	• What would their ideal workflow look like? • What would this enable them to do? • How would they measure this? • Why wouldn't they prioritize this?
Required Capabilities	**Success Metrics**
• What features does their solution need in order to get them from the current state to the future state?	• How will they be able to tell if this trial has been a success? • Can you quantify this?

Figure 5.1: Simple question sheet for a consultative-based sales call.

You might also look at using discovery calls as a means to find new leads. One way to do this is the direct approach, by asking them "Who else do you know who has this problem and might be interested in talking to us?" Another way is to ask people about the sites they read, the communities they belong to, and the influencers they follow, and then use that to find (and reach) more people like them.

This might sound obvious but be aware that the person who has the problem your product solves might not be the actual buyer. As such, while you can learn a lot of useful information from these folks, it might not get you any closer to landing a sale. Your goal with these early calls is to create an internal champion for your product. It's also to understand who has the final say about buying this product, what that person cares about, and what the decision-making process looks like. If you can build a strong enough champion, they should be able to help you get the sale over the line. However, don't make it their responsibility as they definitely won't be able to do your sales job for you, so ask for an intro to the decision-maker and set up a meeting with them next.

Using discovery calls as a lightweight sales process can be a great way for founders to ease into the sales mindset. In fact, experienced salespeople will often use a version of this approach called Consultative Selling or Gap Selling. It's an approach that reminds me of a scene from Enter the Dragon, where Bruce Lee describes his fighting style as "The Art of Fighting Without Fighting." I see sales discovery calls as "The Art of Selling Without Selling." So how do you go about finding the right people to talk to in the first place?

Just Don't Forget to Qualify Your Leads

Remember earlier when I said how much folks like speaking to founders? Founders hold an elevated place in our society, so getting an email from a founder can make you feel special. What if I connect with this founder and they become a useful part of my network? What if the product blows up and I might be able to get a job there one day? Hell, what if they become the next Steve Jobs and I've got a great anecdote to tell about how I knew them when they were working out of their mom's garage? All of this means that people are more likely to accept a call from a founder than a generic salesperson—especially if you harbor desires to become a founder yourself one day. Having the ability to open otherwise closed doors is amazing. However, it comes with some obvious drawbacks.

I've met many founders who love talking about their product to anybody and everybody possible. They gain a huge amount of energy and conviction from speaking to people who get their vision and are as excited by the product as they are. It's hugely motivating. As such, founders will regularly tell me about the amazing sales calls they've had with people at impressive-sounding companies who they feel sure will sign up next month. I check back later only to find that the conversation didn't go anywhere (but there's always a new and exciting person to take their place).

The reason these calls go nowhere is simple: The founder got so tied up in an exciting conversation with an interesting person that they failed to qualify the lead. By this I mean they failed to find out where this person was in the buying cycle and whether they actually had the authority to make a purchasing decision or had influence with the person who did. All too often, founders will end up having an engrossing conversation with somebody who never had any intention of buying the product. While this can be fun at first, these conversations can quickly become demoralizing.

Now I'm not saying you should avoid these calls altogether. They can be educational and energizing and help lay the groundwork for a future sale. Be aware, however, that there are many people out there who work in fairly boring jobs and the most exciting thing that happened during their day was talking to you. As such, get used to asking qualifying questions and be willing to curtail an otherwise fun conversation if it's clearly not heading in a useful direction. Many people mistakenly believe that the job of a salesperson is to convince otherwise reticent people to buy their product. The real skill is to identify potential buyers as quickly as possible—and filter everybody else out. Do this enough and you'll learn to pick up the right signals, allowing you to prioritize your most likely prospects.

Prospecting and Outreach

Remember that slide in your pitch deck where you said how unbelievably huge your Total Addressable Market (TAM) was? The slide that gave your investors the confidence that there were enough potential customers to support a "venture scale business?" This is where you start putting those claims to the test.

Prospecting is about identifying the individuals inside your Ideal Customer Profile (ICP) company, who are looking for a solution to the problem your product solves and either have the authority to buy your solution or the influence to convince somebody else to buy it for them. Sales is a time-consuming process, so the more accurate you can be with your targeting, the more likely people will be to respond positively and convert.

Ideal Customer Profile

Industry	Enterprise SaaS in regulated areas (fintech, insuretech, healthtech)
Geography	USA, UK, EU
Revenue	$2M–$20M
Headcount	20–100 employees
Pain Points	• Low in-house security expertise, causing anxiety • Unable to serve client requests
Business Goals	• Land more enterprise customers (who expect better security) • Raise their next round
Buying Signals	• Recent funding announcement • New CTO hire • Questions around SOC2 compliance
Tech Stack	AWS

Figure 5.2: Simple ICP.

Most founders start by building up a picture of their target prospect, sometimes described as a Buyer Persona. This includes things like their job title or level, the sector they work in, the size of their company, where it's headquartered, and maybe their revenue or funding stage. You can then plug these search terms into a simple tool like LinkedIn Sales Navigator to bring back a list of prospects. With such a huge TAM, this could quickly become overwhelming, so think about segmenting your customers into themed lists of around 2,500 prospects each. I suggest this number in part because it's manageable, and in part because some of the sales tools I'm going to recommend later use this as the upper limit on their free accounts.

Buyer Persona

Title	CTO
Responsibilities	• Managing a team of 2—20 engineers • Ultimately responsible for platform security
Challenges	• Have grown out of AWS inbuilt security features • Is needing to implement SOC2 compliance for the first time
Org Alignment	Company co-founder. Will need CEO approval.
Motivations	• Needs to increase team velocity. Worried about anything that will slow this down. • Realises that cloud security is outside their comfort zone and doesn't want to be held responsible for a security breach
Promotion Path	• Growing the team • Improving team velocity • Making smart resourcing choices

Figure 5.3: Simple buyer persona.

LinkedIn allows you to contact people directly through its InMail feature. However, you're generally limited to between 50 and 150 InMail credits per month, which puts a cap on your outbound messaging. Emails sent using inMail are also flagged as such, which can also set people's spam alarms tingling. As such, many sales executives will use LinkedIn Sales Navigator to create their lists, and then use a host of other tools like PhantomBuster, Wiza, Lusha, Clearbit Connect, Anymail Finder, ZoomInfo, Apollo, or Kaspr to find those prospects' email addresses through publicly available sources and contact them directly. That's great, but what are you actually going to say?

Crafting a Successful Outreach Message

The way you craft your outreach can have a significant effect on the response rate. I've seen good outbound campaigns that have a response rate of 35% or more, while bad campaigns can generate less than half a percent. Some people will claim that a response rate of 1–2% is pretty standard, while other benchmarks suggest an average response rate of 8.5%. As founders who really understand their audience, I know you can do better than average, so I recommend shooting for a response rate of 15% and continuing to iterate your message until you get close to that.

We've all got very good at scanning emails to see if they've come from a real person or a bulk mailout. As such, I'd avoid using things like rich text formatting, tables, images, attachments, or numerous links, and stick to plain text. I'd also avoid sending super long emails that force people to wade through paragraphs of text; keep things fairly short and sweet. The reason most outbound emails fail is because they come across as disingenuous and spammy. This breaks the social convention that we're meant to be polite and respond to people, making them easy for people to ignore.

Often the language people use in emails is too generic and fails to connect with the users on a human level. Other times they try to be clever and end up antagonizing the person on the other end. There's a special place in hell for salespeople who send cute emails saying things like "As you haven't responded to my last five emails, does that mean we're breaking up?" Instead, it's important to adopt a casual, friendly tone, rather than being overly formal, salesy, chummy, or clever. Consider personalizing the email where possible. So do you have a friend or colleague in common? Did you see them at a conference? Did you like something they said on Twitter? Add this in to provide some personal color (and prove you're not a bot).

Starting a Conversation

Novice salespeople will try to get their emails to do the selling for them. However, the goal of that initial email is usually to get a response—not to set up a meeting or close a sale. As such, I wouldn't necessarily even mention your product in the first email. Instead, you want to talk to them about the challenges they're experiencing. So consider opening with a personal message, ask a question relating to a problem you think they might have, and then offer to share something useful or intriguing. For instance:

> Hi [name], I really liked that [article you wrote/comment you made] on [location] the other day. As an [insert role], I was curious about what you're currently doing about [problem]. I've [written an article about this subject/have an idea how to solve it] and I was wondering [if you'd be up for giving me some feedback/sharing your approach]?

This is obviously a super basic script, so I'd expect you to write something a little more tailored. Be human, show interest, mention shared contacts or reference clients the person might know, ask questions and, if possible, have something useful to offer beyond your wonderful new product. It's usually much better to offer something of value first, like an interesting article or an invite to a webinar, than to jump straight into a sales pitch. One of the other benefits of including a link to an article, report, or demo video is it allows you to see who's engaged with your content and might be up for a deeper conversation.

When getting in touch with people, it's also worth thinking a little about sales triggers. These are things going on in your prospects' world that might make them more amiable to your offering. For instance, have they just switched jobs, raised a round of funding, come off of an especially positive sales quarter, come to the end of a big contract, or started a new financial year? Similarly, have they just been through a big round of redundancies, had a poor quarter, or are right in the middle of their busy period and in crunch mode? Essentially—is now the right time to contact them, or would it be better to hold off until a more appropriate time?

In the previous chapter, we talked about the need for founders to do things that don't scale. The founding story of Intercom is a great example of this. Des Traynor, one of the company's co-founders, explains how, in the early days of Intercom, he'd write up to 100 customized emails a day to prospective users. "All day every day I'd email people to tell them about Intercom, show them what Intercom might look like for them, and hear their feedback." Des explains. "I did this 100% by hand, and if I was to do it all again today I'd still do it by hand."

Des goes on to explain why this manual approach proved useful: "The approximately 100 or so emails I sent every day built on the previous day's learnings. When you've read the 40 replies and understood common confusions, you can address them in the following day's new set of emails. Every email was pretty much unique, which meant that the automatable boilerplate was minimal. Doing it by hand helped me avoid all the telltale signs of a bad outbound campaign."

Writing 100 emails a day is tough and likely to lead to a repetitive strain injury if you're not careful. So once you've successfully acquired your first batch of customers manually, you'll probably want to start automating the process. However, don't skip straight to automation, as this is how you end up with a 2% response rate rather than a 15% one.

Automating Your Sales Sequence

Emailing people out of the blue is likely to lead to a fairly low response rate. As such, modern sales teams will typically put together some sort of sales sequence. A sales sequence is the series of steps you're going to take when reaching out to somebody. On LinkedIn, this might be visiting their profile, reading or liking a few articles they've written, following them, verifying their skills, reaching out to connect, sending an initial message, and then following up if they don't respond. The goal is to warm somebody up a little, so the contact request doesn't come entirely out of the blue. Doing all these actions can be quite time-consuming, so early founders will often hire a sales development representative or sales assistant to do the initial prospecting for them. There are also an increasing number of tools like Dripify that will automate this process for you. This allows founders to focus on the highest-leverage tasks: hopping on a call with prospective customers and closing the deal.

Far too many founders send a single email and then give up on that contact if they don't hear back. I get this. We've all been bugged by an overly persistent salesperson. I occasionally get promotional emails that look interesting but I don't have the bandwidth to engage with them right now, so I will save them for later. In fact, it might take a few emails with different approaches before I think, "Hmm, that actually looks quite interesting." As such, you'll probably need to create multiple email templates in order to capture somebody's attention, potentially up to seven. And even though I joked earlier about those annoying "I'm breaking up with you emails," it's often sensible to send one last email letting folks know that you're not going to be bothering them anymore. If they actually were interested in your offering and just got used to the idea that you were always going to be in their inbox, this last email can often be the trigger they need.

Be aware that email providers rightfully try to protect their customers from unsolicited emails, so rank the domains your emails are sent from. If you're interested in seeing how your domain currently ranks, tools like GlockApps can give you a quick health check. To improve the credibility of your domain, you're going to want to be seen to be sending emails that get through people's spam filters and generate a response. If you're sending emails from your main domain, this will happen naturally. However, you might want to be protective of your main domain to make sure it doesn't get downgraded in the future. As such, many sales teams will set up subdomains to use for sending their email communications, inoculating the main domain from any potential blowback. These subdomains need warming up, so there are a number of email warm-up tools you can use like Warmup Inbox, Warmbox, MailReach, Allegrow, or Lemwarm to achieve this. These tools will send out and respond to a bunch of fake email traffic for a few weeks, raising both the reputation and legitimacy of your domain and IP address in the process.

Managing your outbound campaigns requires some sort of Customer Relationship Manager (CRM) to keep track of who has been contacted, how, and when. It also requires specialist tools to manage the sending of bulk emails and help keep them out of people's spam folders. As such, it might be worth exploring tools like Attio, Pipedrive, HubSpot, Streak CRM, Clay, Lemlist, Instantly, and Outreach as you slowly build up your sales tech stack.

While email and direct messages are powerful, it's worth keeping an eye out for new (yet-to-be-exploited) channels. For instance, at the time of writing this book, LinkedIn had just released its voice memos functionality, and several founders I've been supporting have found this to be an effective approach. This is largely because of the novelty factor: This might be the very first voice memo this person has received so they're keen to check it out. This approach won't last long, but it will last long enough for the early adopters who jumped on this channel when it was fresh.

Setting Activity Targets

At the start of your sales journey, activity is key. The more quality emails you send, the more calls you make, the more demos you run, and the more proposals you send, the higher your hit rate will be. As with all sales motions, you'll get many rejections and this can get disheartening. One way to get around this blocker is to set explicit targets for the number of contacts you're going to make each week and carve out specific blocks of time when you're going to focus on this. Otherwise, the tendency is to let this slide in favor of the more fun product stuff.

Let's assume that you've just launched your product, your Average Contract Value (ACV) is $25K and you're aiming to hit $1M ARR by the end of the year. This means you need to close 40 deals a year or 10 a quarter. If we assume that you are able to close 20% of all the people you schedule a demo with, that means you need to schedule 50 demos a quarter. If we assume a 5% response rate to your sales outreach (which is small but not unreasonable), that will mean needing to contact 1,000 prospects a quarter or around 75 per week. These are some sobering figures, but they give a realistic estimate of the sales activity required to hit that $1M mark.

It sounds obvious, but it's important to note that sales targets aren't just passive predictions. Instead, they are something you're actively driving toward. This means knowing whether you are going to hit your numbers for the week, month, or quarter, and doing something about it if you aren't. I'm constantly amazed how many founders see that they aren't going to hit their monthly targets, and just shrug their shoulders rather than getting on the phone. You wouldn't accept this from a salesperson, so hold yourself to a higher standard.

In order to keep yourself and your team accountable, I suggest setting up a weekly sales meeting with your team (or if it's just you, with your investors or sales coach). During this meeting, you should look at the level of activity you're doing, hone your qualification criteria, identify where people are in your pipeline, and most importantly plan what you need to do in order to move them to the next step. If things aren't going in the right direction, make a decision on what you're going to do to turn things around.

It's super important to keep your sales activity consistent. I remember one company pitching for investment that showed 100% Month-on-Month (MoM) growth in their first quarter of operation. With growth like that, I was definitely tempted to invest. However, it was now March and their figures stopped in December. I asked them to share their most recent figures, hoping to see a similar trend. To my surprise, their figures had dropped down to nothing. The founder explained that they'd spent the last three months focusing on the product, and so they hadn't been able to focus on sales. This gave me the sense that they'd really doubled down on sales in order to create a good impression for investors but had failed to build a sustainable Growth Engine. While a bit of variance is to be expected, it's a worry when founders go all in on sales in one quarter and then all in on product the next. It's much better to create a sustainable tempo that supports both.

Sales Velocity

Sales is partly a numbers game. Once you realize that you are generally able to close one in every five demos, there are two obvious things you can do to improve growth. The first is simply to set up more calls. You may struggle to do this on your own but might find help by hiring a founder associate or sales assistant.

The second thing you can do is improve your hit rate, by bringing it down from closing 1 in 5 demos to 1 in 4 (or even 1 in 3). There are plenty of things you can try here: more research up front for better-qualified leads, recording and analyzing your sales patter to smooth out the rough edges, and creating a list of stock responses to common objections you come across so you're not constantly freestyling.

Sometimes it's not about the volume of deals you can close, but the speed at which you can close them. If it usually takes you six weeks to close a deal, but you can get that down to four weeks, you've now improved your close rate by 50%.

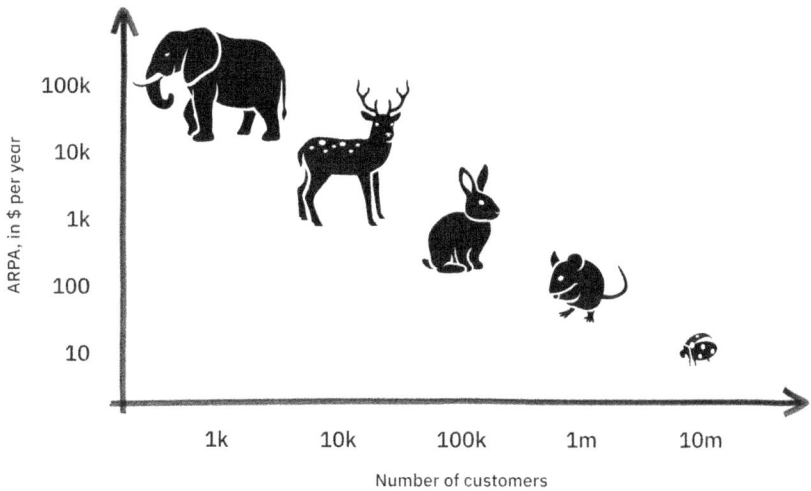

Figure 5.4: Christoph Janz of Point Nine Capital explains how there are five ways to build a $100M business, from the article of the same name.[16]

Deal size should also be considered. If you find that it takes you three months to close a $25K deal, but only three weeks to close a $10K deal, focusing on those smaller but easier-to-close deals might be sensible. Landing a nice juicy deer (sorry to my fellow vegetarians reading this) always feels great, but as a new salesperson, you might find it easier to land a brace of rabbits first.

This general concept is known as Sales Velocity, and founders following a Sales-Led approach should track this metric and do everything they can to speed it up.

Figure 5.5: How to calculate your Sales Velocity.

Your First Sales Hire(s)

Founders often look to hire an experienced salesperson fairly early in the process so they can go back to doing the stuff they love. However, they frequently get a shock two or three months later when they find that sales have gone down rather than up. This is because early stage sales are usually a lot scrappier and more vision-driven than in an established sales team. As a result, experienced sales leads often lack the processes, technology, support structures, internal competition, and brand equity that allowed them to thrive in their previous role. This is especially true if they come from a much larger company that has already found Product-Market Fit. Experienced salespeople will often come with a pre-existing playbook, only to find that what worked in their previous 10-person sales team, doesn't work here.

Instead of hiring a senior sales executive right off the bat, it's usually better if the founder stays focused on closing deals and hires a more junior person to provide sales support. Sometimes this is described as a Sales Development Representative (SDR), who can take manual prospecting work off the founder's shoulders. This includes doing some of the following tasks:

- Using LinkedIn, Twitter, industry news, and other tools to identify and classify prospective customers
- Contacting prospective customers (often logged in as the founder) to introduce your company and set up initial calls
- Creating email and message flows, often with the help of the founder to ensure tone of voice consistency
- Managing the sales pipeline and CRM
- Setting up a good sales tech stack
- Reviewing sales calls and creating sales FAQs, which help the founder answer common sales objections
- Helping the founder close prospects, issue contracts, take payment, and onboard new customers

I think the perfect first sales hire is a bit of a hybrid. They're part salesperson, part SDR, part customer success associate, and part product manager. They're somebody who doesn't mind doing prospecting, talking to customers about their needs, and closing deals. They also understand the product roadmap, can help customers get set up and start getting value quickly, and can use their customer insight to make the product better. Essentially you're looking for somebody who can build the sales playbook while in flight. This might mean looking to hire a founder associate or GTM manager rather than a traditional sales exec. These fairly new (and largely made up) roles mean that the profile can vary widely: Sometimes it's a recent business graduate who is looking to break into the startup space and willing to get their hands dirty; other times it might be a former founder who ran out of runway and is looking for their next gig.

Some people might feel nervous about hiring a former founder—or if you are being ungenerous, a failed founder. Just remember what I said at the beginning of this chapter: Founders are naturally skilled at sales based on the amount of buy-in they need to get up and running. If they have a penchant for early stage sales, they might be a good short-term fit. With these early hires, you're simply looking for someone who can be a multiplier of your time so you can focus on the higher value tasks.

If you do choose to hire a more traditional salesperson, you may be better off hiring two at the same time. I know this might sound expensive, but consider that salespeople tend to be competitive. Having someone to compete with is likely to improve the performance of each person. It's also likely you have never run a sales team before, so it's difficult to know what good looks like. Having two salespeople allows for comparison and for setting a baseline, so you'll know what to do if performance varies wildly between the two.

Money is an excellent motivator (this is not surprising). While founders generally want to treat everybody equally—because we're all in it together—the best salespeople expect a meaningful commission structure. A common place to start for tech sales is to have On Target Earnings (OTE) around 20% of their sales targets: 50-60% of this would be their base salary with the rest coming from commission.

Let's say your new salesperson has a quarterly sales quota of $150K at an ACV of $25K, which means they'll need to close two deals a month (which sounds reasonable). Let's say the average OTE salary for a mid-level salesperson in your area is $120K. You'll set their base salary at $72K (60%), and you'll give them another $48K (40%) if they hit all their targets. This makes their commission 8%, which equates to $2,000 for every deal they land. If your salespeople regularly hit their quotas but don't go over, you might want to consider a tiered model. For instance, any sales over their $150K quota gets paid at 10% instead of 8%. You might also want to add in a four-month "clawback," which basically means that if a customer churns within four months, the salesperson has to give their commission back. This is useful as it helps prevent reps from misselling in order to close a deal.

Getting External Help

Because so many founders dislike sales, there's a tendency to outsource this function to a lead generation agency. These companies offer to do the initial prospecting and outreach for you, before handing over warm leads for you to close. While this sounds good on paper, I've met few if any founders who were happy with the results. Generally companies will use a lead gen agency for three to six months, get a few meetings but no deals, and then finish the relationship no better off. Interestingly, this generally costs about the same as hiring an internal SDR, so I recommend folks do that instead.

Another option could be to hire an external sales coach, who will help a novice founder improve their sales strategy. This will usually include reviewing their ICP, sales pipeline, messaging, sales material, and tech stack, as well as running some demo sales pitches and providing feedback. So if you are struggling with Founder-Led Sales, getting a recommendation for a good sales coach from another founder or VC might be a sensible way to go.

Summary

Founders are generally the best people to run sales in the early days. As such, though it's tempting to try and outsource sales, it's something I'd encourage every founder to own at the start. This is because founders have a clear passion for their product and this passion tends to come through in conversations with prospective buyers. They also have an encyclopedic knowledge of the space, so are generally much better at answering questions and addressing concerns. Talking to prospective customers can also give founders a huge insight into the product roadmap and what to build next. Once founders have understood the sales motion themselves, it also becomes much easier to build and manage a sales team to take over.

Just remember that the modern sales motion has many technical parts, so you might need to get some help optimizing your messaging and setting up your tech stack. You might also benefit from having an SDR or junior person do more of the grunt work, including prospecting, automating sales sequences, and setting up initial calls.

Next Steps

Start by doing a quick review of your current sales motion. Look at your sales funnel to see on average how many outreach messages you need to send for each demo, and how many demos you need to do to land a paying client. Now look at your annual revenue targets to make sure your weekly activity is aligned with this goal. Use this data to create a sales dashboard for yourself and your team. Share this with your investors and commit to specific activity targets and month-on-month improvements.

Now take a quick look at your existing clients to make sure that they are a good fit with your ICP. Often reviewing existing clients will give you a better insight into the types of people who a) truly get value from your product and b) you know you can close. If there's any discrepancy between the two, make sure to update your ICP and hone your targeting accordingly.

Next, review the contact messages you're sending out and how successful they are. Only getting a response rate of a couple of percent? If you're sure that you're absolutely targeting the right ICP, then it's time to tweak your messaging. Make sure you're setting up a good sequence rather than sending a single message. Try experimenting with different messages so that you're constantly pushing your hit rate up. Don't stop until you're regularly getting a 15% response rate from the emails you send.

Regularly record and review your sales calls. Look at the calls that went well, note what you did, and incorporate this info into your sales script. Make note of any common sales objections and the most effective way you've learned to deal with them. Now look at some of your near misses. When did the conversation turn? What would you do differently if you could run that call again? See every sales call as a learning opportunity. If you can improve by just 1% after each call, you'll be doubling or tripling your hit rate in a matter of months.

Capture the above information in some sort of sales playbook. It doesn't have to be fancy. A simple Notion document will do. If your sales motion is written down it becomes much easier to improve. It's also the perfect onboarding tool for your first few sales hires.

If you think of your sales motion as a machine, your job is to make sure it's humming. So do you have the right fuel? Is it well lubricated? Are the spark plugs firing at the optimal time? And are you constantly tweaking your sales engine in order to improve week-on-week performance?

CHAPTER 6

Founder-Led Marketing

I f Founder-Led Sales is an outbound approach, then Founder-Led Marketing is an inbound approach. The basic principle is the same—you're trying to connect the value your product delivers with potential early adopters. The main difference is that you're doing this by broadcasting rather than narrowcasting. To put it another way: Rather than finding individual prospects, you're finding (or creating) the places where your prospects hang out, and then sharing messages on those channels in the hope it will resonate with prospective customers and draw them in.

Early stage Founder-Led Marketing generally works best if the founder already has clear channels they're comfortable with. Many would refer to this as having a strong personal brand or being a thought leader. Maybe they have a large following on Twitter or LinkedIn, are frequently speaking at conferences, or have a popular newsletter or blog. Maybe they have already earned credibility as a member of an existing community relevant to their product. Either way, the founder's first job is to find the product's audience and start telling people what they're doing, which generally means creating content that connects.

Finding the Right Acquisition Channel

Even if, as the founder, you already have a large personal following, you'll eventually need to grow your reach beyond your network alone. As such, many early acquisition experiments center on finding an effective acquisition channel—and by effective I mean a channel where you are able to connect with a sizable number of prospective customers (the A in The Growth Equation) in a predictable and cost-effective way. Sometimes the right channel is obvious. Other times you might have to experiment to see which channel performs best.

The most common promotional channels for early stage startups tend to be social media (including content marketing and influencer marketing) and paid search. Tactics like Search Engine Optimization (SEO), traditional advertising, event marketing, direct mail, flyering, and public relations might also be part of your marketing mix. For certain products, partnerships and re-sellers might be worth exploring.

While many startups will attempt to engage across every distribution channel possible, this tends to spread resources far too thin. As PayPal founder Peter Thiel explains in his book Zero to One: "The kitchen sink approach doesn't work. Most companies get zero distribution channels to work. If you get just one channel to work, you have a great business. If you try for several but don't nail one, you're finished."

In my experience, marketing tends to follow a Power Law Distribution, where the bulk of your customers come from a single channel. The CEO of Hotjar, Mohannad Ali, agrees: "In almost every business, when you look at the success of marketing channels, it's a Power Law Distribution. You have one primary channel where most customers are coming from, then you have a second main channel and then you have a long tail."

Most of the channels you're considering will work to some degree. The goal of your early marketing activity is to figure out which ones work best for you, your product, and the skills you have within your team; once you find a channel that starts delivering traction, you should double down on it.

When evaluating potential channels, it's worth considering the maturity of the channel, what the competitive landscape looks like, and thinking about the following questions:

- Will it be relatively easy to break through, or is the channel already awash with brands trying to connect to your customer base with similar products and messaging?

- How easy is it to get up and running on that channel, and do you have the necessary skills in-house to make it a success?
- How much of your market is already on the channel, how easy is it going to be to connect with them, and how quickly are you likely to see results?

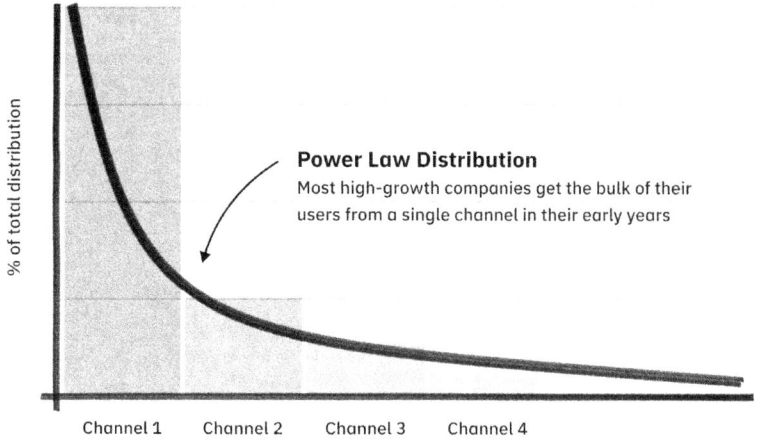

Figure 6.1: Chart showing the effects of the Power Law Distribution.

You can glean some of these answers from publicly available data or simply by spending time on the channels; for other info, you'll need to rely on segmentation tools like the ones Facebook and LinkedIn provide.

It's also worth making sure that your brand makes sense in the context of a particular channel. You might think that TikTok or Reddit would be good places to promote your company, but do you understand the unique culture of each, and do your brand and messaging fit with the community standards and values that have emerged? Are you able to craft a campaign that makes sense for the particular channel, or are you going to come off as clumsy and inauthentic—like a politician pretending to support a popular band or football team in an attempt to appear more likable? It's far easier for founders to promote themselves on channels and to communities they are already members of. They've built a reputation and learned the cultural norms, which allows them to post authentic content.

When exploring different acquisition channels, it can be helpful to segment them into four different groups.

1. Channels in which you have a high degree of confidence and are likely to show results and ROI quickly
2. Channels in which you're less experienced or confident and require some experimentation
3. Channels that are likely to have a high impact but take time to set up and start seeing results (SEO, for example)
4. Channels that take a long time to see results and you're uncertain about.

| **Always on** | **Test & learn** | **Long-term** | **Disregard** |
| Short payback, low risk | Short payback, higher risk | Long payback, high impact | Long payback, low impact |

Figure 6.2: Four ways to categorize your acquisition channels.

Managing Your Marketing Spend

Deciding where to put your marketing efforts will depend in part on how cost-effective a particular channel or approach is when it comes to acquiring customers. This is where the concept of Customer Acquisition Cost (CAC) and Payback Time become useful.

As you probably know, your CAC is the total amount of money you spend on marketing (including salaries for your marketing team) divided by the number of customers you acquire over a specific time period through your marketing efforts. So if you spend $5K on staff and $3K on advertising to acquire 200 paying customers a month, your monthly CAC is $40. Most startups focus on their blended (or total) CAC, but this can hide problems. For instance, let's say that $4K of the salary goes to producing social media content and that generates 160 customers. That means your CAC for the social media channel is $25. If the rest goes toward advertising, your CAC for that channel is a whopping $100. As such, separating out the CAC for each channel can really help determine which channels are working and which might need to be retired.

A related concept is Payback Time, which is the time it takes a company to pay back its customer acquisition costs. In the above example, if the company makes $5 a month per customer, the blended Payback Time will be eight months ($40/$5). However, the Payback Time for ad-based sales is actually a whopping 20 months ($100/$5). If your customers stick around for only 18 months, this means you're actually losing money from your ad-acquired customers (more on this in the chapter on retention). This is obviously not ideal, and it might get even worse if you segment churn based on acquisition channel. You may find out that customers acquired through social media stick around for 18 months, while those acquired through ads stay for only 12. This is one of the reasons why marketing teams tend to get into analytics fairly quickly in order to track exactly what's working and what isn't.

CAC Payback Time is a handy metric, and recent research on SaaS companies shows that high-performing products tend to have a CAC Payback Time of 5–14 months depending on the sectors they serve.

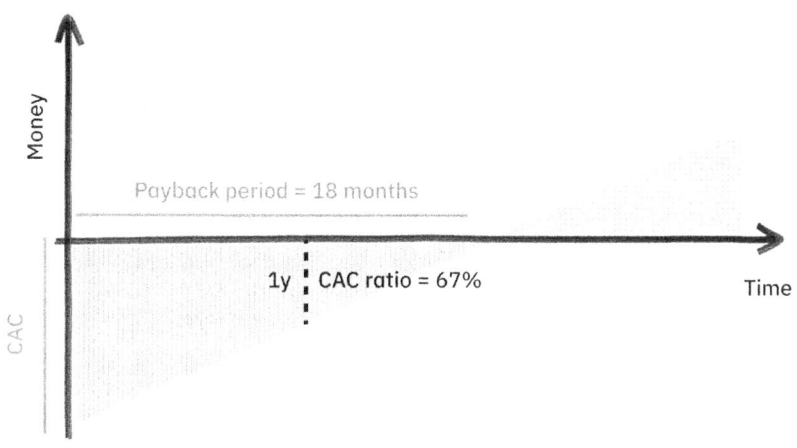

Figure 6.3: Example of CAC Payback Time.

It's worth noting that most channels won't deliver results straight out of the gate, so don't abandon the channel prematurely. Instead you want to try and understand what is and isn't working. Did you get the messaging right? Was the creative on point? Did you post at the right time and with the right frequency? Did you have the right people with the right skills to make the campaign land? Is the reason you're failing to connect with people because it's the wrong channel for your product—in which case move—or because you've yet to figure out Language-Market Fit (more on this later in the book)?

Be aware that new channels emerge and old channels fade away. At one point, companies relied on placing newspaper ads to get customers. Search marketing effectively decimated that channel, killing newspaper ad revenue in the process. As such, it does make sense to keep an eye out for emerging channels and not put all your eggs in one basket. Twitter has been a huge channel for many founders looking to engage with their community. However, at the time of writing this, the future of Twitter is looking uncertain, so if you are reliant on a single acquisition channel, it might be time to diversify your strategy.

How to Build a Following on Social Media

Social media platforms like Facebook, YouTube, TikTok, LinkedIn, and Twitter allow individuals and brands to build a following to which they can market directly (and generally for less money), rather than having to pay to access someone else's audience. Picking the right social media channel will depend in part on who you are trying to connect with. It might also depend on the channel, however, in which your founders are most active, if any.

Building a social media following from scratch is hard, which is why I see so many startups with follower counts in the low hundreds. It can take years to build a meaningful following you can market to, which means the Payback Time can be fairly long. If you have a founder with a few thousand followers (or better still tens of thousands), it makes sense to piggyback on their existing profile. Otherwise, there are some obvious tried-and-tested ways to build your profile and find your audience.

I see too many brands producing bland, copycat content—something I generally describe as background radiation. This is often the result of hiring a social media marketer who is being judged by output (how many tweets they post) rather than outcomes (Are you connecting with the right audience? Is that audience growing fast enough? Are they converting into users?). It's not uncommon for novice social media marketers to spend a ton of time creating mediocre content, which results in only five new followers that week.

I also see many startup social media accounts that start with a flurry of promotional material, get very little traction, and then tail off almost immediately. There's nothing sadder (or that instills less confidence in a brand's future) than a social media account with half a dozen posts, the latest being over two months old. As such, posting high-quality content on a regular basis is table stakes.

The exception to this rule is having static content on platforms where you don't plan to be active but still need to have a presence—possibly for the purpose of being tagged by others, the opportunity to comment and engage as a user, or just to plant a flag until the budget (and the strategy) support consistent content on the platform. For example, many brands for which Instagram is not an ideal use of time or energy still find it important to claim an account name, fill out a bio line, and post static content. This static content would cover the 3x3 grid (for a total of nine posts) and would exist as a sort of mini website, providing a little information.

Having a complete profile on a platform also allows you to run ads on that platform with increased credibility—no one wants to click on an ad to find out more about the company, only to discover an empty bio and a sad gray placeholder avatar. So, if you don't plan to be active on a platform but want to at least create a presence, static content that is strategic, well designed, and evergreen (e.g., able to last without going stale) is your best bet.

For platforms you do plan to be active on, you'll see results quicker in the earlier stages by daily activity—at least an hour per day—by the founder themselves, rather than by a full-time social media marketer. This activity includes thoughtful comments, shares, and engagement in other people's content in addition to posting your own. And if you do hire a marketer, their job should be making it easy for the founder to produce high-quality content, rather than doing that themselves. So how do you create content that people find interesting enough to follow you?

Creating Interesting Social Media Content

For early stage founders, it makes sense to lean into areas you're especially passionate about that align with what you're building, who you're building for, and that you have a particular stance on. Think about: What are the big annoyances people have in the space you're serving, what incumbent attitudes are you pushing against, or what sacred cows are you trying to topple? Most founders are trying to build a meaningful product that upsets the status quo, so this should be a great source of content.

I know one founder who is trying to revolutionize the hiring space. We've all had terrible hiring experiences in the past, so there's plenty of opportunity for creating interesting content. Sharing what you think is broken and how you think the industry should change is likely to encourage people who have had a terrible hiring experience to follow along. It's also likely to pique the interest of hiring managers and HR people who see this as a problem—exactly the sort of people my friend is trying to market to. As such, taking a mission-driven approach to your social media output can be highly effective.

It's important to be genuine and avoid being too salesy on social media. Social media is meant to be about making human connections. As such, let the people who find your thoughts interesting discover your background and products organically, rather than filling their timeline with overt marketing messages. If you do want to foreground what you're working on, consider taking a "building in public" or behind-the-scenes approach where you show interesting demos of things you're noodling around with, including bugs, issues, and dead ends. If things look too glossy, people will interpret it as a sales pitch. So a quick Loom video might feel more real than an artfully staged demo, and a two-minute video of the founder captured on their phone is likely to do better than a slickly edited studio shot interview. You want to communicate with authenticity, which has the tendency to disappear when content is overproduced.

Marketing-Led accounts tend to be fairly insipid and often one-way. When the person managing the account does interact with a follower, it's usually to thank them for the follow or for sharing their thoughts. As a result, you can spot these sorts of accounts from a mile away. It's much better to get into a deeper conversation with folks, and don't be afraid to disagree where necessary—just as long as you do it in a way that doesn't make the other person feel foolish.

Social media accounts shouldn't be just about acquiring followers, however. Go out of your way to follow other interesting accounts in your space. I always find accounts that don't follow people to be highly suspect. A great way to get noticed is by reposting interesting content they share, tagging them in conversations, or adding your own thoughts to comments and threads. Just make sure this comes across as genuine rather than needy. Nobody likes a sycophant.

One of the great benefits of building relationships with people via social media is that it makes it much easier to reach out to them later with a specific ask. On several occasions, I've had a high-profile founder (or more likely one of their sales associates logged in as the founder) reach out to me asking if I'd like to get a free trial of their product, to hop on a demo, or to take a look at what they're working on next. For whatever reason, I'm a lot more receptive to people reaching out to me like this on social media than via email—especially if I already have a relationship with them, they have a good number of followers, and are generally well respected.

This might sound obvious but I think the key to success on social media is to be interesting, helpful, and genuine. The goal isn't simply to acquire users and post content, but rather to build meaningful connections with people; connections that allow you to grow your reputation, gain people's trust, and ultimately earn the right to share the things that matter to you most. If you can do this, you'll be able to leverage your social media network in a way that can positively impact your business.

The Basics of Content Marketing

Social media relies on content to drive interest. Often the content that appears on social media is short form (in the case of sites like Twitter) or in a particular medium (like videos on TikTok or YouTube). One way to build a deeper relationship is to create longer content that allows people to interact with you directly, maybe through blog posts, email newsletters, white papers, or podcasts. This approach is typically described as content marketing.

Content marketing has been the secret sauce behind many successful startups. One company that has excelled in this area over the years is Intercom. The idea around content marketing is super simple: Create useful content that connects with your core audience's needs and either educates, entertains, or hits a nerve in some way. So what are the things that keep your customers up at night, but nobody else is talking about? What do they hate about existing solutions and the companies that provide them? What are the industry "sacred cows" that are ripe for disruption? You then share this content through a wide range of channels (social, newsletters, online communities, and organic search) and start building a relationship. By engaging with this content, users become aware of your company, your product, your values, and your brand, and are more likely to become customers.

I think there are a few things that companies regularly get wrong with content marketing. The first one is being overly focused on your solution, to the point of it becoming a hard sell. If people aren't getting value from your content or if they feel overly pushy or disingenuous, they will disengage quickly—and it'll become super hard to get them back. So instead, your focus should be on talking about the problems your customers have, delivering advice that your customers find useful, and positioning yourselves as experts in the field. This allows you to draw in customers who have the problems your product solves. When they are finally ready to buy a solution to their problems, your name is at the top of their mind.

Much as they do with their social media output, many early stage companies produce a ton of low-value background radiation–type content that is frankly a waste of time and energy. This is often because the founder or marketing person doesn't really know what resonates with prospective customers, so they are simply throwing things against the wall to see what sticks. This is why founders tend to do a better job at early content creation. They're the ones talking to customers, understanding the market, and setting out their vision for a better future. Who better to articulate this than the founders themselves?

If you find that your content really isn't landing, it's worth taking a step back and defining what "good" looks like to you and your audience. You should then undertake a content audit and remove anything that isn't up to scratch. You might want to create a set of content themes you know your audience cares about. This can be drawn from the sales discovery calls you've been having. You might also want to create a content guide to help your authors maintain quality and tone of voice. Creating great content is surprisingly difficult, so if it's not working you might need to reassess your existing capabilities and get external help.

One of the reasons Intercom has been so successful with content marketing is their ability to create evergreen content that taps into their customers' hopes and fears. In the early stages of the company, this content was primarily created by the founders. In fact, co-founder Des Traynor wrote 93 of the first 100 blog posts on Intercom's site. They were able to produce such high-quality content by understanding the jobs their customers wanted the product to do (known as Jobs to Be Done or JTBD for short).

Intercom's former VP of strategy, Matt Hodges, explains how this approach informed their entire Go-to-Market Strategy "from the way we position our products, to the audiences we target and the content we produce." As a result, the Intercom blog became the company's primary acquisition channel, helping them grow from $1M ARR up to $50M ARR. Even today, with a sizable marketing team, Intercom's founders still regularly post articles, share videos, and host podcasts. They do this because high-quality content has become a primary driver of Growth, and it's just too important to palm off to a junior marketer.

Making the Most of Your Content

One of the great things about content marketing is that good content is easy to repurpose. If you begin with a long-form piece of content (e.g., a long video, podcast, article, or webinar recording), you can effectively break it down into several smaller pieces of content for much more mileage. A long video interview could be turned into an article; soundbites from the video could be shared with graphics and subtitles on Instagram Reels and TikTok; key quotes could be made into visuals for LinkedIn and Instagram feeds. Suddenly a single piece of content has become a month's worth of assets. This sort of snackable content is also more likely to get shared by your followers, introducing you to a whole new audience of potential customers.

Social media marketing supremo Gary Vaynerchuk is a big advocate of this approach. "Since I start from video, my team is able to repurpose that one piece of content into dozens of smaller pieces of content, contextual to the platforms that we distribute them to," Gary explains. Gary does a range of other things like screenshotting Tweets and reposting them to Instagram, screenshotting notes and posting them to Twitter, or screenshotting articles and posting them to LinkedIn (so, a lot of screenshotting). In a presentation he posted online a few years ago (and probably screenshot the hell out of), Gary detailed how you could potentially create 64 pieces of content in a single day[17]—enough content for several months' worth of activity.

While that's quite a lot, you'll be amazed at how much traction you might be able to get from just one or two high-quality pieces of content. Even if you're following a Sales-Led approach, it's super useful to be able to offer up an interesting and relevant piece of content to a prospect as an excuse for getting in touch, or as a potential secondary call to action if they're not quite ready to take your call. Good content can also give you an excuse to connect with a prospective customer you might not have spoken to in a while. As such, I think content marketing is still an important tool in many companies' arsenal, and a few well-placed pieces of content are sometimes all you need. However, some days it does feel like social media is awash with marketing content and

---

[17] https://garyvaynerchuk.com/how-to-create-64-pieces-of-content-in-a-day/

we're closing in on "peak content." So while it's still an important part of your marketing mix, it's getting increasingly hard to stand out in this space.

Use Free Products as Lead Magnets

The internet is arguably drowning in low-quality marketing content at the moment, and generative AI is only making this worse. As such, it's getting increasingly hard to stand out. One way around this is to create content that delivers actual tangible value. More traditional consultancies or B2B companies might do this by releasing a report or white paper. Payment company Stripe went one further by creating a whole book publishing arm.[18] Others might create some kind of free canvas or template to give away, often in exchange for your email address. I'm starting to see more and more companies create lightweight tools (sometimes called "sidecar products") as part of their marketing efforts.

Shopify is an excellent example of an ecommerce company using sidecar products to great effect, offering a range of free tools including a company name generator, a privacy policy generator, and a logo maker. Ramp is another company that has invested heavily in marketing products including a VC database, mission statement generator, and burn rate calculator. These sidecar products have helped propel Ramp into becoming one of the fastest-growing tech companies in history, growing from zero to $100M in revenue in two years.

Security startup Snyk has seen impressive traction thanks to its Vulnerability Database, a free tool targeted to its core audience of security-minded developers. The database is constantly updated and allows people to search for vulnerabilities at no cost. Snyk then uses this tool to drive visitors to their core product, which automates these checks in the background.

---

[18] https://press.stripe.com/

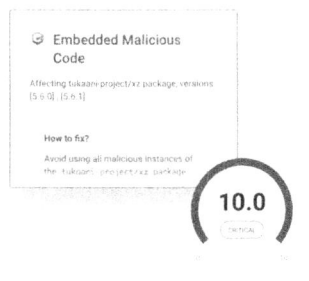

Snyk Vulnerability Database

The leading database for open source vulnerabilities and cloud misconfigurations.

Embedded Malicious Code

Affecting tukaani-project/xz package, versions [5.6.0], [5.6.1]

How to fix?

Avoid using all malicious instances of the tukaani-project/xz package.

10.0
CRITICAL

Search by package name or CVE

Figure 6.4: A free security tool Snyk provides to help with user acquisition.

As you can see, free tools are a great way of delivering value to your customers as quickly as possible. If the experience is positive, people are likely to assume that your paid tools are even better. Free tools are also a great way of driving traffic by aligning your brand with the "Search Intent" of prospective customers—something we'll touch on shortly. To demonstrate how powerful this is, there are supposedly over 70K search terms you can type into Google that will return a link pointing you to a free Shopify tool.[19]

Community-Led Growth

Another popular marketing approach is to get your community to create the content for you, often described as User-Generated Content (UGC). Dating app Bumble has done a great job of encouraging its user base to share both positive and often amusingly negative dating experiences while tagging the company on social media. So if you go online, especially on TikTok, you'll see users sharing good (and terrible) opening lines, funny conversations, touching interactions, embarrassing experiences, and general dating advice. Getting your user base to do the marketing for you creates a real sense of authenticity and buzz around a product—something that many marketing teams struggle to replicate.

---

[19] https://foundationinc.co/lab/the-growth-toolkit/

Influencer marketing relies on finding people who are willing to connect you with their existing community. (We saw earlier in the book how GymShark sent free samples of their product to prominent fitness YouTubers and how Bumble set up an ambassador program on university campuses.) But what if, rather than relying on other people's networks, you could build a community of your own? A marketing channel that you owned, that grew organically through recommendations, and allowed you to gain customers at a super low CAC?

This is exactly what my friends at Butter have been doing. Butter—a cool video conferencing tool aimed at folks running collaborative workshops—set about building a community of some of the best workshop facilitators in the world, creating a space where expert facilitators can share approaches, ask questions, and network.[20] You don't need to use the tool to be part of the community, and there's little if any hard sell. However, Butter has positioned itself at the heart of a community made up of its target customers. This allows them to learn what the community needs from a tool like Butter, connect with influencers and superusers in order to create collaborations around content, and create a space where they have permission to share what they are working on with potential users. Is it any wonder that Community-Growth strategies are popping up in more industries?

In order to build a community, you need a couple of things. First, you need a loose connection of people who are actively looking for a home. It's useful to understand who that community is, where that community hangs out, what's currently missing, and what they are looking to get through community membership. Often these communities exist on social media and form pockets of activity around well-known figures, so it's worth creating a map of who and where those influential people are. Other times they might live in private groups on platforms like Slack and Circle. Often these smaller communities are run as hobbies in peoples' free time, and, as such, are generally composed of friends and friends of friends. Wherever and however these communities form, if you find a patchwork of disparate

---

[20] http://community.butter.us

groups, there might be an opportunity for you to bring them together under one roof.

Seeding Your New Community

If you're able to connect with existing community leaders and bring them (and their network) into your platform, you're in a good position. You might find, however, that people who already have a sizable community might be resistant to joining your group—not least because they might feel like they are giving up a certain amount of control and handing it over to a commercial entity with an ulterior motive. As such, having established credibility in the community is super important. One way to do this is to be seen as an active member of the community, especially one that gives more to the community than it takes. Organizing conferences and events can help here, as can sponsoring community groups. Another way is to form friendships with respected community members and have them vouch for you.

This is exactly what InVision (the now defunct design tool) did when it created its Design Leadership Forum. InVision had found early success through its excellent content strategy. This included hiring well-known community leaders to write blog posts, create podcasts, and publish books on subjects close to the design community's heart. Looking to make inroads with design leaders (presumably because they saw them as the ultimate buyers of their software), InVision set about hosting a series of leadership dinners around the world with well-known designers. I was lucky enough to be asked (and paid) to host several of these myself, in places like London, Stockholm, and Berlin. Off the back of these dinners (and the reputation of the hosts), InVision quickly built a Slack community of over 2K heads, directors, and VPs of design, which is still going to this day. Such a shame then, that the product failed to keep pace with the company's excellent marketing strategy.

Community Leadership

Early stage products might have a hard time bringing well-established community members onto their platform, as there's some nervousness around joining something that has an uncertain future. What you can do, however, is use your platform to find upcoming voices and elevate them. This is exactly what Notion did when Ben Lang discovered the product, started tweeting about it, and created a fan site getting about 80K visitors per month.[21] Notion hired Ben to be their first community manager when they were around 10 people.

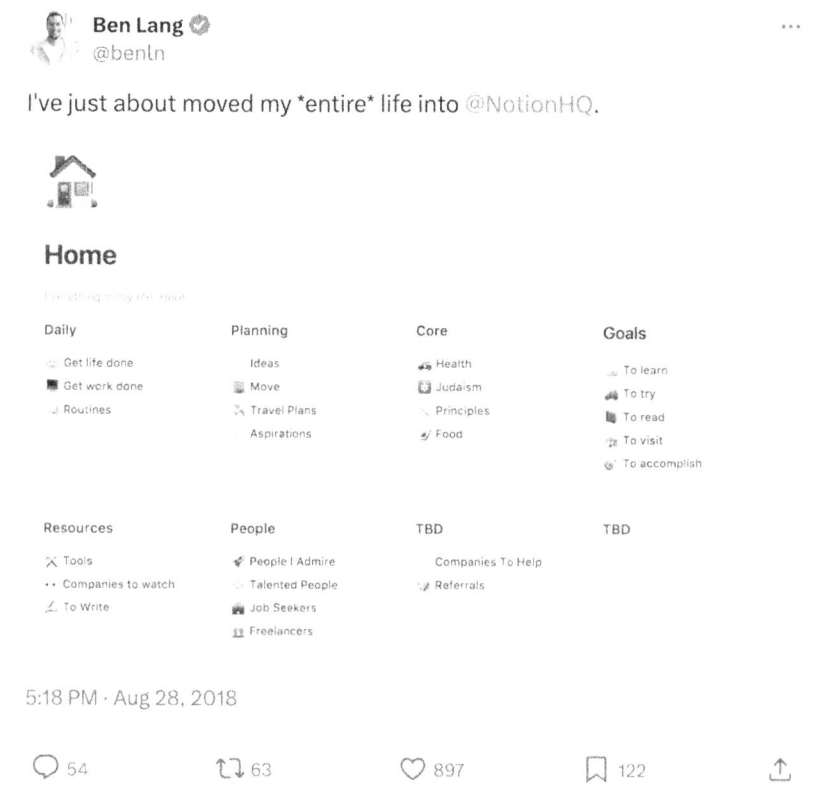

Figure 6.5: Ben Lang, the first community manager at Notion, tweeting about his use of the tool.

One of the company's early initiatives was to create the Notion Pro Community. It started with around 20 members, giving them access to exclusive founder Q&As and making them feel like part of the family. They also provided them with early access to new features, company swag, and funds to run their own meetups. Being invited into a private

---

[21] https://x.com/benln/status/1749815485716430933

community like this confers a certain status to its members, making them much more likely to become advocates for your brand. For some, this sort of access might even be the start of a new career, allowing them to talk at conferences, offer consultancy, or sell products like paid templates, and ultimately tie their personal goals to the success of your business.

Notion Pros

Apply to be a Notion Pro 🌐

Notion Pros are Notion enthusiasts who lead local communities, organize online and offline events, and showcase best practices to inspire and educate other users. They represent Notion as ambassadors around the world and the Internet.

Does this sound like you?

- I love connecting people, both online and off.
- I want to create a community of kindred spirits with shared values around productivity, great design, and the future of work.
- I enjoy helping people set up their Notion workspaces.
- I spend a bunch of time teaching folks how to use Notion and building templates.

Just a few ways you can create and participate as a Notion Pro:

- Organize local gatherings for fellow Notion enthusiasts to share habits, productivity hacks, cool things they've built, and more. Meetings are online or in person.
- Showcase your Notion superpowers –- help us broadcast the neat things you've built yourself, and inspire others to follow in your footsteps.
- Get your community excited about what Notion can do for them through social media, videos, and other content.

What we provide

- Access to a closed group with other Notion Pros so you can meet and chat.
- Training and tools for representing Notion.
- Swag to share with your community.
- Direct connection with the Notion team and insight into what's up next.
- Access to upcoming features.

Figure 6.6: How Notion uses the Notion Pro Community to stimulate Growth.

Notion has really doubled down on community-building efforts since those early days, creating ambassador programs, supporting community-driven events, and setting up a template market that allows community members to profit from their association with Notion. You see a similar focus on Community-Led Growth across a range of categories, but especially in the no-code space. In fact, Community-Led Growth and Product-Led Growth (which we'll talk about later) often go hand in hand.

Building a strong community is a great signal that you're committed to a particular group of people. It allows you to build up trust and connection by delivering value to that group. That value creates brand equity, which is likely to pay off at some stage in the future when people start looking for the sort of solutions you provide. It also builds up goodwill, which the members of the community are likely to pay back through recommendations and referrals. Finally, it provides you with a marketing channel that you own, one that directly links to a highly engaged and influential audience. This is really powerful, but as Spider-Man's Uncle Ben once said, "with great power comes great responsibility." Communities can take a long time to build up but you can lose trust overnight, so it is important not to abuse this responsibility—one reason why hiring community managers like Ben (from Notion, not Spider-Man) is so important.

Some people liken community management to gardening. You need to tend to the medium, plant multiple seeds, and nurture the community as it grows. As plants mature, you need to do more pruning and weeding and protect the community from bugs and other annoyances. If gardening isn't your thing, I also like to think of running a community like throwing a fancy cocktail party. You get to choose your initial guest list, where the party will be held, and the environment, music, food, and entertainment. As people start slowly drifting in, it's on you to greet them, introduce them to other guests, and get folks talking. As things start to build momentum, conversations will start to happen naturally, so you can now turn your attention to making sure folks have drinks in hand and are having a good time. As the night goes on, they might need to smooth over an argument, clear up the odd spill, or help somebody get a taxi home. Hopefully, your guests will see the effort you've put in, appreciate the new connections you helped them make, and think fondly of you as a result. This is what community leadership is all about for me.

Using Existing Communities

The good news is that you don't necessarily need to build your own community in order to benefit from Community-Led Growth. Sometimes it's easier to join existing communities. This is especially true if those communities are already well established. However, much like starting your own community, you'll need to build up credibility among a community before they'll let you engage in promotional activities.

In order to build credibility among a community, you really do need to be a member of the group it serves. To do this, you'll want to spend time getting to understand the community standards and norms, including common memes and hot topics. You'll want to start engaging in conversations, befriending regular posters, commenting on others' messages, and starting your own threads. Generally, you want to add value to the conversation and grow your reputation over time. If you're seen as a valuable member of the community, folks will generally be receptive if you ask for help or make the occasional self-promotional post. I generally think you need to give at least 50 times what you take from a community, which means that only one in 50 posts should be promotional in nature. If all you do is post self-promotional content, you'll end up annoying the community and probably get yourself banned. So tread with caution, and don't palm this work off to a junior.

Online Advertising

I think one of the reasons founders are drawn to online advertising is that the other marketing approaches are super hard and take a lot of time and effort to get right. So if you have a good amount of VC money sitting in the bank doing nothing, it can be tempting to throw money at Google and Meta in the hope they'll take care of customer acquisition for you, allowing you to focus on the fun product stuff.

Just bear in mind that most online advertising is sold via auction these days. This means that you have to be good at picking the right target groups and keywords, as well as writing attractive copy. Running an effective ad campaign takes skill, and it's easy to burn a ton of time and money with a poorly optimized campaign. This is especially true if you're targeting a highly contested domain or have well-funded competitors with deep pockets. So, while I believe founders should be driving outreach and acquisition in the early phases, it's generally better to get expert help when it comes to running paid campaigns.

If you do choose to lean into online advertising (and especially social media advertising and paid search), you'll see much greater results if you've created a knowledge base of highly targeted and specific blog posts relevant to your customers in their search for a solution like yours (effectively, establishing a solid SEO foundation). Adding a little paid budget behind these already helpful and audience-relevant posts will get you more bang for your Search Engine Marketing (SEM) buck. We'll cover that in the next section.

For social ads, on Instagram, LinkedIn, Twitter, and Reddit, great creative (that is, solid copywriting and good visual design) is key. As the influx of ads between organic posts has increased, so has a user's ability to ignore them. Think about your own scrolling behaviors. What makes you want to click "learn more?" Reddit does allow you to reach highly specific audiences and may do well in your early adopter audience, but Redditors tend to be highly suspicious of marketing that smells like marketing, so authenticity and realism are crucial to an effective ad on the platform. Test your ads with different copy, visuals, and audience demographics until you find what works. Kill the underperformers, double down on what's proven to work, and keep your testing budgets low. The worst mistake you could make is to invest your entire monthly ad budget into the first ad you create. Experiment small and apply the same principles to building and testing your ads that you do to your product.

Most platforms offer free training and extensive knowledge bases to help you get better results with your ads. Take advantage of these. The paid social landscape changes rapidly, and what worked a year ago will most likely not work now.

Ultimately I think targeted advertising can act as a good stopgap, while you get your acquisition engine set up and figure out a more cost-effective acquisition mechanism. It can also be a cheap way of testing different messaging by running a few different campaigns at the same time to see which performs best. However, it can be very addictive over the long term. If you're not careful, you might find yourself with a really bad Customer Acquisition Cost to Lifetime Customer Value ratio (CAC/LCV). So proceed with caution.

Search Engine Marketing

Companies will pay large amounts of money to get their ads placed at the top of the Search Engine Ranking Pages (SERPs). But there is a much cheaper way to do this, and that's through Natural Search. This means your site is one of the first results returned for search terms meaningful to your product. It's worth noting that search engine marketing is a winner-takes-all approach, with the first three listings taking about 70% of the traffic. However, if you manage to get in the top three listings for your preferred search terms, it can drive a ridiculous amount of free traffic your way.

Over the years, a whole industry of Search Engine Optimizers (SEOs) and Search Engine Marketers (SEMs) has grown to help companies capitalize on this "free" search traffic. In the early days, these approaches often relied on slightly hacky techniques like doorway pages and keyword stuffing. The search engines really care about the quality of their results, so every time one of these hacks became popular, the search engines would respond, causing a bit of an arms race.

While some search firms still maintain they know the secret sauce of getting a good ranking, the reality is fairly simple. Search engines are looking to rank sites that seem authoritative for a range of connected terms. Authoritative sites have generally been around for a while, contain content that talks about the searched for subjects in depth, and have lots of other authoritative (and relevant) sites pointing to them. As such, the best way for early stage founders to benefit from organic traffic is to write plenty of useful content (content marketing) and have plenty of high-quality sites linking to you (link building).

If you hire an SEO company, they will almost certainly recommend you do both these things; and if they are any good, will help you do them in a way that search engines typically favor. However, if the SEO companies are starting from scratch, it can take quite a bit of time and effort to build a presence, so I think it's generally a good idea to start your content marketing and link-building activities early on, in order to give yourselves a head start.

Creating Content Around Search Intent

As the name suggests, Search Intent is understanding what jobs your users are searching for help to complete. If you understand your prospective users' Search Intent, you can then create content that ranks highly, meets those needs, and positions your product as a possible solution.

Canva has done an excellent job in this area. They've really thought about Search Intent and produced a whole range of interlinked content to match. For example, Canva has a bunch of category pages for people looking to design things like a certificate, greeting card, or invite full of great examples, advice, and (most importantly) Canva templates. As a result, their general certificate design page gets around 16K visitors a month while their template page gets 33K visitors a month.[22]

However, Canva doesn't stop there. They've also created pages for specific types of invitations: for weddings, birthday parties, conferences, etc. There are 73 in total, all containing practical advice, examples, and links to even more templates. Canva's search team then trawls the web for people talking about those subjects, contacting the authors to suggest they include a link to the page, using specific language in the link. This backlink strategy raises the authority of these pages, making them much more likely to appear at the top of the results pages for searches like "How do I design a wedding invitation?"

Picking the right search terms is super important. For instance, Grammarly could try to rank for terms like "grammar correction software" or "AI writing assistant." However, the people most likely to benefit from the software probably aren't aware of these categories, aware they could benefit from something like this, or aware of what to search for if they did. So instead Grammarly tries to be the canonical answer to common grammar questions like "When should I use there, their, or they're?" As such, it's worth having a good understanding of

---

[22] https://foundationinc.co/lab/canva-seo

the jobs your software helps people get done (JTBD) and write helpful content around those themes.

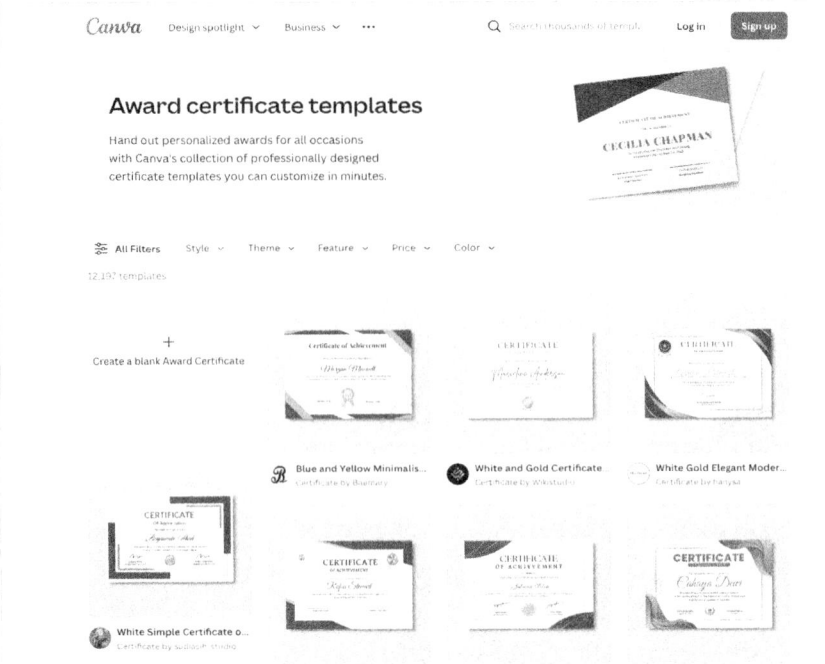

Figure 6.7: Canva has dozens of different certification template pages.

Figure 6.8: How Grammarly uses SEO to drive growth.

Another approach many product companies take is to create a series of comparison posts, demonstrating how their product stacks up against others in the market. For instance, a search for "Loom vs" brings up suggestions for a variety of video tools. Some of the top results come directly from Loom, some come from competitor sites, and some from third-party publishers. Ranking highly for these comparison searches is a great way to attract people already considering your product, as it allows you to control the framing.

It's even better if you can get your product to appear in the search recommendations dropdown next to a big competitor as it might allow folks who didn't know about you to discover a potential alternative. Make sure you have content on your own site referencing these comparisons, and even more importantly, make sure that you're appearing on the key comparison sites as well. You can also leverage your friends and network who blog (or produce YouTube content) on similar topics, by reaching out and asking them to write these articles with backlinks to your site. You may also find an opportunity to guest blog or post on a platform that hosts content like this, where your audience is likely to read.

Figure 6.9: Other comparisons shown when you type "Loom vs" into Google.

Along with content and link-building activities, some SEO companies also specialize in something called technical search: making sure that your site is easily accessible to search engine crawlers. Though I wouldn't jump deep into technical search on day one, it might be worth doing a spot of reading or hiring a consultant. You want to make sure that your promotional site isn't doing anything that's likely to negatively affect your search rankings, like having many low-value doorway pages, which might potentially get you banned. Tools like Ahrefs, HubSpot's Website Grader, Google Search Console, Screaming Frog, and Moz Pro (to name a few) can be used to analyze your site and suggest improvements.

Hiring Your First Marketer

As we've mentioned before, founders tend to focus the bulk of their energy on product and outsource growth to somebody else on their team. This happens with sales, and it also happens with marketing. As a result, a marketing executive is often one of the first non-product hires a startup will make. However, I've seen this go wrong more often than it's gone right, so I recommend proceeding with caution.

I generally see a pattern of founders hiring senior marketing executives from much larger startups. The logic is often "If that person helped company X grow, they'll be able to do the same for me." Unfortunately, marketing execs at large companies are generally managers and strategists. They've inherited an existing (and working) marketing playbook, and it's their job to optimize it and keep it running. As such, they're great at writing marketing plans, hiring teams, and engaging external suppliers. All things you'll need eventually.

In the early stages, however, what you really need is somebody who can roll up their sleeves and get stuck in. Somebody who doesn't mind writing content marketing articles and can do it quickly and knowledgeably. Somebody who is happy creating quick and dirty social media assets, and posting to Twitter, Instagram, and TikTok multiple times a day. Somebody who is happy to join tons of different communities and engage in conversations with members. And somebody who is happy to experiment with online advertising, update website copy, tweak your SEO, design discount tokens—and hand them out at conferences and events. In short, you need somebody who can get stuck in and create a new playbook from scratch, based on your unique needs and circumstances, rather than recycling something that worked at their last company but might not work for you.

The other mistake people make when hiring an early marketing person is to hire somebody with a specific specialty: a content marketer, a social media marketer, or a community builder. All these things are valuable and you'll probably need to hire specialists in all these areas once things take off, but in the early days, you need a generalist to experiment across a range of channels, rather than focusing on one. Or to put it another way, you need your hire to help you find the right channel, rather than having the person you hire dictate your acquisition channel.

I often think it's better to hire a junior person to help with marketing. Maybe a recent graduate who has dabbled in a bunch of different areas but has yet to specialize in one. Whoever you hire, you want to make sure that they have a strong writing ability and can turn out high-quality content on a dime.

Summary

It's tempting for founders to pass on the responsibility for customer acquisition in the form of sales or marketing to a member of their team, so they can focus on the product. In the early stages of a company, however, finding your first customers is probably the highest-leverage thing you can do as a founder. As such, it's important for founders to get over their natural reticence toward sales and marketing.

One way to get over this inertia is to carve out dedicated time in your calendar for sales and marketing activities and set yourself goals for the number of outreach emails you're going to send or articles you're going to write each week. Once you get your sales or marketing motion going, you can maximize your impact by hiring a junior person to cover the support work. This tends to be more efficient than hiring high-end sales or marketing execs, who often struggle with the scrappier, hands-on nature of early customer acquisition.

Driving traffic to your site is a major part of customer acquisition. It's the top of the funnel, but all the traffic in the world is valueless until they become customers. This requires a level of nurturing and guiding through the rest of the funnel. It's also where marketing efforts join with sales efforts. We'll need to take the visitors and activate them into paid users, which is what we'll examine in the next chapter.

Next Steps

I recommend doing a quick review of the different marketing channels you are using to attract new customers. Start by listing all the channels you're currently using, along with a couple of sentences to describe the strategy you're adopting for each. If you find yourself struggling to articulate the strategy, there's a good chance you don't have one and are simply throwing content at the wall in the hope that some of it sticks. Next to each channel, list a few key figures like the number of followers you have, the amount of content you're publishing, the frequency of your posts, the amount of engagement you're getting, the amount of traffic this is sending to your website, and if possible, how many sign-ups each channel is actually generating. Try to determine if the audience is actually made up of buyers and decision-makers or just fans. Use this to identify your most effective acquisition channel.

For each channel, identify your top 10 pieces of content. What is it about these pieces of content that resonated so well? What can you learn from these pieces that you can roll into your general content strategy? And—just in case—was the engagement for these pieces largely from your buyers and potential customers?

Now take some samples of your average content. How do they stack up? What's the quality like? What's the engagement like? Is your average piece of content still driving meaningful engagement, or are you spending too much time producing mediocre content, which is failing to move the dial?

Next, do the same with your closest competitors. Select companies who are a few years ahead of you, rather than a tech unicorn with a 30-person marketing team. What do you like about their content and could emulate? What positions are they taking that you disagree with and could create Counter Positioning around? What channels are they hugely successful on? What channels are they weaker on? Use the intelligence you've gathered to hone your own marketing strategy.

If you have a marketing strategy document, update it with your findings now. If you don't, put one together. It doesn't have to be huge or overly complex. Just a few pages outlining the channels you're planning to invest in, the angle that you're going to take, how frequently you plan to publish, and some examples of what great, good, and not-good-enough content looks like. Attempt to explain the gap in the market you're trying to take advantage of and how you're going to win in this space.

What most people do at this stage is to create their marketing strategy and then completely ignore it. Don't be that person. Instead, treat your marketing strategy as a hypothesis that you're going to spend the upcoming months testing. Starting to see results? Great. Double down. Not going according to plan? Review what's not working and iterate. A great marketing plan is all about execution and acquiring new customers in a sustainable way. This is the highest-leverage thing you should be doing right now, so don't leave it to chance.

CHAPTER 7

Converting Prospects To Users

You've built an amazing product that offers a ton of value, and you've managed to convince a steady flow of people to check out your website or hop on a sales call. How do you then move these people down your acquisition funnel, from curious tire kickers to registered users?

Many founders assume this happens naturally: that the value of the product is so obvious that as soon as people encounter it, they'll immediately sign up. Of course the value of the product is obvious to you because you conceived it, built it, and have experienced that value firsthand. Unfortunately, most prospects won't even understand what the product is yet, let alone feel its value.

It's also worth noting that we all have busy lives. We've been sold plenty of dud products before: products that promised the world but failed to deliver. So even if they have a "hair on fire" problem, most people won't have anywhere near the level of time or motivation needed to consider your product. Switching products is a laborious process and involves a huge amount of risk, especially if the product is new and relatively untested. As a result, prospects will approach your product with a high degree of skepticism, and it's your job to help them over this hurdle.

How People Evaluate New Products

When people encounter a product for the first time, they'll have a rather blurry and incomplete idea of what the product is and whether it might meet some implicit need. If users have a fairly low level of motivation, they'll be looking for an immediate hook to draw them in, and if they don't get this in the first few seconds, they'll be tempted to click away. This is where things like a compelling design, a strong tagline, and an identifiable brand can get people over the hump. In Daniel Kahneman's book *Thinking Fast and Slow*, this is described as a "system 2 decision." We have hundreds if not thousands of these decisions each day, so we tend to make them quickly and instinctively so as not to overtax our cognitive system.

Highly motivated users are usually a little more forgiving. They'll want to close the information gap in their heads, so they can make a more informed judgment (a "system 1 decision"), and this naturally takes a bit of time. This is one of the reasons why Audience Motivation features heavily in The Growth Equation. The way you talk to users can tap into their existing motivation and either grow that motivation further or (if you're not careful) frustrate and demotivate them. As such, getting this right becomes a difficult balancing act.

$$\text{Growth} = f[(A, \textbf{M}, \Delta V/t, S, K) / (\mu, C)]$$

Figure 7.1: User Motivation plays a core part of The Growth Equation.

A curious and motivated user will see their early interactions with you as information-gathering and sense-making exercises. They'll pose a series of questions to themselves (and potentially to your salesperson) that will start quite high level and generic and then get increasingly more detailed. What exactly is this product? What does it do? Who does it do it for? How is it better than what I'm already using? What superpowers will it give me? How will this help me excel at my job?

Smart founders use these common questions and clarifications as the foundation for their marketing and positioning content. As your prospective customer answers each of their questions, they start to build up a better picture of what it is you do—or at the very least what they think you do. This will either give them the confidence that they're on the right track and to dig deeper or they'll decide to cut their losses and look elsewhere. User researcher Jared Spool calls this "the scent of information." Your job is therefore to leave a strong enough scent trail to lead them into the sign-up process.

Understanding this mindset is vital. Many founders assume what the product does is obvious—because it's obvious to them—and jump into a confusing level of detail or jargon far too quickly. This can make your prospects feel overwhelmed and when that uncomfortable feeling becomes too great, they'll abandon the process. This is why getting the right framing is key.

Getting Your Framing Right

When encountering your product, the first thing a prospect will do is try to figure out the right bucket to put you in. This is their way of answering the first question: "What is this thing I'm looking at here?"

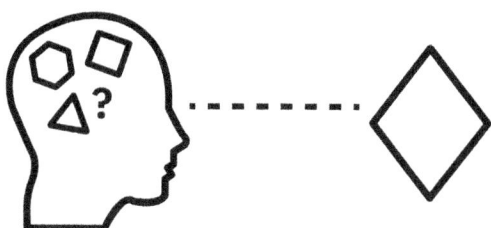

Figure 7.2: Users try to classify your product based on their existing mental model.

Established industries will already have a series of common categories they use to describe products. For instance, the sales software space has tools for CRM (Customer Relationship Management), Lead Generation, Analytics, and Sales Enablement to name just a few. So if you're launching a product aimed at knowledgeable salespeople, don't be surprised if they try and assign an existing category to you. This can be both helpful—as it gives you a shortcut to explaining what you do rather than having to explain everything from first principles—but also potentially unhelpful if you're doing something fundamentally different or new.

Of course, you might not always be selling to somebody with a good understanding of the current market categorizations. For instance, you might be selling a sales tool to a first-time founder who has never done sales before. They might have a general idea of what a CRM is but might have no clue what Sales Enablement means. As such, it's important to understand your user's Frame of Reference and pick the most appropriate framing.

In the design and product world, we talk about a user's Mental Model. This is the internal image they have built up in their heads about how the world is classified and interconnected. If you present them with a new product, the least cognitively stressful thing for them to do is to figure out which of their existing buckets to put it in. If there are multiple existing buckets to choose from, understanding their Mental Model allows you to frame your product so they categorize you in the most beneficial way. As such, it's important to understand your users' Mental Models—usually through research and direct conversations—and frame things in a way they understand, rather than trying to impose your own Mental Model on them.

One of the problems with allowing users to categorize you through their Mental Model is that they might make a mistake and put you in a wrong or overly competitive bucket. As such, founders often want to create a new category in their users' minds where they are the sole inhabitant. Dana Publicover, a marketer and friend of mine, has been known to tell founders, "You're not famous enough to invent a new category." While it sounds a bit direct (she's American, after all), the sentiment is quite accurate. If you're already a well-known market leader, you may be able to get away with creating a new bucket. The rest of you will be much better understood by a prospective customer if you stick to their Mental Model and position your product in terms they already understand.

If you are truly disrupting an existing category, but need to stick to an established Mental Model, one way of doing this is through the old

"It's like X for Y" trick: "We're like Uber for Air Travel" for instance. Customers who understand how Uber's ridesharing works can apply that to this new industry—air travel. However, I've seen many companies positioning themselves as something random like "Uber for Pets," which doesn't make as much sense. Are you renting pets by the hour? Having people walk your pets on demand? Or are you just a pet food delivery company referencing Uber because they got big and you want to get big as well? Choose your metaphors wisely.

Another approach is to create a new subcategory in people's minds. For instance, "We're a CRM aimed at founders doing their own sales." Or to bundle several categories together: "We're a single sales tool that combines Lead Generation, CRM, and Analytics in one place."

The Fine Art of Product Positioning

What we're essentially talking about here is the concept of Product Positioning: your ability to explain clearly and concisely what your product does and how it differs from the competition in a way your audience understands and cares about. If you can do this well enough, prospective users will experience the first of many aha moments. They'll really "get" what you do and, more importantly, how it will benefit them.

There are numerous templates around to help founders come up with a basic positioning statement. The most popular one is sometimes called the Mad Libs Elevator Pitch, because you're intended to fill in the blanks as in the game of the same name:

> For (target customer) who (has problem), (product name) is a (product category) that (key benefits/compelling reason to buy). Unlike (primary competitive alternative), our product (primary differentiation).

While these statements tend to come out sounding a little robotic, it does help describe some of the key components of a positioning statement. Namely:

- A well-defined target customer
- A well-defined problem or opportunity this product aims to address

- The category this product sits within
- The main things this product allows you to do
- How people currently solve this problem
- Why your approach is better

The main benefit of doing something like this is less about the deliverable than the act of thinking through the answers in detail. So who is most likely to get value from your product? Especially at this early (and probably yet to be feature-complete) stage, what is truly valuable and unique about this product? Which features do your users love that are genuinely 2–10X better than what's currently on the market? What class of product do people generally liken you to, and is this a fair comparison?

The job here isn't to come up with a bunch of marketing hyperbole and unprovable claims. For your positioning statement to be meaningful, you need to be brutally honest and willing to go back to the drawing board if things don't stack up. Fortunately, this is a relatively easy thing to fix. We'll go into some of the ways to do this in more detail next, however, for a comprehensive guide on the field of positioning, Obviously Awesome by April Dunford is a great primer on the subject, so well worth the read.

A Quick Note on Counter Positioning

In fairly crowded markets, it's sometimes easier to explain what a product isn't than what it is. This is sometimes called Counter Positioning, and it generally works best if there are a few large incumbents in the market that people are clearly frustrated with but feel trapped into using. People often like rooting for the underdog, so it can be a smart approach to position yourself as the scrappy upstart taking on the lazy incumbent.

Rahul Vohra, founder of luxury email client Superhuman, took this exact strategy, positioning his product as "the fastest email experience ever made. It's what Gmail could be if it were made today instead of 12 years ago. And unlike Gmail, Superhuman is meticulously crafted. So that everything happens in 100 milliseconds or less." This positioning statement (which leans heavily on the Mad Lib template) takes a bunch of digs at Gmail for being old, slow, and poorly crafted while positioning Superhuman as the exact opposite. It also aligns perfectly with the Mental Models and sense of identity exhibited by many engineers, who aspire to create well-crafted, performant software.

Notion has used similar Counter Positioning on its website, explaining how its product means you can do away with a whole raft of other tools like Confluence, GitHub, Trello, Asana, Jira, Google Docs, and Evernote—many tools developers would be only too happy to ditch in favor of a new and scrappy upstart. This comparison has the added benefit of allowing Notion to explain what its product does without going into the details. They simply say (or at least imply) that they do all the things these tools do and more.

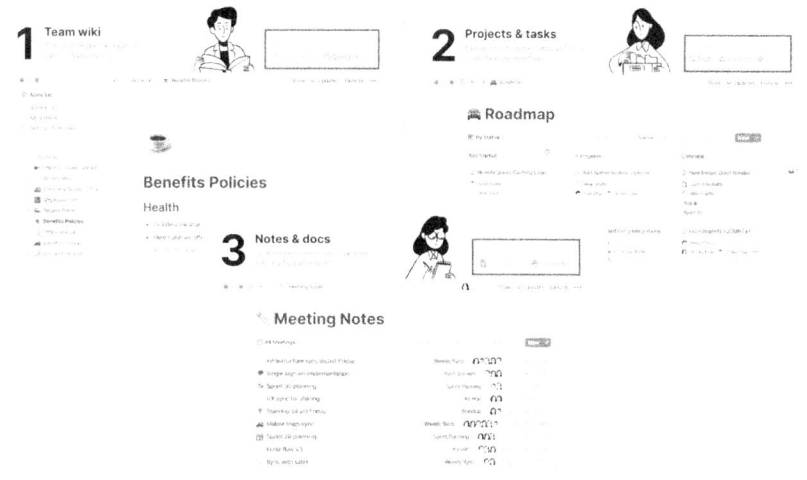

Figure 7.3: How Notion describes what it does in terms of other products.

Ditch the Jargon and Use Plain English

Despite all the amazing advice there is about nailing your positioning, I still see a surprising number of startups pitching services I don't really understand. "We deliver end-to-end marketing solutions" they'll claim, "leveraging customer intelligence in a multichannel world." I'm sure the founders know exactly what that means, but as a visitor I'm generally left feeling baffled. "That's nice," I'll say to myself, "but what is it you ACTUALLY do, and how is that relevant to me?"

Whenever people are asking "What is it you ACTUALLY do?" you have a communication problem—something that desperately needs to be fixed.

Some of this confusion might come from founder insecurity. The product is new. There's plenty of well-established competition out there. If I throw a lot of jargon around, it might make me sound more established, serious, and impressive. This approach reminds me of some former classmates who always used overly florid language when answering the teachers' questions (think Russell Brand but without the problematic backstory). They thought their over-preponderance of obtuse verbiage made them sound super intelligent, but I honestly didn't have a clue what they were saying (and I don't think they really did either). It was all a bit of a smokescreen. It turns out there's a word for this practice: "sesquipedalian"—from the Latin for using words that are "a foot and a half long."

I remember working with one founder who had an amazingly clear and concise investment memo. It was a simple two-pager that clearly outlined what the company was doing, why they were doing it, and why it was better than what was out there. However, every time they attempted to take this simple and concise vision and apply it to their website or sales deck, the core message got lost in a confusing word jumble.

If you know a little about the history of the English language, you might know that we developed two parallel languages as a result of the Norman Conquest. We had the high language of the aristocracy, which developed from French and Latin, and the original Anglo-Saxon language of the peasants, which had Germanic roots. This is why we say "cow" and "pig" to denote animals, while we use "beef" and "pork" to denote food. The Saxons farmed the animals, while the Normans ate them at fancy court banquets.

Something odd happens when we write pitch decks or websites. We find ourselves switching from the more casual and straightforward language of the Saxons to the florid and formal language of the

Normans. It sounds more sophisticated, but the clarity gets lost and we end up sharing a meaningless word salad.

There's also a tendency for newer companies to try and ape the language of their more successful competitors. While I get the desire to fit in, this results in whole sectors looking and sounding the same. This makes it harder for new entrants to stand out from the crowd, ultimately benefiting the incumbent companies they find themselves copying. For a sector that's all about making bold, disruptive decisions, this feels anything but. As such, I highly recommend that you Keep it Simple, Stupid (KISS) and use plain English.

Language-Market Fit Leads Product-Market Fit

One of the most useful concepts I've come across when it comes to startup positioning is the idea of Customer-Language Fit or Language-Market Fit. We're all familiar with the idea of Product-Market Fit by now: finding that perfect combination of features that solves a meaningful problem for a sizable chunk of the market in order to drive sustained and cost-effective growth. For many startups, Product-Market Fit feels a bit like an Easter egg hunt—trying a bunch of different things, almost randomly, in the hope that one of them works and creates traction.

One thing I feel many startup founders miss is that before you can reach Product-Market Fit you first need to convince people to try your product. And to do this you first need to figure out Language-Market Fit: the right language and framing of your product to make your customers go, "Oh, I get what this is. I need something like that." Because, unless you can position your product in such a way that it attracts the right users to sign up, those users will never get to experience the value your product delivers. To solve this problem, you need to experiment with a range of different ways of articulating your value proposition until you find the right combination of words (language) that meets the needs of a specific segment of your visitors (market) in order to drive acquisition.

Language-Market Fit is essentially the process of understanding your users' Mental Models and using Frames of Reference that resonate with them. If you fail to do this properly, you can literally end up speaking a different language than your customers. It's like being stuck talking to somebody at a party who you're struggling to understand. You nod politely but you're comprehending only about 10% of it so you feel awkward, and maybe a little stupid, and try to extract yourself from the situation as quickly and politely as possible.

In many cases, your promotional material or sales spiel is that dull or confusing party guest—and it's never a good thing to make your audience feel dumb or confused. Now, think about those conversations when you meet somebody and you immediately gel. They speak the same language as you and share many of the same cultural references. Conversation is super smooth and you leave feeling smarter as a result. That's the effect you want your promotional material to have on people.

Stop Talking About Features

When it's clear I'm struggling to understand what a startup does and why it's better than what's already out there, the founder will usually switch into feature mode. This can work if done well. "We're like X, but we do these two or three things better than anybody else can. Here's how and why." However, more often than not the founder will dive into a long list of seemingly marginal features, which you'd only know or care about as a user if you'd already signed up (aka the typical superuser mindset). When founders start reeling off these lists, I can feel my brain shutting down almost instantly.

As we mentioned earlier in the book, founders regularly fixate on features. I get this. Some people might indeed buy your product based on the existence of certain features, but it happens less often than you'd think. Consider the last TV you purchased. Did you buy it because of a specific set of features or because you saw a review saying it was great for gaming and had the best picture quality for the price?[23] Being able to clearly articulate to people why your product is better is a skill. If you find yourself listing out a dozen small features, you've probably already lost them.

---

[23] https://www.smashingmagazine.com/2024/01/feature-centricity-harming-product/

148

I remember seeing somebody talk about features in terms of Super Mario (although I'm racking my brain to recall who). They explained how product features were essentially power-ups: things that give your users some new capability. The skill at selling your product isn't to focus on the power-up itself, but to explain what it unlocks in your users: "If I eat that flower I can shoot fireballs. This makes it easier for me to complete the level and beat my high score." As such, it's usually smarter to focus on outcomes than features.

Jobs to Be Done

This is where the concept of Jobs to Be Done (JTBD) comes in super handy. As we've talked about previously, the idea of JTBD is that people "hire" products not because of their "features" but for what those features allow them to do (i.e., the job to be done). The canonical description is that "people don't want a quarter-inch drill bit, they want a quarter-inch hole." The problem most promotional material makes is either to list out all the features a product has—without really describing what people can do with those features or why they care—or to try and boil all those features down into a single pithy concept, often losing the necessary clarity and specificity along the way.

This is one of the reasons I love the approach Intercom took in the early days of their business. They spoke to 40 customers to understand the different jobs they wanted to get done, and then they reflected these needs and desires on their homepage. If you read these different package options, you're left with no doubt who the product is for, what problems it solves, and what value it delivers to customers. So much clearer than "We're a 24/7 customer service platform that allows ambitious brands to create closer connections with their customers through context sensitive just-in-time interaction."

The easiest way to do this is to listen to how your existing customers describe your product. It often amazes me how rarely founders really understand what they've built. They'll have many rather mechanistic assumptions about who will use their product and where the value comes from. However, if you watch users interact with the product and ask them about their experience, they'll often cite things the founders never really thought of. Usually, this is less about specific capabilities or features, but how those features have been designed and grouped together in a logical workflow. Users will say things like, "I really like how I can see X and Y at the same time. It means I've got a much better overview of Z." or "This product makes it really easy for me to do A and then B, without having to worry about C." Being able to capture these sentiments and communicate them to prospective customers in their own language is super powerful—especially because it happens so infrequently in the software world.

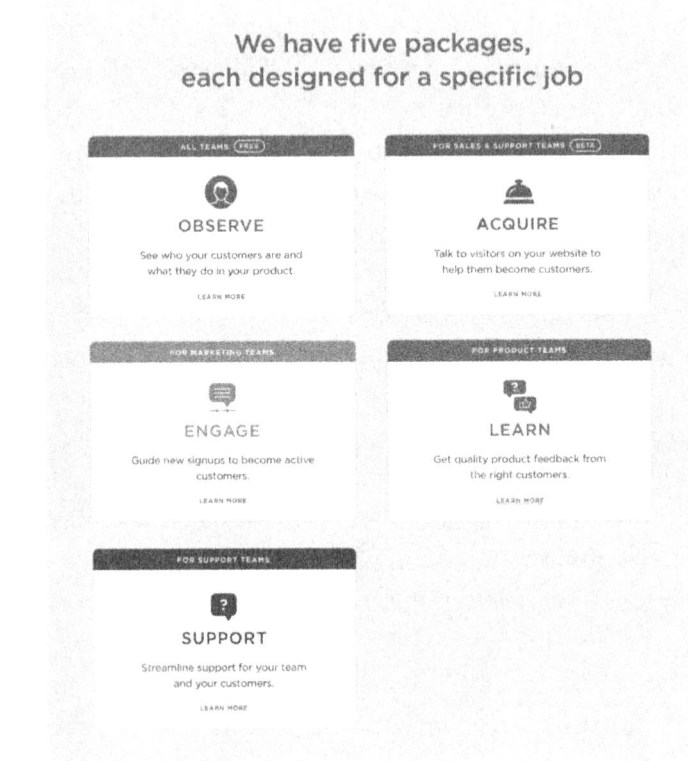

Figure 7.4: The Intercom website positioning its product in terms of Jobs to Be Done way back in 2015.

Experiments With Framing

Sometimes the changes you need to make to the way you frame your product are embarrassingly trivial. Take for instance Popsa, one of dozens of photobook apps on the market. By talking to their customers, Popsa learned that people really appreciated how fast their product was, so they used the tagline "fast easy photobooks." Sure it's descriptive, but it's also pretty boring, right? Diving deeper into their prospective customers' Frames of Reference through a series of JTBD-based interview questions, the team realized that folks had no idea how long it would actually take to create a photobook. For all they knew, fast might have meant it would take only three hours. They decided to try a new headline, initially with paper testing, before trying it out on the app store and seeing the results. The results were impressive, increasing conversion by a factor of four. The change they made? The new tagline was "Photobooks in 5 minutes." This simple change created a new Frame of Reference in their prospective customers' minds, while hinting that their competitors' products took longer.

The brilliant thing about Language-Market Fit is it's super easy to test, without having to devote costly (and often wasted) development cycles shipping features that end up delivering little in the way of value. A really simple way to experiment with Language-Market Fit is to create a handful of Google Ads using slightly different framings, in order to see which one drives the most clicks or registrations (this is why in the online advertising section I mentioned dividing your budget across a few different messaging options). This can be a good way to test your category definition and value proposition. You could also create a series of different landing pages to see which framing performs better. Do customers respond better when we say that we're an X or a Y? Do they respond better with this list of problems or that list of features? How does changing the length, complexity, and specificity of our language affect sign-up? All these things can help you hone in on the optimal framing and find Language-Market Fit.

One of the brilliant things about Language-Market Fit is that you can do this before a single line of code is ever written. And if you do it well, it can help you shape your product direction. Stripe Advisor Patrick McKenzie says it best: "Before you write a single line of code, start verifying that you can connect to the target audience and their understanding of the problem. If you can't write Why Hiring for QSRs

Is Broken, then you have absolutely no business trying to solve that problem. So write it."

Aha Moments and Time to Value

If you get your Language-Market Fit right, people will quickly experience their first aha moment: that flash of insight where they understand exactly what your product does, and, more importantly, how it can make their lives better. The quicker and more effectively you're able to deliver that first aha moment, the more likely someone is to take your product for a spin. What you're effectively doing here is trying to turn a curious visitor into a motivated one. Motivation is a precious commodity and something that can disappear just as quickly, so it's funny seeing founders put artificial speed bumps in the way of such users. One such speed bump is the humble waitlist.

Don't get me wrong, waitlists can work really well if there's some buzz around the product, the need is clear (and hopefully immediate), and people see their friends being slowly onboarded, sparking social proof and FOMO. Superhuman does this spectacularly well. However, there is also the chance that by the time you get back to somebody, they've forgotten they signed up, lost interest in the product, or found a reasonable alternative. As such, if you are going to run a waitlist program, at the very least you need to keep the people on your waitlist engaged and eager to participate.

For many early products, waitlisting and manual onboarding are necessary because the product is still a little complicated and self-service may be a way off. However, I'm a big proponent of showing rather than telling, so if there's any way you can give people a cut-down demo of the product without having to wait (or force them onto a demo call), all the better.

$$\text{Growth} = f[(A, M, \Delta V/t, S, K) / (\mu, C)]$$

Figure 7.5: How the delivery of Value Over Time fits into The Growth Equation.

One way of looking at this is to reduce your visitors' Time to Value (TTV). The quicker you can get them not only understanding but also experiencing the value of your product, the more desire they'll have to stick around. This is one of the reasons why Freemium models and Product-Led Growth models are so successful. It's because they reduce the TTV down to the absolute minimum—sometimes a matter of minutes.

As an example, have a think about how you first discovered a product like Notion. I remember going to their website a few times and thinking "that's cute, a modern wiki" and then immediately forgetting them. It wasn't until somebody sent me a link to a Notion page with a request to collaborate that I really got what it was all about. I'd experienced the value firsthand, rather than relying on the website copy to explain it to me.

Operating in Stealth Mode

I come across many startups operating in stealth mode with little more than a logo, an obscure description, and a sign-up form for a website. This is probably OK if you're a few months into your startup journey, are mostly talking to people you already know, and aren't looking for customers or investors just yet. It can also work if you're a super well-known founder with a strong social media presence and a good track record. The mystery around what you're doing next might be enough to get people to join your notification list.

Of course most founders aren't Jack Dorsey and being in "stealth mode" feels very 2010. As such, you're probably missing a great opportunity here. Somebody has taken the time to click on a link: maybe in your social media bio, as a result of a talk or blog post, or from the credentials page of your pitch deck. They're keen to understand what it is you're doing, and you're being deliberately coy. As somebody who has been on the receiving end of these sorts of websites, all this unnecessary cloak-and-dagger is somewhat frustrating.

I think one reason founders have such minimalist websites is that they haven't really figured out what they're building yet. Despite the received wisdom, most early products are emergent. They start with some vague idea and then iterate to something useful. Only once the product is finished can founders truly understand what they've built, who they've built it for, and why it's any good. I get that. I really do. However, I think it's much better these days to be clear about what you're doing, plant a flag in the sand, and ditch stealth mode altogether.

Getting Your Early Website Right

It sounds obvious, even trite. However, for most startups, your website is your primary shop window. It's the destination the bulk of your outreach will be driving people toward and where people go to in order to understand who you are, what you do, who you do it for, why you're different, and ultimately why they should care. It's also where they usually go to take the next action in becoming a customer, so it's amazing how little attention early founders pay to this crucial acquisition tool.

One reason for this lack of attention is that the founders are usually busy building the product and plan to come back to look at the marketing site once they start nearing launch. However, we all know the product work is never done, which means the promotional site often ends up languishing unloved for a significant amount of time. And when the product starts shaping up, there's usually a mad rush to get a promo site up quickly. I think this presents a missed opportunity. All those people who could have potentially discovered your site, got excited about what you were building, and signed up for notification over that period have now been lost, so it's best not to waste this one-time opportunity.

I also meet plenty of founders who claim that they don't need a "nice looking website" because they are following a Founder-Led Sales approach. This sort of response demonstrates some major red flags to me. Firstly, the use of the term "nice looking" indicates to me that the founder really doesn't understand the importance of Product Positioning (or design) and has dismissed their website as mere window dressing. Secondly, they haven't realized that the first thing a prospective sales lead will do is check out your website, and if they can't understand what you do or why they should care, they're not going to respond to your beautifully crafted outreach email. As such, a well-written and well-designed website is a crucial part of any sales motion.

Another excuse founders have is that they simply don't know what should go on the website until the product has been built—they are waiting for the product to inform the marketing. While this makes logical sense, I think it's much better to have a vision for what you're building first. Amazon is famous for writing press releases for products that have yet to create, in order to understand what it is they're building. I think the same argument can be used for your promotional website. Having to create a simple landing page before product work has started forces you to answer key questions around what you are building, who you are building it for, what value it will deliver, and how it will deliver it. Ironically, I've seen founders do an amazing job of encapsulating all this stuff in their fundraising deck, but completely drop the ball when it comes to their website. It's as though they are trying to mimic what they think a professional website should sound like, but in doing so they lose everything that's interesting and unique about their proposition and end up sounding the same as everybody else.

Now I'm not saying that the website needs to be super flashy. I've seen my fair share of early stage founders who go the other way, get obsessed about the design of their website, hire a world class agency, and spend the next six months on a fun, but often distracting design journey. Your website needs to clearly encapsulate your positioning, connect the value you have to offer to your visitors (through Language-Market Fit), and remove as many barriers to them hitting that aha moment as possible. Most importantly, it needs to encourage users to take the next step on the journey to acquisition.

Perfecting Your Call to Action

A lot of promotional websites for early stage startups focus on driving people to a single Call to Action (CTA); be that joining a waitlist (if the product is super early), requesting a demo (if it's a little further along) or signing up for a free trial (if it's self-serve). I think it's important to think carefully about how you frame that CTA, as it can have a big effect on your conversion rates.

Founders will often opt for "book a demo" as the primary call to action because it maps to their internal sales process. Demos can work if you have a highly motivated visitor. However, many people will see a demo as an unnecessary barrier they need to get over in order to start using the product. Demos take time, and there's always a fear that you'll be given a hard sell. This is the perfect example of the interplay between Motivation and Friction in The Growth Equation. As such, you might want to experiment with different calls to action like "join our waitlist," "join our beta," or simply "join" (which takes you into a flow to set up an onboarding call) in order to lower the friction. The former feels lower stakes while the latter feels like a step closer to trying the product out.

$$\text{Growth} = f[(A, \mathbf{M}, \Delta V/t, S, K) / (\boldsymbol{\mu}, C)]$$

Figure 7.6: How Motivation and Friction affect The Growth Equation.

Despite your best efforts, a good proportion of your visitors won't be ready to commit just yet. If they leave your site without taking some sort of action, all the effort (and cost) of getting them there has been wasted. This is why secondary and tertiary calls to action are so important.

As the name suggests, a secondary call to action is essentially the thing you want your visitor to do if they're not quite ready to start using your product. This often includes things like playing with a live demo, watching a product walk-through, viewing a product detail page, signing up for a webinar, joining your community, or anything else you think will advance somebody along the acquisition journey. Website homepages tend to be super generic, so I'm personally a big fan of use case pages. This is where you demonstrate how your product works for different types of users like founders, marketers, or product managers. These sorts of pages allow you to focus on the individual anxieties different types of users have and showcase in more detail how your product actually addresses these issues. They're also great for SEO.

After secondary, we have tertiary calls to action: things you might want to get your users to do if they're still not ready to sign up, but before they leave your site (potentially for good). In many instances, this might be signing up for your newsletter or following you on social media. While these activities are obviously less valuable than a straight-out acquisition, they give you permission to contact prospective customers later on; ideally with useful information or updates that slowly, over time, turn a cool prospect to a warm one.

I see far too many early stage websites with a single call to action (sign up for a demo) at the top of the page, and no secondary or tertiary calls to action. I can't tell you the number of times I've visited a site, thought it looked interesting, and wanted to keep track of their progress, but wasn't quite ready to jump on a sales call with their founder. I'd scan around looking for a newsletter to join or a Twitter link to follow, but nothing. So I'd leave the site, never to return. This really is web design 101, so it's amazing these sorts of mistakes still happen. Fortunately these are super easy issues to fix, so I suggest you take a look at your website right now to make sure you're not losing the slightly-intrigued-but-not-ready-to-buy audience.

Trust and Social Proof

One of the problems with a new product is it's hard to tell if it's any good. Will it really solve my problem? Will it still be around in six months? Is it even legit, or is this some clever scam? These are all the sorts of questions that go through people's minds when they encounter something for the first time, so these are all concerns your website needs to address.

One obvious way to demonstrate trust is to show who is behind the product. So include prominent contact information, details of the team with links to their social profiles, and maybe links to your prominent investors. You'll also want to add some legal disclaimers like your terms and conditions or data protection policy.

Another way to instill a sense of trust is to include trust badges people recognize. On a very basic level, you'll want to have an up-to-date SSL certificate. If you're taking money you'll want to include the credit card logos and maybe the logo of the payment provider if it's recognizable like Stripe. For more established companies, you might want to show that you're SOC2 or ISO 27001 compliant.

While the above are table stakes, the best way to show trust is through social proof: essentially demonstrating that high-profile brands already trust you. So share the logos of some high-profile clients. Share quotes and case studies from folks people recognize. If you have a badge from a Product Hunt launch or a good Trustpilot rating, throw that in as well. Anything that can help give the impression that people believe in you, and so your visitors should too.

Conversion Rate Optimization (CRO)

The ultimate purpose of your website is to convert visitors into customers or users—or at the very least to convince them to sign up for a demo or join your waitlist (if you've yet to launch). As such, your website conversion rate is the percentage of your visitors who complete your primary CTA. This figure essentially describes your website's effectiveness.

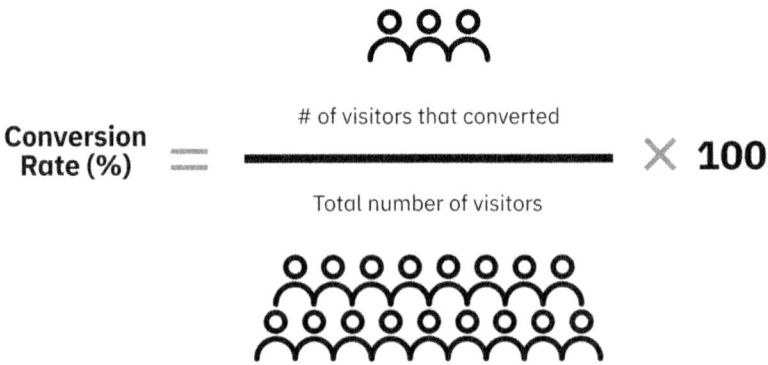

Figure 7.7: How to calculate your conversion rate.

While conversion rates vary from sector to sector and product to product, average conversion rates for SaaS products tend to fall in the 2-5% range, while 8% would generally be considered high. I personally wouldn't worry about the absolute number, especially in the early days when that number might be fairly low. Instead, I'd set targets from how much you're looking to improve things.

Conversion Rate Optimization (CRO) is the practice of doing just this: optimizing your website, and especially your landing pages, in order to maximize the number of people who sign up for your product. In the early stages, when your website is getting only a few hundred visitors a day, the rewards for doing CRO are fairly small. As your traffic builds, it makes sense to try a range of techniques and experiments to help you nudge your conversion rate upward.

Sometimes this is as simple as experimenting with different headlines and calls to action to see which performs better: a practice known as A/B testing or multivariate testing. Other times you might want to test entire pages to see which performs better. For SaaS companies, the most important page to test tends to be your pricing page—something we'll touch on in a little more detail in the chapter on Behavioral Design. For ecommerce companies, optimizing your product pages, category pages, and checkout flow can be super impactful.

Tools like Crazy Egg and AB Tasty are an easy way to start exploring multivariate testing. People often graduate from these to more sophisticated tools like Optimizely, while really large companies like Booking.com—a company famous for running hundreds of multivariate tests at any one time—might end up building their own custom tool sets.

Conversion rate optimization grew out of the search engine marketing world. SEO and paid search practitioners got very good at driving traffic to websites, but they realized this work was in vain if people didn't convert. If this is an area you'd like to lean into, there are plenty of SEO consultancies out there who will be more than willing to help (for a fee).

Be Careful About Over Promising and Under Delivering

Marketing teams do an amazing job of generating desire by positioning your product as the very best way (sometimes the only way) to meet your customers' needs. If they do their job, visitors will get over their natural sense of friction and skepticism in order to test out your product. As such, making big claims about what your product can do is a great way to turn an interested visitor into an activated one.

However, marketing hype also creates a set of expectations for users—expectations that your product really needs to deliver on. If it doesn't, you'll end up with customers who feel let down, disappointed, and in some cases hoodwinked. This gap between what you claim and what you actually deliver is known as the Expectation Gap and often happens when marketing teams are given unrealistic acquisition targets that are disconnected (or siloed) from the product team. To paraphrase a famous quote from a well-known marketing Maverick (sorry), you need to avoid having a marketing team write checks your product can't cash.

As such, try to be realistic with your marketing promises. Otherwise you'll do a great job driving awareness and acquisition, only to lose people further down the funnel—something we'll see in our chapter on retention and churn.

Summary

Founders often spend a lot of time building the best product possible under the belief that "if you build it they will come." However, no one will experience that value if you're failing to position the product effectively. As such, you need to get inside the heads of your customers in order to deliver Language-Market Fit before you can deliver Product-Market Fit. You then need to make sure that all of your touchpoints (most notably your website) do a great job of communicating your value proposition, in order to remove friction and get people to that aha moment as quickly as possible. This all comes under the heading of positioning and isn't something you should leave to chance.

You can improve your conversion rate even further by testing out different headlines, calls to action, layouts, and even whole pages. It's tempting to believe that getting users to sign up to your product is the end goal. However, as we'll see in the next few chapters, this is really just the beginning.

Next Steps

This chapter was all about nailing your Product Positioning: being able to clearly articulate the type of product you are, the problem you solve, who you solve it for, how you solve it, why your approach is fundamentally different and better than all the other products out there, and why anybody should care. You need to do this in language your users immediately get, rather than hiding behind fancy sounding words and marketing jargon. So what language would your customers use to describe your product? What would they say to convince a friend to give it a try? What do they like so much? What does it allow them to do that other products don't? If you can do this well, then congratulations, you've just found Language-Market Fit and are well on the way to Product-Market Fit.

If you're like most founders, you probably think that the superiority of your product is self-evident, and that you're already doing an amazing job of positioning. I'd advise you to try and forget everything you know about the product already and review your offering from a beginner's mind. Is the proposition truly clear and compelling, or can you understand why potential visitors might be confused? Try sitting down with people who don't know your product. Ask them to look at the website and explain what they think the product does. What makes it different? What makes it special? Are they right? Do they get to that aha moment quickly, or are they missing something important? You'll probably find your users scrolling up and down the page, really trying to understand what the product is, but more often than not failing. Jot down all the words people use to describe your product; understand where folks get stuck and then use this to strengthen your proposition.

To do this, try creating a bunch of different positioning statements, each of which focuses on different aspects of the product. These should be relatively short one-pagers that try to describe the product in different ways. Use a short headline, a paragraph or two introducing the product, and three key benefits. Then add more details about who the product is for, how it works, why it's special and why anybody should care. If you're getting stuck, consider how boxed products describe themselves. On the front: higher level information, the core value prop, a few key features. More details on the back: longer descriptions, pictures of the product in action, testimonials. Even more in-depth details on the side. Consider using popular writing frameworks like AIDA, which encourages you to first grab people's Attention, appeal to the reader's self-Interest, convince them to Desire your product, and then drive them to the next Action. Think about the gap your customers currently have in their lives and how your product fills that gap.

Consider trying on different product categories for size. Are you a CRM? A one-stop sales tool? An AI-powered SDR? Something else? What problem do you solve? Do you help manage the end-to-end sales process? What does that really mean? Do you simplify the sales pipeline? Help founders land more sales? Is there a better way to describe the problem? Who do you do it for? Is it for ambitious founders? Maybe a bit too generic? How about first-time founders doing their own sales? Founders who are overwhelmed by all the complex sales tools out there? What about the key features? Or better yet, key outcomes? Also, what makes you better than the rest? Is having all your data in one place really that meaningful? What ability does this actually unlock? How about being able to automate a bunch of common sales activities so you can focus on talking to your customers? Or maybe using this tool means you won't have to hire an SDR for another six months, if at all?

Try stress-testing some of your claims with the five whys: Keep asking why something is important until you get down to some sort of fundamental truth. Why is having all your sales data in one place important? So you're not having to switch between different tools. Why is that important? So you don't waste time, lose track of prospects, or let a sale go cold. Why is that important? To make sure that your customers have the best sales experience possible. Keep digging until you find a really meaningful insight you can use (that your customers really care about).

Try getting at least four or five fundamentally different positions together and test them on prospective customers. Which resonates the best? Try turning these into landing pages and push a bunch of traffic their way using Google Ads targeted directly to your customer to see which version of your proposition performs best. Take these learnings and update your homepage accordingly. Once you truly nail your positioning and find Language-Market Fit, you'll suddenly find growth starts to happen automatically and everything starts slotting into place.

CHAPTER 8

Successfully Onboarding and Activating New Customers

L et's assume you have a steady stream of people discovering your product and signing up. What happens next? In the early stages, onboarding will probably be you or your customer success manager walking early adopters through the setup process. This can work for a while. However, if the Average Contract Value (ACV) or Lifetime Customer Value (LCV) is low, this quickly becomes unsustainable.

There is also a bigger problem in store, as a registered user isn't necessarily an activated (or active) user. Many startup founders are shocked to find out how few of the people they've onboarded end up becoming truly active users. For many companies, having 5% of people active after the first 30 days (D30) is considered a success. That means that potentially fewer than 1 in 20 of the people you walked through the onboarding process will be there in a month's time. I call this The Activation Gap.

I'm currently working with a founder who is suffering from this problem. Their product launched a month ago and already has 14K registered. However only 1.5K have completed their sign-up process and done anything meaningful, and only 500 are actually active each month. That's quite a drop-off. As such, anything you or your product team can do to close this gap will have big downstream effects. Activation has been shown to have a significant effect on revenue, with a 25% increase in activation yielding a 34.3% lift on MRR over a 12-month period.[24] Clearly it's well worth founders spending time nailing their activation.

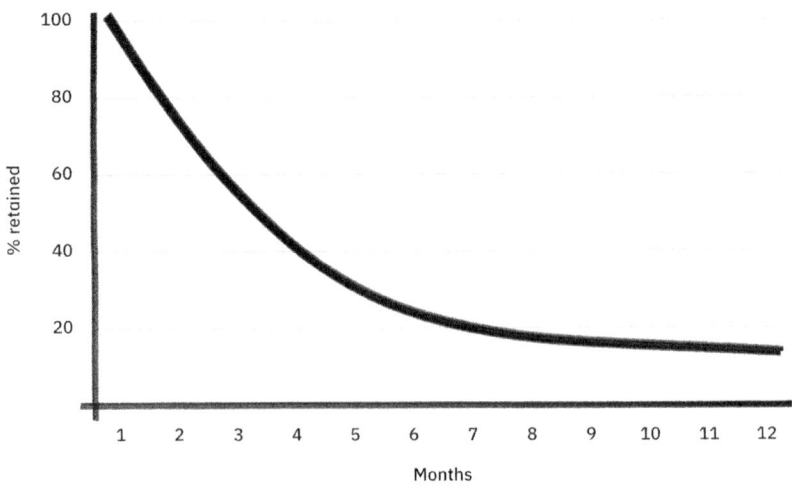

Figure 8.1: An example of a common startup retention curve.

While activation and retention are super important, I do occasionally come across founders who obsess over activation and retention figures when they have only a handful of customers. Don't spend three months building the world's best automated onboarding process when you only have a few sign-ups per month. At this level of growth, it makes more sense to have a more manual, non-scaling process. Ideally, you should start by driving acquisition and only then switch your focus to activation and retention.

Fortunately, a lot has already been written about onboarding, including Better Onboarding by Krystal Higgins. So as your customer acquisition starts to kick in, allocating product, design, and engineering resources to increasing activation and retention rates becomes increasingly valuable.

---

[24] https://www.appcues.com/blog/pirate-metric-saas-growth

Onboarding New Customers

Onboarding is the process of getting new customers set up on your system and ready to start using and realizing value from your product. The goal with onboarding is therefore to reduce your users' Time to Value (TTV) as much as possible so they can start building up positive usage behaviors.

Good onboarding processes have four steps:

1. Getting set up and situated
2. The aha moment (where they understand the value)
3. The eureka moment (when they start actually experiencing the value)
4. Habit building or stickiness (when the product becomes embedded into their workflow)

Some products are useful as soon as you've signed up. For instance, you can start creating designs in Canva straight off the bat. Other tools like email and calendar apps require a small amount of configuration, such as connecting to your email or calendar servers like Apple or Gmail. Then there are tools like CRMs that might require you to import your whole email history and address book, create a list of all your current prospects, customize process flows to match the way you currently work, and start tagging prospects and conversations. All this might mean that you need to spend weeks or months of effort before you start seeing any value.

Some products are relatively familiar. If you've used a calendar or email client before, you probably have a pretty good Mental Model of how they work. However, even fairly standard tools are likely to do some things differently, so your goal is to break people out of their old Mental Models quickly and help them form new understandings. This may look like helping them understand the benefits of tagging, smart inboxes, reminders, AI composition, and other workflows that will enhance their basic experience.

If you've used other drawing tools, getting accustomed to the quirks of something like Canva or Miro might be fairly straightforward (although there are still things about Miro that annoy me coming from Figma). But what if you've never used a design tool before? Looking at a blank page can be scary, which is why tools like Canva and Miro offer a range of different templates to get people started as quickly as possible as well as articles to help close the knowledge gap.

You might think that tools like calendars and email clients would be the easiest to onboard people to, as they're known entities with minimal setup. Almost all of your users will have an existing set of tools they use, and with them a powerful set of embedded behaviors. Getting people to switch their habits—from opening up their default email client, calendar app, or browser to yours—can be a real challenge. As such, tools like this really do need to have some sort of hook that makes them immediately better than their competition in order to solidify new behaviors. This is one reason why some companies use metrics like D30 to see how many people are still using their product after 30 days and have started forming new habits. Tracking Daily Active User (DAU) or Weekly Active User (WAU) rates might also give you an indication of how many people have become habituated to using your product.

Ultimately, the harder your product is to use, and the longer it takes for users to derive value, the more likely it is that they'll break their onboarding up over multiple sessions. And when people are forced to come back later to complete tasks, there's a good chance they'll forget, get sidetracked, or simply give up. As such, effective onboarding typically involves some of the following activities:

- Making it easy for users to get set up and import all their data
- Removing unnecessary conceptual or usability friction that might slow or frustrate new users
- Explaining to people how the product works so they can start getting value quicker
- Highlighting the most valuable parts of your product so they can experience those first
- Allow people to start playing with the product in order to understand its capabilities in a risk-free way
- Getting people to experience that first aha moment where they begin to understand how the product might be helpful
- Driving that eureka moment by delivering early value

- Creating hooks and loops that bring users back to the product and cement new behaviors

Some Common Onboarding Techniques

It's quite common to see established products offer things like product tours, where you get an animated walkthrough of all the features of the product. While these are nice, I'm sure we've all come across similar tours and simply skipped past them. This is because we assume that modern software has been built with ease of use in mind, and we assume that we're smart enough to figure things out. We're also just coming off that sign-up high and don't want any barriers in the way of exploring the product and getting all that amazing value we've been promised. I think these sorts of tours are generally overkill for early stage startups and might actually backfire. If you feel like you must have some sort of tour, showing tooltips when people first use a feature is generally less of a blocker than forcing people through a 10-step animated walkthrough of the whole interface.

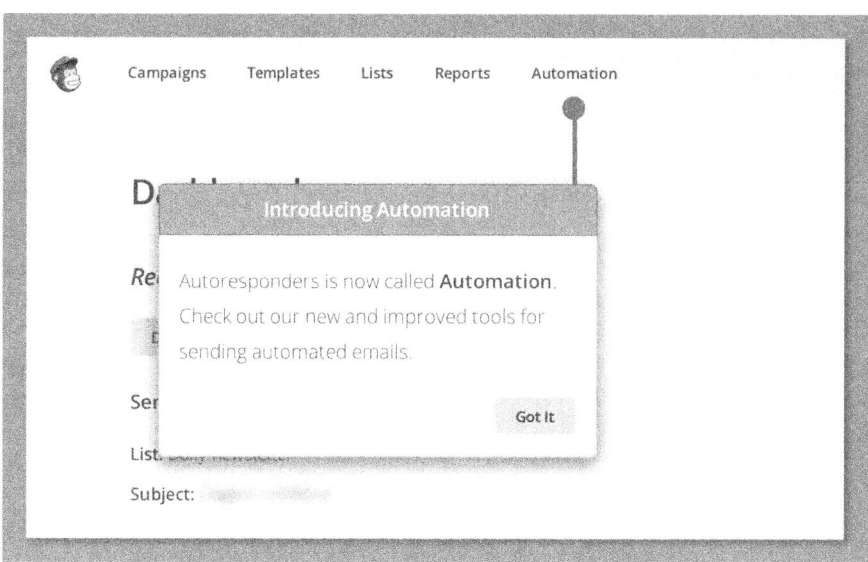

Figure 8.2: Mailchimp onboarding feature tour.

Instead, the first step to automated user onboarding is likely to be a series of emails you send out every few days (or when a user has, or maybe hasn't, completed a specific action) in order to create a new habit and level them up. Sometimes called a Drip Onboarding Campaign, these emails will usually be based on the questions people asked and the challenges they faced when you were onboarding them manually. You might start with a simple welcome message, along with a follow-up message a few days later to help orient people and see how they're getting on. I recommend sending out your welcome email within the first hour of people joining. Thank people for signing up, provide helpful tips to get them started, and let them know they can ask for help if need be.

In the first few days of onboarding, you might want to offer new users the opportunity to speak with a customer success manager to help them get started, or at the very least, point them to a live webinar. Doing this for every customer can be expensive, so security company Auth0 decided to share the onboarding booking form only to people with a corporate email account (rather than a Gmail address), leading to a sizable uplift in account activation.

As we mentioned earlier, the setup is just the start. If the user hasn't done anything since joining, you might want to give them a tiny nudge, perhaps by suggesting they create their first project or invite a collaborator. As people start using the product more, you might want to switch into education mode: highlighting features they've yet to use or helping them master the ones they're using regularly. And of course, if activity goes quiet, you might want to try and reactivate them in a timely manner.

Written content is great, but short Loom (or similar) videos can work even better. As you become more sophisticated, you'll start to see from usage data which parts of the product are getting used, which parts are being ignored, and where people tend to drop out along the way. The more you learn about your users, the more you'll be able to improve your onboarding emails, add contextual cues to the interface, and make the necessary product tweaks.

A lot of founders take user onboarding for granted at first. They understand the value of the product they've built, so they assume everybody else will, too. It's only when they see just a tiny proportion of registrations turn into activated users that this becomes an issue. Fortunately, you can get surprisingly large upticks in activation by doing simple things like testing out the content and cadence of different onboarding emails or switching from text to video, so it's worth putting early effort in here.

Checklists and Progress Bars

Another common onboarding technique is to give people a series of tasks they need to complete in the form of a checklist or progress bar. For example:

- Fill Out Your Profile
- Add a Picture
- Create Your First Project
- Upload Your Data
- Invite a Collaborator (this one is also a good Product-Led Growth technique)

This allows users to explore the interface by themselves, in whatever order they like, at their own pace. If they miss a few steps or go cold for a couple of days, this gives you the opportunity and permission to get back in touch and remind them that they still have a few more steps to complete.

This sort of checklist-based approach encourages users to start adding content into the product. The more content they add over time, the more likely they'll be to become an activated user. This is in part due to the idea of Sunk Cost. If you've invested a certain amount of time into a product, you're more likely to stick with it and less likely to churn. As such, some products will use checklist completion as a proxy for activation.

It's also worth noting that people generally have a natural inbuilt desire to complete things, especially if doing so is relatively easy. So if a user logs in and sees that 60% of their profile has already been completed (possibly automatically through social sign-on), there's a good chance they'll fill in the other 40% to remove the reminder and get a sense of completion. This feeling of progress taps into the idea of Gamification, which we'll discuss in the chapter on Behavioral Design.

The Cold Start Problem and the Blank Page

As we mentioned earlier in the book, there are many products like marketplaces and social media sites that need other users in order to be useful. Back in the day, it was quite common for new services to ask users to import their address book to see who else they knew was using the product. This was a good way to speed up the creation of a meaningful network, rather than forcing users to search for friends manually. However, this technique was often abused, with some of the big social networks spamming your address book, or at the very least, creating shadow accounts for users without their permission. As such, users have become more wary and protective of sharing this information.

That being said, many people are happy to sign up to new services using social sign-on: allowing the product to use your Google or LinkedIn credentials instead of having you choose yet another password. These services will often ask for additional permissions, like looking through your contacts, so in a weird way, startups are still doing the old contact book trick—just now by stealth.

Another way to get over the Cold Start Problem is to make suggestions for accounts new users should follow. Twitter realized that its early adopters were joining the platform because they had a bunch of friends already using the app; but later majority users would turn up wanting to see what all the fuss was about, be greeted with an empty feed, and quickly leave. So as part of the onboarding process, the designers asked some questions about the sort of topics new users were interested in and then gave recommendations on who to follow. This meant that once folks had finished the sign-up process, they were taken to a feed already populated with tweets, so they could understand the value and how the product worked much faster.

The Blank Page Problem is very similar to the Cold Start Problem in that you sign up for a new product based on a number of bold claims, only to be dumped into an empty product not knowing what to do next.

One of the easiest ways to tackle the Blank Page Problem is to fill it with some useful, instructional content. As such, this can often act as a mini product tour.

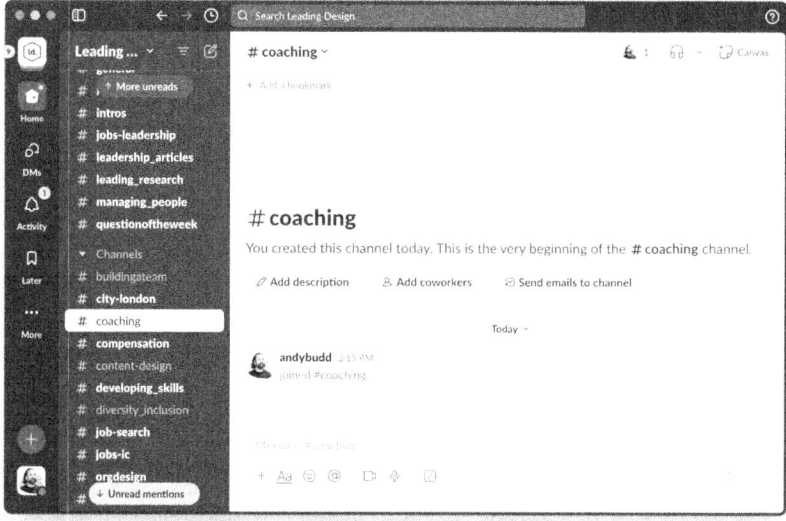

Figure 8.3: Slack new channel page.

However, let's be honest: People don't read instructions. Instead they want to get stuck in and start exploring what the product can do straight away. That's why it's often better to provide some demo content people can start playing with, as is the case with project management tool Trello.

Playing with demo content is a great way to understand what a product does in a low-risk environment and reach your first eureka moment. However, it doesn't necessarily get users closer to deriving value. This is where templates come in.

Staring at a blank page in Miro or Canva can be intimidating—all this flexibility but no clue where to start. Templates are a great way to shortcut this process by offering up premade solutions to common problems. Want to map out your org structure? No worries, Miro has a template for that. How about creating a workshop activity? Well, Miro has a bunch of suggestions for that as well. Templates are a great way of introducing new users to all the things you can do on a tool like Miro or Canva—and hopefully have them create something valuable right out of the gate.

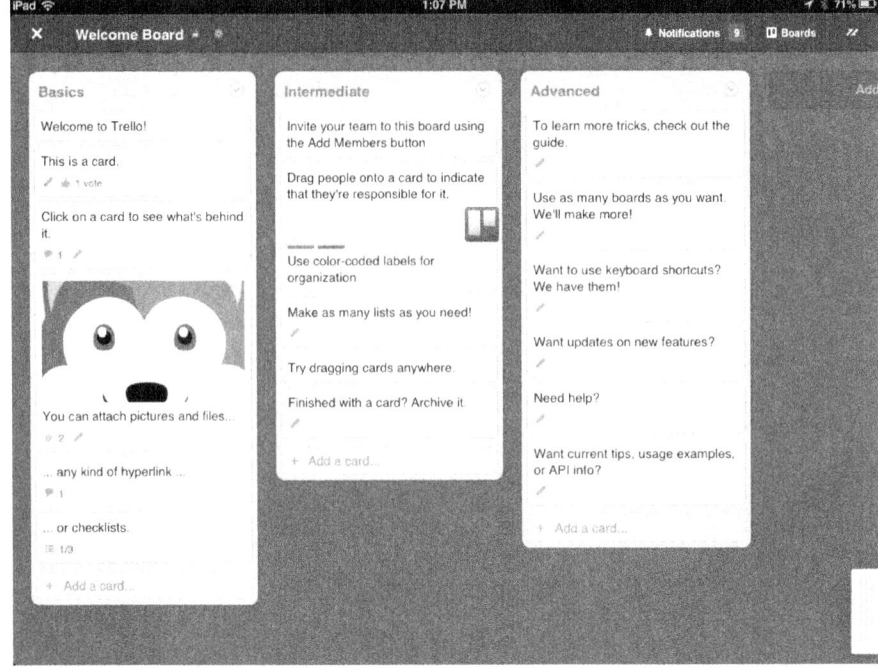

Figure 8.4: The Trello sandbox project allows new users to start playing with the tool without needing to input data.

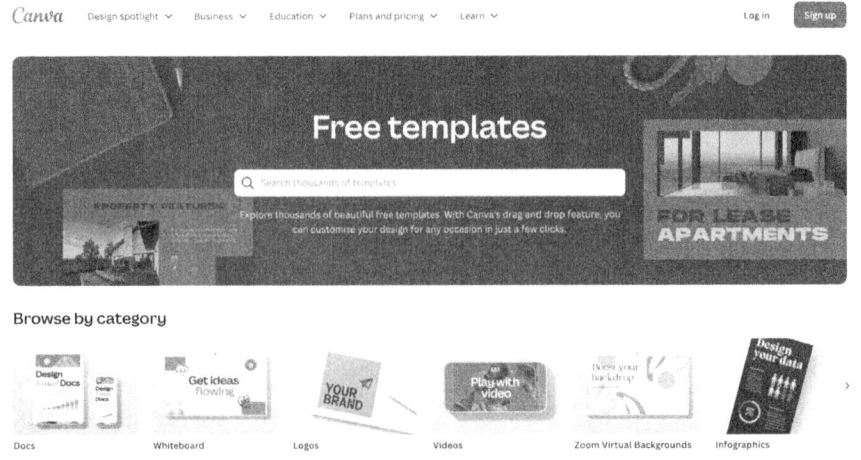

Figure 8.5: Canva template page.

Rather than forcing new users to find relevant content through a template store, it's become quite popular to ask users a series of onboarding questions and then present them with a landing page tailored to their needs. Typeform, for instance, will ask some questions about your background and take you to the templates it thinks are most relevant. Shopify does the same, asking new users about their sector and then taking them to themes and templates that best fit. They'll also ask users if they are already selling and push them into a migration flow if the answer is yes.

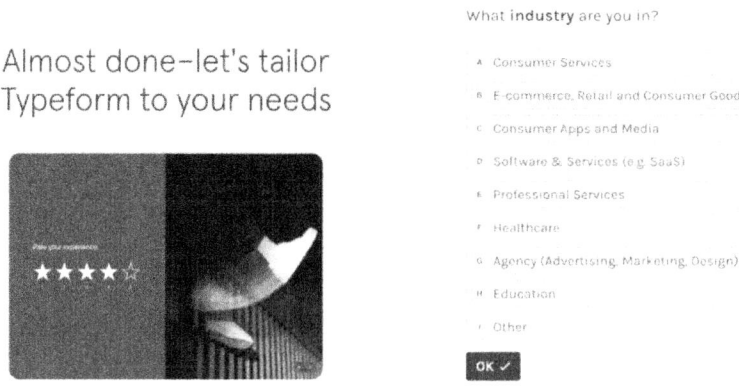

Figure 8.6: Typeform's customized onboarding flow.

Usability and Friction

One major reason people drop out of an onboarding process is experiencing unnecessary Friction (μ). Having to create yet another account and choose yet another password, rather than using social sign-on. Having to answer a bunch of seemingly irrelevant marketing questions when you just want to kick the tires. Getting all the way to the end of the sign-up process only to be told that you need to provide your credit card details to join the "free trial." Being forced to then validate your email address before you're allowed to go any further and having to wait ages before that validation email arrives. When it does arrive, being forced to fill in a CAPTCHA to log in. And when you finally do make it through all those hurdles, being deposited on a blank page with no indication of what to do next.

$$\text{Growth} = f[(\text{A, M, } \Delta\text{V/t, S, K}) / (\mu, \text{C})]$$

Figure 8.7: The role of Friction in The Growth Equation.

Often, the solution is equally simple: Run usability tests to identify these pain points and get your designer to remove as many usability blockers as possible—this is one of the things you pay your UX designer to do, after all. Some of this might involve clever staging, so think about what you absolutely need to ask up front in order to create the account and what you might hold off asking until later, once people have started deriving value from the product.

Even if you're able to remove all the obvious usability blockers, some processes are innately complicated, especially if they involve an initial setup process. Hotjar is a great example of a company that has gone out of its way to reduce the barriers to use. Hotjar is an analytics tool that requires users to add a snippet of code to their website before they can start getting value. As you can imagine, this either requires some technical ability on behalf of the person using the product or access to a helpful developer who can do it for you.

The team at Hotjar have thought deeply about how they can reduce the innate barriers to use in their product. For smaller customers, they've built tools that allow non-technical users to add the snippet into their platform themselves via Google Tag Manager. For larger enterprise customers, they've looked at ways to bring developers into the platform, share the snippet with them directly, and provide all the support and information they need to get it live quickly. As an aside, making the process happen inside the platform rather than through emails or personal conversations is a great way to keep the product front of mind and keep everybody focused on the task. The results have been impressive, giving Hotjar a strong competitive advantage. "If you look at the time of first value," explains CEO Mohannad Ali, "67% of users get to the point of value within 15 minutes. It's really quick because over the years we've done a lot of work to make it a very, very frictionless process."

Of course, not all friction is bad. In fact, people generally like there to be a bit of a learning curve in order to develop a sense of mastery and progress. This is something game designers and e-learning designers know only too well. In fact, we'll touch on the issue of Gamification later in the chapter on Behavioral Design. The goal is to remove unnecessary usability blockers and cognitive load, without making the process so simple as to be dull and unengaging. Despite sounding simple, it's actually quite hard to deliver and generally requires a high level of design talent.

Enterprise Activation and Concierge Service

It's much easier to activate self-serve customers in some ways, as you can automate the process through messaging and prompts. Conversely, it can be surprisingly hard to activate larger companies, especially if onboarding requires any manual setup or technical integration.

If your product requires a lot of setup, you might need to offer your earlier customers a white glove or concierge service (meaning you'll do the work for them). This can be challenging if your customers need to give you sensitive data, or if the setup is highly customized and specific to them. In some instances, it might end up being more like a two-week consultancy project where you ask questions, try to track down the people with the necessary data, perform a manual setup in the back end, and then walk your customers through the process.

Using a concierge approach can be costly (recall earlier in the book when we discussed things that won't necessarily scale). In the early stages, you might need to do this to win some design partners (companies who have agreed to use the product in return for giving you a ton of feedback) and well-known customers who will give you credibility among your market (logos you can put on your website). Long term, a concierge approach only makes sense if you have customers with a high ACV (Average Contract Value) or LCV (Lifetime Customer Value).

Onboarding can be especially hard if it requires technical integration and needs to rely on the goodwill of the customer's engineering team. Often, the people who bought the product aren't the ones doing the integration. The folks who are doing the integration already have a big backlog of work and don't see your project as strategically or politically important to them. As such, part of your onboarding strategy needs to be figuring out how to create a sense of importance and urgency.

One obvious way around this is to have a contract that allows a short set-up window, after which you start charging. The idea is to create some sort of time imperative to get your project bumped up the backlog. You need to be careful here, or you might find yourself in a situation where you've been charging customers for a few months, they're still not set up, and decide to cancel. As such, this might be more effective as a negotiating tactic than something you regularly implement. Going back to the client to let them know that you're meant to start charging but are happy to give them a two-week extension and asking, "Is there anything we can help you with here?"

The other way is to make integration as easy and beneficial to the people doing the integrations as possible. This means having great documentation, great technical support, and potentially some sort of developer relations manager (DevRel) who can befriend the team managing the implementation and use their relationship as a way of getting things over the line. For instance, if you've invited the CTO to an interesting seminar or treated them to lunch (yes, I know this is very old-school), they might be more inclined to help chivvy the project on.

It's also important to make sure you have the right relationship with the right people. In my experience, founders are great at selling enterprise products to executives but can often be a little brusque and impatient with those doing the onboarding or implementation. As such, it's often better to separate these roles and hire a customer success manager or developer relations manager to take over. This then gives you the ability to apply influence on several fronts and play good cop, bad cop where necessary.

Regardless of approach, it's important to get your new customers onboarded as quickly as possible or they might lose interest—so do everything you can to get the set-up and integration times as low as possible.

Bottom-Up Onboarding

When it comes to enterprise sales, it's tempting to want to get the whole team signed up and onboarded in one fell swoop. However, sometimes it's easier to take a bottom-up approach to onboarding. Tools like Dropbox and Figma have done this very effectively by making their tools free for individuals. Those individuals will start deriving value from those tools in single-player mode. They'll soon start sharing files and folders with peers to collaborate on. These tools can very quickly propagate around a whole organization, with the data being added by individuals over time, rather than through one big onboarding process. Eventually the organization gets wind of this emergent behavior and formalizes the process. Sometimes it's because they need to see the value before having to go through a trial or an onerous onboarding process themselves; sometimes it's because folks are using it anyway and they need to put some formal control in place around who can share what and when.

As such, if you find yourself struggling to get organizations to invest the time needed to set up your product, you might want to explore a single-player self-serve Product-Led approach instead.

Another approach is to sign up a single team, possibly on a trial basis. If you have a product that encourages cross-functional collaboration, you can quickly see how a single trial can work its way around an entire organization and embed itself in other people's workflows. Ideally by the time the trial comes to an end, so many other people in the organization are deriving value from the product that the team running the trial will get pressure to keep using it. This sort of behavior is at the heart of Product-Led Growth, a topic we'll dive into shortly.

Calculating Your Customer Activation Rate

One important thing to understand is what actually constitutes an activated user. This may sound simple, but there are many different ways you can measure this, and the activation metric you choose might have a profound impact on your focus as a team.

Activation metrics are generally tied to some sort of activation milestone: the action a user takes that flips them from testing the waters to being a user. Activation milestones are often unique to the type of product, the type of users, the market, the founder, and the team. They are also somewhat subjective, which means you can decide whether to set a high or low bar.

It's been said numerous times that Facebook's early activation metric was getting seven friends in 10 days. Hubspot has a similar target of getting customers to use five out of their 25 features in the first 60 days, while Dropbox is aiming to get customers to upload one folder on one device within the first hour. I'd argue that some of these are closer to North Star metrics, as they hint at a target that's likely to turn somebody into an activated user, but I'm probably splitting hairs here. Loom's activation metric is a little clearer—when a user shares a Loom video with somebody else—while Zapier's is somebody setting up their first "Zap."

Here are a few more examples of activation milestones that different companies might choose:

- First virtual event with more than three attendees
- First five survey responses collected
- First video with a view
- Third order placed
- First 20 minutes of content streamed
- First design shared
- First invoice sent
- 10 contacts added
- First meeting scheduled
- First job application published
- Bank account connected
- Javascript code snippet is added

Ideally you'll pick a milestone that has a strong correlation to sustained use and is highly actionable by your team. Start by listing a dozen common actions users can do on your site and then look at your data to see which ones a good proportion of your users can achieve and which are somewhat predictive of longer term retention. All these actions should tie back to the core value your product offers. For some of these milestones, it might be debatable whether you choose five or six survey responses or whether you choose 15 or 20 minutes of content streamed. The key is knowing that increasing the number of survey responses or the length of tracks listened to is a strong predictor of retained use and is something your team can help improve.

Once you've decided on the activation milestone, coming up with your customer activation metric is pretty simple. It's just the number of people who reached your activation milestone in a given cohort, divided by the number of people who signed up in that cohort. You can then multiply this by 100 to get your activation rate.

For instance, let's imagine that 1,000 people signed up to your product in January, 60 hit your activation milestone within a week of signing up, 30 within two weeks, 10 within three weeks, and none for the rest of the year. That's 100 activated users divided by 1,000 sign-ups, multiplied by 100, which is a 10% activation rate.

What constitutes a good activation rate is somewhat subjective. I saw a survey of 500 tech companies recently that claimed an average activation rate of 30% for SaaS companies, while the median activation rate for B2C marketplaces and ecommerce was 16% and 15% respectively. Though SaaS companies might be looking at people using a Freemium version of their product, ecommerce companies are more likely to be looking at their first sale. I wouldn't worry too much about industry benchmarks here; instead, focus on where you currently are and what you can do to improve that number—which is essentially what we've been talking about in this chapter.

In the early stages of your product, measuring cohorts by time will probably be sufficient. As you get more sophisticated, you'll probably want to break down cohorts by user profile and acquisition method. That way you'll be able to tell if one sort of user is gaining significantly more value from your product or whether one acquisition channel is driving a lot of sign-ups but not turning them into activated customers. Although it's common for marketing teams to be judged on conversion rate (as we saw in the previous chapter), we're starting to see more and more marketing teams be judged on activation rate, as a way to prevent them from throwing lots of low-value traffic into the top of the funnel or encouraging the wrong type of people to sign up and immediately churn.

Other Common "Activation" Metrics

While the above approach is probably the most helpful and accurate way of tracking activation, there are some common shortcuts people use. For some products the ratio of visitors to sign-ups might be enough. For others, you might want to track the trial-to-paid conversion rate. Both of these are fine metrics, but they're really conversion metrics rather than activation metrics and might hide the fact that people have signed up but have yet to figure out what your product is about or derive any value.

Another common approach is to track the ratio of Daily Active Users (DAU) to Weekly Active Users (WAU). This is a way to see how many of your customers are still active (i.e., deriving enough value from the product that they come back on a regular basis). However, not all products make sense to use on a daily basis, so this is another one of those metrics that, while interesting, might not be super helpful.

The best way to tell if previously activated users are still active is to have some hypothesis around frequency of feature use. To do this you can pick a single feature (i.e., an active user is a user who posts a minimum of five messages a month). Or you can measure activity across a whole range of different features to see how your product stacks up.

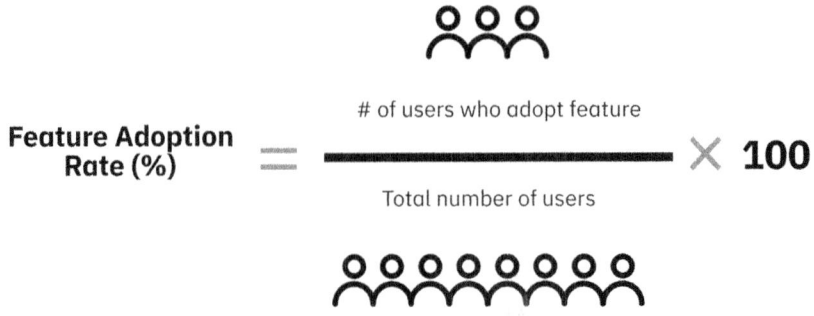

$$\text{Feature Adoption Rate (\%)} = \frac{\text{\# of users who adopt feature}}{\text{Total number of users}} \times 100$$

Figure 8.8: How to calculate your feature adoption rate.

This will help you track how much value your customers continue to derive and whether there's a chance they might churn (which we'll be discussing next).

The Role of Onboarding in Retention

In the next chapter, we're going to look at the importance of retaining previously activated customers. It's worth noting that if you start to see retention drop, it doesn't necessarily mean that you have a product problem and it isn't delivering the necessary value. It might be that the product is there, but the user hasn't been able to discover it properly during their onboarding process. As such, you often find that improving the onboarding process can have a dramatic effect on retention as well.

Summary

Good onboarding flows don't just happen. Instead they are considered and designed, converting as many of your hard-fought prospects into active users as possible. Product teams need to work closely with marketers to make sure they aren't over promising. However, they also need to make sure that they can deliver the promised value as quickly as possible. There are usually plenty of places you can lose prospective users during onboarding, so design and product teams need to identify these problem areas and plug as many holes as possible. Effective onboarding can lead to higher activation, higher retention, and ultimately higher revenue. As such, nailing your onboarding process can deliver outsize effects and shouldn't be ignored.

Next Steps

Once you have a reasonable flow of new sign-ups, it makes sense to turn your attention to onboarding and activation. Start by doing a quick audit of your site onboarding flow. Imagine that you're a brand-new user who knows nothing about the product. Try signing up afresh and note all the points of friction. Can people register using social sign-on or are you forcing people to pick a new password? If so, is the process as smooth as possible? Are you forcing people to wait for an email verification message to come through and does that happen instantly or take a few minutes? If you are doing this, is that really necessary or can you remove this potential barrier altogether? When people are going through the sign-up process, what information are you requiring and does this feel reasonable? What can you do to streamline the process and get people in and using your product as quickly as possible?

When people finally get access to your product, what's the first run experience like? Are they dropped onto a blank page, or are you providing clear signposting? Is it obvious what to do next? Are you providing templates, sandboxes, or other forms of scaffolding to make things clear? Don't just stop at the sign-up process. Are you sending useful emails that encourage repeat use? Do you have a clear activation KPI? If you don't, you really need to come up with one stat! What do you do when new users fail to meet that KPI during the initial window? And if you send follow-up emails, are these actually effective?

Have your designer, product manager, and engineer go through the process. What have they seen that you haven't? Maybe get on a call with some new users and watch them go through the onboarding process. What barriers do they face, and how do they find the experience? Maybe follow up with them in a week's time to see if they activated and ask good questions to find out why some didn't.

Getting your onboarding right can be surprisingly time-consuming. I'm starting to see the emergence of companies like Dopt that offer both a visual onboarding flow builder and a series of common components via an SDK, which can help speed things up. The real trick is making sure that your product team is given enough space to properly address these problems. This will be almost impossible if they're drowning in new feature requests. To avoid this, set a clear objective, like increasing activation rate from 20% to 30%. Give them the flexibility to figure out how to achieve this, and don't fill their plate with too many feature extensions until they do. Time-boxing activity can really help here. Just remember that there is very little point in adding additional functionality if new users are struggling to use the features you already have. Once you have a good number of users signing up, focus on improving activation before worrying too much about retention.

CHAPTER 9

The Importance of Retention

Most early stage startups are understandably fixated on acquisition and activation. This is especially true if user account numbers are starting to resemble that hallowed hockey stick graph. However, fast growth can conceal a multitude of problems, including equally fast churn.

Startups like Clubhouse, which exploded overnight and generated a ton of buzz, acquired lots of customers very quickly, and then—just as quickly—fizzled out. When was the last time you logged into your Clubhouse account? As with many products, users sign up in order to understand what all the fuss is about but fail to understand the point of the product, discover any meaningful value, or develop lasting usage patterns. As a result, they leave almost as quickly as they joined.

Our friend Des Traynor from Intercom explains that "Customers gradually stop using products, from using it every morning to every week to once a month. At some point down the road, you'll remember you're paying for something you don't need and don't use, and then you 'churn,' even though the decision was made months ago." As such, churn has the tendency to sneak up on you unawares.

Much has been written about the concept of Product-Market Fit (PMF): the point where you know you have a product that meets a meaningful need and starts to take off. The challenge with PMF is it's difficult to pinpoint exactly when you've achieved it. Some people will claim that if you're wondering whether you've reached PMF you almost certainly haven't, because it's one of those things where "you'll know it when you see it." While this might be true, I think it is fairly obvious whether you have PMF from your retention curve. Does your curve shallow out relatively quickly, indicating that a meaningful proportion of users are finding value from your product? Or does usage drop off steadily (as we saw in the early days of Clubhouse)?

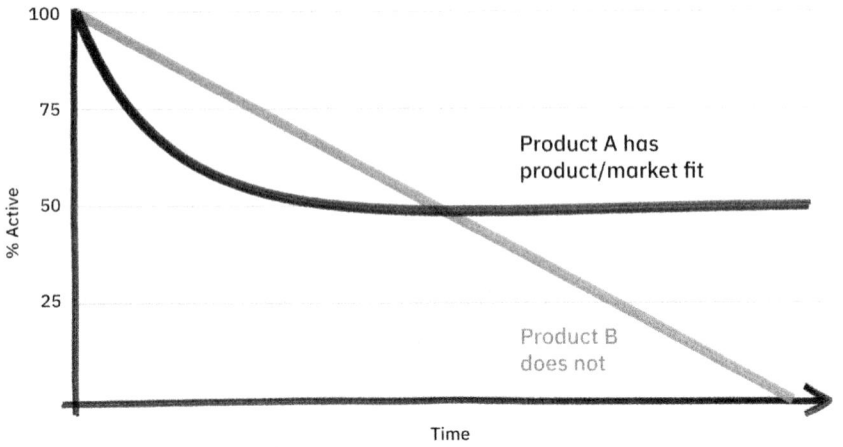

Figure 9.1: Comparing the retention curve of a product with PMF to one without.

Marc Andreessen from investment fund a16z sums this up perfectly:

> "You can always feel when Product-Market Fit is not happening. The customers aren't quite getting value out of the product, word of mouth isn't spreading, usage isn't growing that fast, press reviews are kind of 'blah,' the sales cycle takes too long, and lots of deals never close. And you can always feel Product-Market Fit when it is happening. The customers are buying the product just as fast as you can make it—or usage is growing just as fast as you can add more servers. Money from customers is piling up in your company checking account. You're hiring sales and customer support staff as fast as you can."

While people might debate the numbers, there is one school of thought that suggests that a 90% annual retention rate is a sign of having reached Product-Market Fit. The logic is that this demonstrates a significant proportion of your users are gaining enough value from your product that they're willing to sign up for another year. Whatever the actual figures, I tend to agree that retention and PMF are highly correlated.

Acquisition vs. Retention: A Cautionary Tale

Imagine there is one startup, we'll call them Avocado Co., growing at 10K users per month, while another, Banana Co. is growing at 20K per month. It would be fairly easy to assume that Banana Co. will massively outperform Avocado Co. However, let's assume that Avocado Co. has a monthly churn rate of 5%, while Banana Co. has a monthly churn rate of 15%.

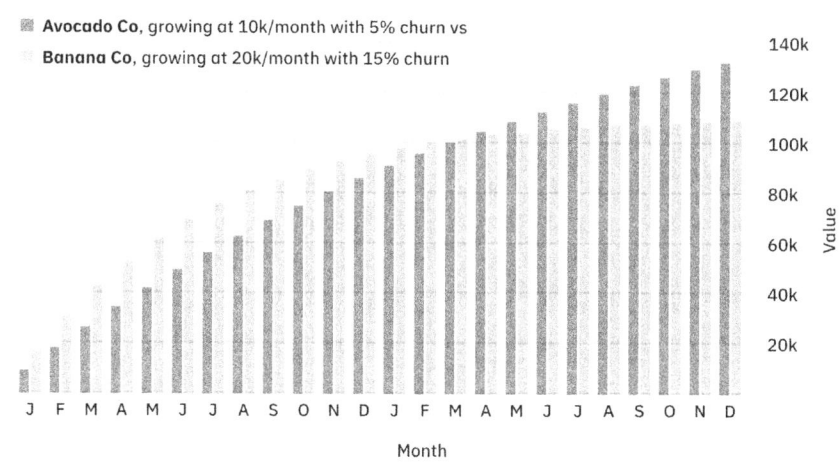

Figure 9.2: The effect high churn can have on a high-growth product.

With these numbers holding steady, Avocado Co. will have lost all the people in their first cohort within 20 months, while Banana Co. will have lost 20K users in just eight months. That suddenly looks a lot less promising—especially if you consider that highly effective startups generally have a Customer Payback Time (the length of time it takes for a user to pay off their acquisition costs) of 5-7 months. This leaves

Banana Co. almost no time to make any money, while Avocado Co. has a full year or more of profit.

If we look at absolute numbers, after the first year, Avocado Co. will have 87,332 customers, while Banana Co. will have 97,213. By the second year, things will have flipped, with Avocado Co. having 134,522 active customers while Banana Co. has only 111,040.

The high acquisition rates have effectively masked the fact that retained customers have actually dropped much faster than at the competition. The company with the higher retention has had to acquire much fewer customers than their competition, presumably costing them a lot less. At the same time, they've actually managed to end up with more retained customers over a longer period, which means significantly more profit; profit that can be spent on acquiring new customers in the future.

The Business Case for Retention

As we've seen, it can be difficult and costly to attract new customers. Therefore, if you can retain customers for longer, you can earn more money for each customer at the same customer acquisition cost. This additional money can then be spent on acquiring even more customers, effectively optimizing your sales costs.

If customers stay engaged for longer, there's also more opportunity for them to introduce new users to your product. Users can do this in several ways, which we'll discuss in more detail later in the book. First off, there's more opportunity for them to make direct recommendations and referrals. If you have a collaborative tool—like Figma, Miro, or Dropbox—the longer the user is on the system, the more opportunities they'll have to invite people to collaborate. Lastly, with social media and user-generated content products like Twitter or Pinterest, they'll have more time to create more content, which might get picked up by search engines or otherwise shared.

Because retention can help increase both acquisition and monetization, it's become a popular topic in startup circles of late. In fact we're seeing more and more companies align their teams around retention. Ruairí Galavan, Intercom's director of customer engagement explains:

> "Half our team is focused on conversion and activation while the other half is focused on retention and expansion. Each half of the team works closely with marketing, product, and sales; and within each half of the team we work on two types of projects. On the one hand, we create product education content that aligns with whatever the product team is shipping or launching. And in between all of that activity (which is a lot), we work to proactively and strategically broaden and deepen our customers' usage of Intercom."

How to Improve Retention and Reduce Churn

Retention is a challenge for most early stage companies (and some later stage ones as well). Although there's no single way to plug a "leaky funnel," there are a few common approaches. The first step is to understand why customers are churning. If you can understand where the holes are and why people are dropping out, you can plug the gaps and hold onto more users (or, to stick with our leak metaphor, keep more water in the funnel).

As we saw at the end of Chapter 7, one common reason for high churn is when your sales and marketing team end up "writing checks your product can't cash." (For those of you who aren't fans of Top Gun, this means promising things your product doesn't currently deliver.) While this is sometimes a result of marketing teams highlighting features that might be months (if not years) away in order to hit their targets, it's not necessarily driven by dishonesty. Usually they're sharing an ambitious vision that the founder really does believe in but doesn't quite match the current state of the product. Overselling the value, the quality, the experience, or the delivery will cause a customer to churn quickly when they arrive to discover a poor design, poor experience, or a lack of what they were promised.

New customers trying a product for the first time have much less patience for finding what they are looking for and will often give up when met with even small barriers to completing their task (the μ in The Growth Equation). If the value really is there, but users struggle to connect with it fast enough (think back to the Time to Value section in our chapter on onboarding), they will quickly abandon the product never to return—no matter how many feature update emails you send them. Whether these barriers are a result of poor onboarding or a poor experience guiding them toward the features, an overly complicated product requires investment in a better experience.

To help your users access value quicker and easier, you can guide them directly to it with better onboarding, setup wizards, shortened user flows, or other UX improvements. These are all issues a UX designer can solve, and a good UX designer will build (and test) MVP versions of these features before you invest too much design and development time.

It may be easier (and less costly) to manage the expectations up front instead. If you are claiming your product is better than it actually is—if your sales and marketing teams are over promising—adjust the messaging to better fit what the product actually delivers. This may cause a reduction in acquisition (more users are ruled out before even trying the product), but those who come in will be more likely to stay, having found what they were looking for.

Encouraging Regular Use

If the product is delivering on the promises made by your sales and marketing teams and the value is there, customers may be churning because they just aren't using the product frequently enough for it to become part of their workflow. Regularity of use plays a huge role in retention. Products that retain customers the best are either products people use so frequently that they become a core part of their workflow (like an email client) or products that need only to be set up once to run in the background, continually adding value (like security software).

Products that sit in the middle and get only limited use generally struggle the most to retain customers. Sometimes people take these sorts of tools for granted or forget about them between periods of use, so it's important to remind people of the value they are getting out of the tool—perhaps by listing usage in the monthly billing email or by sending a timely "usage review" email[25] if you notice a drop in engagement. If people engage with the product more regularly, you increase the opportunities users have to experience value and become a key part of their workflow. When irregularity of use is your cause for churn, you might need to explore using some of the Product-Led Growth strategies we'll discuss later in the book—such as collaboration and messaging—to bring users back to the product more regularly.

This is where we get to the concept of Stickiness: your product's natural ability to engage, entertain, delight, and ultimately retain customers beyond the core value it delivers. Designers are especially good at creating products that are a delight to use due to their superior user experience.

$$Growth = f[(A, M, \Delta V/t, S, K) / (\mu, C)]$$

Figure 9.3: Stickiness is a major component of The Growth Equation.

While I think it's best to focus on delivering as much value as early as possible to your customers, companies have a number of techniques they can use for improving Stickiness and reducing churn. We'll touch on some of these in our later sections on Gamification and Product-Led Growth, however one I want to mention now is the role of inertia.

User Lock-In, Switching Costs, and Inertia

We all know that people are less likely to switch tools if they've invested a significant amount of time and energy into the tool already (Sunk Cost). Sunk Cost can take a few different forms: actual setup costs or the manual effort to get up and running. It could also be familiarity with workflows or the hassle of exporting and re-entering data. For instance, I've been wanting to switch from Evernote for quite some time, but can't face having to export all my data, import it to a new tool, and then tidy everything up. The work required to make this

---

[25] https://medium.com/boldstart-ventures/improving-adoption-with-the-product-usage-report-email-573dadd3c6ef

switch just doesn't feel worth the effort involved, so users end up feeling "locked in." I similarly feel locked in to Twitter because of the number of followers I have on that platform.

Sometimes this lock-in comes from the amount of time and effort you've invested in mastering a specific tool. For instance, designers are so locked into Figma that it's hard for them to consider other tools. If you're Figma, you can double down on this by adding ever more complex features and investing heavily in user education, while as a competitor you might want to copy as many of the core features as possible to make switching easier (as Figma did with Photoshop). Or, you can do what Canva did and remove the learning curve altogether.

Personal identity and status can be a big motivator. If people have invested a ton of time into your product, their identity might be intrinsically tied to your offering. This is true for professional tools as much as it is for social media sites. Think back to the section on design partners in Chapter 6, and Notion's Pro Community. It's especially hard to leave a product if that's where your community hangs out, which is why we've seen a rise in community features and community-led retention strategies.

An equally powerful motivator is money. If your product helps users generate income, they will be much less likely to churn. In fact, even if a competitor offers similar benefits, as long as your product continues to deliver value, they may use both products in tandem. Many course creators, for example, host their courses on both Coursera and Udemy, since there are no rules against unique content (although Udemy's rules state that a course hosted elsewhere cannot be free there if it is listed as paid on their own platform).

When I think about the tools I use on a regular basis (Slack, Figma, Miro, Twitter, Evernote, Notion, Google Docs), most of them get harder to leave as the years progress and more and more of my knowledge, data, network, and income becomes associated with them. The idea of starting afresh with a clean slate feels that much more daunting. This is one of the main reasons people stick with older tools, even if there are now better ones on the market. Past a certain point, data lock-in and switching costs (both financial and time) create a powerful disincentive to leave.

Unintended or Accidental Churn

Churn isn't always a direct result of experience. Sometimes it's as mundane as the credit card you have on file going out of date or the person who was originally responsible for the account leaving the company. If a payment doesn't go through and no one notices, your product might not be delivering that much value. In fact, some customers will deliberately let payments fail because it's easier than unsubscribing. However, for subscription tools that run in the background, this can be a big problem. ProfitWell argues that between 20-40% of MRR churn[26] is a result of failed credit card transactions, so having a good process for dealing with failed payment is essential— especially if your tool is securing someone's cloud infrastructure.

Lots of product companies will wait until payments have failed before getting in touch with the potentially churning customer. Generally, it's better to be proactive and warn people in advance that their card is about to expire and they need to update their payment information. You might want to do this a month in advance and again two weeks in advance. If a payment does fail, don't just email once and then close the account. Consider sending several reminders and giving people a reasonable grace period (along with plenty of in-app messaging). And above all else, make sure it's super easy for people to give you their new payment details.

Consider Different Pricing Models

It's safe to assume that some people will churn from your product because they're not getting quite as much value from it as they'd like. That doesn't mean they aren't getting *any* value, however—just not enough to justify either the hassle or the expense. This is a common problem if you are using some kind of banded pricing. Some of your users are using the product every day and getting a ton of value out of

---

[26] https://www.profitwell.com/recur/all/youre-handling-delinquent-churn-incorrectly

it. They might even be getting too much value, and you might be able to move them to the next price band (more on this in the monetization section later). Others might be sitting at the other end of the spectrum and debating whether or not it's worth continuing to be a user.

You see this sort of behavior in all sorts of subscription services. Gym memberships are an obvious example: If you take out a monthly gym membership, you want to "get your money's worth." You'll go four times a week, sign up for loads of classes, and use the sauna and steam room as much as you can. However, maybe you have a busy period at work or go on holiday for a few weeks and fall out of the habit. We've all been there. You still want to maintain the "potential" to use the gym. You're now using it just twice a month rather than every other day and starting to feel a little disgruntled about the cost.

One way around this problem is to offer some kind of Usage-Based Pricing model, where the usage metrics you choose are tied to customer value. In the above model, you could charge a smaller membership fee plus a per-visit fee. This means that if the customer's usage drops, so does their bill. It also means that customers can quite happily go dormant for a few weeks or months and won't feel the need to unsubscribe, because they're not being charged as much.

You sometimes see a variation of this for enterprise accounts. They still use a Per-Seat Pricing model, but you only get charged per "active seat." That means somebody at the client organization doesn't need to constantly keep an eye on the number of users they have and change the account every couple of months. It also reduces the urge for users to share accounts. You simply get charged based on the number of people getting value from your product over a set period.

Improved Customer Offboarding

Despite all your best efforts, people will quit using your product if they no longer feel they are getting enough value. If this happens, you still have a small window of opportunity to change their mind.

In the old Growth Hacking days, teams would deploy Deceptive Patterns making it difficult for people to unsubscribe, in the hope it would deter people. For instance, they would make it super easy to sign-up online, but force people to call a phone line that was poorly staffed during core work hours and hard to get through to (in the hope people would give up trying). When they did eventually get through to someone, they'd be forced to go through a long series of scripts with a customer service agent trained to talk people out of canceling, often by using highly emotional language.

These days it's still quite common to see cancellation flows use language intended to trigger feelings of loss or guilt. "Remember that you're going to lose access to all your data" they'll say, or they'll show photos of some of your contacts on the platform and say, "you'll be missed." People use these techniques because they're effective. However, they're also emotionally manipulative—which isn't a good look for any brand—and increasingly being legislated against.

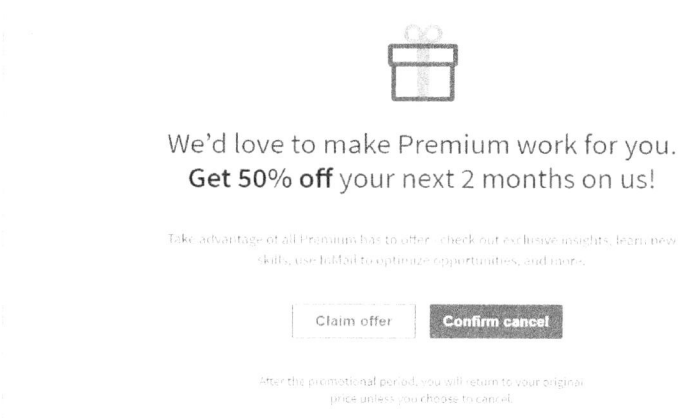

We'd love to make Premium work for you.
Get 50% off your next 2 months on us!

Take advantage of all Premium has to offer - check out exclusive insights, learn new skills, use InMail to optimize opportunities, and more.

Claim offer   **Confirm cancel**

After the promotional period, you will return to your original price unless you choose to cancel.

Figure 9.4: An example of how LinkedIn offers customers a huge discount when they try to downgrade their accounts.

I prefer to make the offboarding process as simple as possible in order to maintain a good relationship and the chance that the customer might leave with enough goodwill that they'd be willing to come back someday. One of the easiest ways of doing this is to realize that the reason the customer might be churning is the fact that they're not getting enough value: Consider offering them a reduced cost contract, offering to pause their account for a short period of time, or putting them back on the Freemium contract if you have one. LinkedIn does this by offering users a 50% discount for two months as part of the cancellation flow. Just be aware that if you do this for every customer, some who have no actual intention of leaving might threaten to leave just to get the discount.

Reactivating Dormant Customers

There's an old adage in sales and marketing that it's 10X harder to find a new customer than it is to sell to a past one. As such, while it's understandable to continuously invest energy into acquisition and filling a sales pipeline, don't forget about the people who started on that journey but never made it through—or made it through but eventually churned.

We often discount these people, assuming that they made a conscious effort not to engage, and sometimes that's exactly what happened. Maybe they wanted a particular feature that your product didn't yet have. If folks got this far, they'll often make a mental note to check back in six months but then fail to follow through. Because of this, it makes sense to try and understand why people have churned (possibly through exit surveys), note their reasons, and then actively get back in touch when those features have been added or issues have been solved.

For other people, they really intended to use your product but life got in the way. They had a big project they needed to deliver, they just moved into a new house, or went on vacation and simply forgot. Sometimes sending a simple follow-up email a few weeks or months later is enough. If you're lucky, this gentle reminder will land at a time when they have a little more bandwidth. If you know your customers well, you might be able to predict when this is likely to be—maybe the first few weeks of the calendar year, once the financial year has finished, or in the runup to the holiday season when things are starting to ramp down a little.

You might also want to give folks a little nudge to get them back on track. This could be a carefully worded email explaining how the product might be able to help them (or is helping other people), a link to a helpful onboarding email, an offer to set up a customer discovery call with them, or some sort of free inducement (an extra month of a free trial, additional features, 20% off).

Don't Confuse Happy Customers With Happy Users

An interesting thing to consider is that the people who are using your product might not be the people paying for it. This is especially common in large enterprises. One person is responsible for assessing whether your product has all the features it needs, but someone else is responsible for using it day-to-day. If the product is doing what it needs to do, users will stay engaged. However, if frustrations start to build up, users will start complaining to their managers about the tool, and eventually the pressure will build so much that the organization switches. I say this primarily as a warning. Just because your sales contact seems happy with things doesn't mean that your users are—and things can go south very quickly.

I remember hearing a story about the CEO of a well-known design tool company making an emergency visit to one of their biggest customers to plead with them to stay on their platform. Discontent had been growing among their users for years, which the company had largely ignored because there wasn't a credible alternative. And then, along came a credible alternative, at which point folks started to churn en masse. The CEO offered to discount the product heavily, but to no avail, and the client left. A few years later the company in question attempted to buy their competitor for a record price because it had started eating into their lucrative enterprise base; something they could have avoided if they had listened to the feedback and acted accordingly. This is one of the reasons why having a strong design and product team who are in regular contact with customers can be so important.

Don't Focus on Retention Too Early

I've met a few founders who have been obsessed with retention from the outset, often when they only have a handful of customers. While retention is important, worrying about retention before you've really cracked acquisition and activation is probably a case of putting the cart before the horse. As user numbers grow, so does the importance of retained revenue. And in some cases, as you've seen, a really effective acquisition team can hide the fact that users are churning at an alarming rate.

It's also worth mentioning that your early customers, made up of friends, family, and fans, are likely to dismiss the odd annoyance or outage. That's the benefit of having early adopters. As these early adopters start drying up, however, later cohorts will be less forgiving. As such, retention becomes both a bigger issue and a harder issue to solve as time goes on. Eventually you'll hit the classic "crossing the chasm" problem that's beset many fast growth startups. Because this book is all about early stage growth, it's not something we're going to cover in detail. However, I'd highly recommend reading Crossing the Chasm by Geoffrey Moore for more details on this common and well-documented phenomenon.

Measuring Retention

We've spent most of this chapter discussing how to increase and improve retention because it's important to understand how good retention works and see how yours stacks up. Identifying causes of churn and exploring some of the solutions I've outlined in this chapter should help you begin to keep more of your customers. However, in order to know if any of these solutions have been effective (or if they are needed at all), you need to know how to measure your current customer retention rate.

Customer retention is essentially the ratio of the number of customers you had at the end of the measured period to the number you had at the start. If you're examining a period of three months—perhaps since you introduced a new onboarding process to now—you would take the final number of paying customers at the end of the period (say 200), divide that by the number of customers you had at the start (say 300), and multiply that by 100 to get a customer retention rate of 66%—because 66% of the people you started with are still here three months later. To simplify, 200 ÷ 300 x 100 = 66%.

User retention is similar, but you need to be able to determine what an active user is. Is it someone who logged in once during that period, someone who performed a specific action, or someone who performed a whole set of actions? Once you've decided what constitutes an active user, the calculation is the same. Churn then becomes the inverse of this figure: how many customers you've lost or how many users have failed to interact over that same period.

One of the challenges with retention and churn is that it's a lagging rather than a leading indicator: Once someone has churned, it's too late to do anything about it. As such, it's common for startups to track metrics that they believe have a high correlation with retention.

Many startups measure Daily Active Users (DAU) versus Weekly Active Users (WAU) or Monthly Active Users (MAU) to get a sense of how regularly users interact with their product, and hopefully receive value as a result. This is especially true for social networks or business tools that form a core part of your workflow (like messaging apps). Slack found that if a user was active only three days out of the last seven (known as 3d7), there was a 50/50 chance they'd churn the following week. For these sorts of apps, companies are looking for almost daily use throughout the workweek (5d7).

Net Revenue Retention (NRR) is another popular retention metric among many SaaS companies. Rather than simply measuring the number of accounts retained, as the name suggests, NRR looks at retained revenue. This allows you to factor in both the Expansion Revenue you get from happy users increasing the amount they spend with you each month (by using additional paid features, adding more users, or upgrading their account) as well as the revenue you lose when customers downgrade or churn.

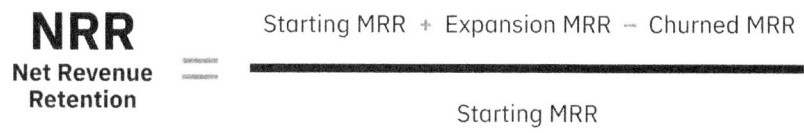

NRR
Net Revenue
Retention

$$\frac{\text{Starting MRR} + \text{Expansion MRR} - \text{Churned MRR}}{\text{Starting MRR}}$$

- MRR: Monthly Recurring Revenue
- Expansion MRR: Upselling, cross-selling, price increases
- Churned MRR: Cancellations, non-renewals, account downgrades

Figure 9.5: How to calculate net revenue retention.

NRR is a useful metric to track as it provides companies with a little more nuance when it comes to retention. You might find yourself with a relatively comfortable customer retention rate of 95%, but it turns out that many of those customers are downgrading their accounts, leading to a NRR of just 75%.

In general, an NRR above 100% means that you're growing the revenue from each account, while companies with less than 100% NRR are earning less revenue from customers as a result of downgrades and churn. Typical SaaS companies aim to position themselves somewhere between 90%-125% NRR, and ideally on the higher side if possible. Below this, and you likely have a retention problem.

Lifetime Customer Value (LCV) and the ratio of this to Customer Acquisition Cost (CAC) is often used as a proxy metric for retention, largely because a high LCV is an indication that customers are either retaining for longer or the value of their accounts are growing. Net Promoter Score (NPS) is another metric that some companies use as a proxy for retention. NPS is a slightly oddly calculated metric intended to assess customer sentiment: a measure of the number of fans or promoters you have minus the number of detractors. An NPS of 50 or more is generally considered good, while lower than zero means you have more people who actively hate your product or brand than love it. As a result, unless you have some kind of market lock-in, a low NPS might be a leading indicator that users are unhappy and likely to churn.

Summary

Poor retention is the silent killer for many startups. They might be succeeding at user acquisition, but those users are churning almost as fast as they're acquired. If this happens, there's a good chance that your product either isn't delivering the value you think or claim it is, or it's hidden by poor onboarding, bad usability, and little or no new behavior formation (the Stickiness part of The Growth Equation). As such, it's important for you to track the necessary data and get your design and product team to plug the gaps fast.

As Des Traynor from Intercom mentioned earlier, churn generally doesn't happen all at once. Instead, engagement slowly drops over time.

If you have the right tooling in place, you can track users who are at risk of churning and help nudge them back on track. This might include sending them an email with helpful advice or suggestions around how they could get more value out of the product, an invite to an event or a training session, or a timely offer like free AI credits. Anything that inspires them to return to the product and delivers fresh value has the potential to improve their opinion of the product, which will help encourage them to continue to use it. It might also be that the value is there, but the pricing plans you currently offer aren't working as hard as they should; something we'll be discussing in more detail in the next chapter.

Next Steps

It's really tempting to try and improve retention and stem churn by throwing new functionality at the problem. This often comes as a result of asking existing or potential users what they want and then adding those features in the hope it'll help. However, as we saw earlier in the book, 80% of new features have little or no impact on key metrics. This is because humans are generally poor predictors of future behavior and struggle to understand why we act the way we do. So what's a founder supposed to do?

As with onboarding and activation, improving retention and stemming churn is a complex problem, which requires you to adopt a scientific approach. You can't just throw things at the wall to see what sticks. Unlike onboarding and activation, the issue of retention and churn isn't bounded by a particular part of the interface or moment in time, which makes it much harder to solve.

The first step in solving a churn problem is realizing that your product isn't delivering enough value to users. As we mentioned above, the knee-jerk reaction is to add more features under the belief that more features means more value. This might hold for a while, but it often covers up deeper problems. Like any scientific process, you need to come up with a hypothesis around what you think is happening. This usually involves looking at the data to pinpoint where in the user journey your product is coming up short, then either talking to or watching users (user research and usability testing) to figure out what's going on and what you might do to fix it. These are all challenges that good, experimental, growth-oriented designers, and product managers can help address.

If you have a retention problem, you can't just brush it under the carpet or double down on acquisition. Instead, you need to dedicate resources to solving it. It might be a little too early for you to hire a dedicated growth team (more on this later in the book), but you do need to invest resources in solving the problem. Start by building a hypothesis for what you think might be going on based on your research, set a target KPI you're aiming for, and then allocate a couple of sprints to get it solved.

A simple place to start is to improve your onboarding. Make sure users understand how the product works, can access the value your product offers quickly, and start showing repeated signs of use. Also make sure that your sales and marketing teams are telling an accurate story and that your onboarding is setting people up for success. Next, consider an assessment of feature usage frequency (we saw this in Chapter 1) to make sure that you have the right spread of features and they're delivering enough value. If the value is there but users aren't finding it, consider investing in better messaging, user education, and offers to get people back on track.

If you've tried everything and users are still churning, consider improving your user offboarding and offering payment holidays and discounts to folks on their way out. And finally, make sure that you have the right pricing model. You might need to add additional tiers, move pricing boundaries, or consider other options like Usage-Based Pricing to satisfy customers who are still getting value from the product, just not enough to justify the price they're paying.

Improving retention and reducing churn isn't a onetime thing, but rather an ongoing challenge. Once you have acquisition working it's arguably your product team's primary job. So hire well, set good targets, optimize your product management process, give your team agency, and don't overwhelm them with new feature delivery.

CHAPTER 10

How to Price Your Product, Monetize Users, and Expand

I n the early stages of a startup's life, it's often enough just to show that a few users are willing to pay for your product. When raising pre-seed or seed, this might be all the signal your investors need. It shows that you have a product people are happy to commit time to, are getting value from, and that you are heading toward Product-Market Fit (PMF). However as you scale, hitting certain revenue targets becomes increasingly important: Growth means nothing if you can't convert at least some of that goodwill into revenue.

The first revenue milestone is always going to be getting your first paying customer, and this can take longer than many founders expect—especially if you don't actually ask people to pay. I see many people holding off on monetization until they have a robust automated payment system in place, which can take several months. However, if your goal really is to test willingness to pay, there's nothing stopping you from asking people for their credit card details or processing their payment through PayPal or a Stripe link. I've seen several startups prove that customers are willing to pay using this approach a good six months in advance of having their payment system in place.

Once you have a few paying customers, the next major milestone is hitting $10K in Monthly Recurring Revenue (MRR). If you can do that in the first 12-18 months of operation, you're in a good place (though if you can get there sooner, even better).

The next financial milestone will probably be reaching $100K MRR or $1M ARR (Annual Recurring Revenue). Being able to do this in the next 12 months tells investors that you have a product people want and have started to figure out your Growth Engine on a relatively small budget and team. This is a good indication that if those same investors commit a decent amount of cash, you'll be able to turn that $1M in revenue into $2.5M next year, $6M the year after, and be hitting at least $12M the following year. As such, getting good revenue growth sends a strong signal to investors that you're on the right track to the ultimate goal of $100M ARR: a figure that will likely secure you the $1B "unicorn" valuation your investors are hoping for.

Don't Get Stuck Undercharging Your Customers

The first monetization challenge is figuring out what to charge. Many early stage founders are used to paying between $5 and $40 a month for the SaaS products they use, so there's a tendency to pick a number in a similar ballpark. Since the founders feel comfortable paying that much for products they use, they feel their customers will as well. This makes sense if you are the target customer, but this approach can lead many founders to significantly undercharge their early users. As such, it's important to understand your users' buying patterns and compare your offering with those of your competitors.

At this stage, the first pricing model you launch is merely a hypothesis and you should be testing and tweaking it constantly—maybe as often as every few months. Don't get too obsessed with nailing your pricing straight out of the gate. The key is getting the ballpark right, so figuring out whether you're a $10, $100, or $1,000 a month product, rather than debating whether your pro account should be $95 or $120.

Going in low might be a great strategy for securing your first few reference customers, however it can also anchor expectations. As such, I'm usually tempted to charge slightly higher than you think the market will bear and offer your early design partners, beta testers, and anchor clients a generous (but not public) discount. Often it's better to charge your first design partners than to give them free use, even if it's at a

90% discount. This is because people are likely to value it more (and subsequently use it more) if they are paying for it.

One reason founders constantly undercharge is that they've been so focused on asking customers what features they want in the product, they haven't thought to find out how much they're willing to pay. As a society we've been taught not to discuss money, so founders often feel shy asking these sorts of questions. This is understandable, as asking prospects "What should this cost?" feels quite blunt and unsophisticated, so we'll discuss more subtle ways of exploring Price Sensitivity in the next section.

The idea that early stage founders regularly undercharge is backed up by research from Openview Partners, which saw average contract values for enterprise SaaS companies jump from $20K to $32K from seed stage to expansion stage and then up to $45K when hitting their growth stage.[27]

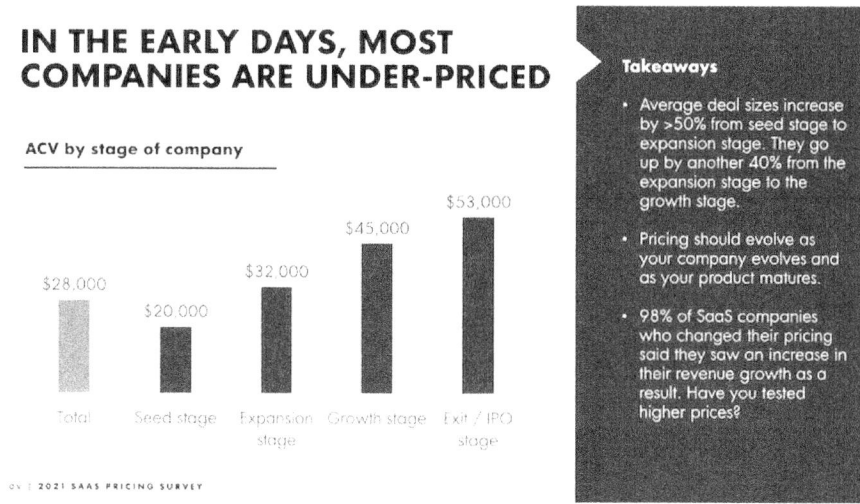

Figure 10.1: Report showing how most early stage startups underprice.

I recently coached a team who had this exact Mental Model. They thought $40 per month per seat was too high, based on what they personally pay for their own software products. As such, they went into every sales pitch feeling slightly embarrassed about their pricing—

---

[27] https://openviewpartners.com/blog/saas-pricing-insights/

something that clearly showed. But their experience as individuals was not their clients' experience. Their (enterprise) client was accustomed to paying high salaries for their staff, was familiar with other enterprise SaaS fees, and knew the founder's product would save them a significant amount of wasted time. As such, I had a hypothesis that their clients wouldn't blink at $100 or even $200 per seat. A $60 (or even $160) difference might feel a lot to an individual but is trivial for a company used to paying thousands for other tools. I encouraged the founders to experiment with different price points in their next few conversations, and to their surprise, their prospects didn't bat an eye. If anything, a higher price made the product seem like a strategic purchase, rather than a discretionary one.

That being said, I wouldn't worry too much about price optimization in the early days—especially if you have only a dozen customers and churn is the main problem. Your goal at this stage should be delivering value to your users, so it's OK if you leave some money on the table. You can always claw this back later. Start by getting Product-Market Fit and acquiring a good customer base. Once you have enough people getting value, switch your attention to optimizing revenue.

Figuring Out the Right Amount to Charge

As you might have gathered from the previous example, one of the best ways to determine your early pricing model is to test a range of different prices on your sales calls to see how people react. Do they seem outraged and slam the phone down in horror? Do they seem a little uncomfortable but are still happy to keep chatting? Or do they carry on without skipping a beat?

The price people are willing to pay for something—called Price Sensitivity—is related to a few different things, and these early conversations will help you start to gauge where different folks sit on this spectrum and allow you to put them in different pricing buckets.

The first and most important consideration is understanding the size of the pain point that your product solves. If it's a small pain (a vitamin, not a painkiller), customers will not pay very much. However, if it's a significant blocker—especially one that costs them money, keeps them from reaching goals, or impacts team engagement or happiness—you'll be surprised how much they are willing to fork over. Because of this, the received wisdom is to structure sales conversations around the problem prospects are experiencing and what it will mean to them if it goes away, and then price accordingly.

The next consideration is what anchors them to their current pricing model. If you're selling to freelancers who are used to paying $20 a month for their software, trying to charge them $1,000 won't work. However, if you are selling to a large company or team who are happy paying hundreds of dollars per seat, you can get away with charging more. This is why asking sales prospects about equivalent software products they use, and how much they pay for them, is a smart idea. This not only tells you how much people are happy to spend, but also how you stack up against the other products they use. This brings us onto the topic of positioning.

Before people commit to buying your product, they have some vague idea of what your product does, what problems it solves, and how much value it delivers. This primarily comes from you, your sales team, your website, and any other marketing collateral you share. How prospective customers perceive your product will play a big part in how much they're willing to pay (and if it adequately meets that perception, how likely they are to churn). If you want to change your pricing, you may also need to change your positioning so that you more closely align with other expensive purchases. For instance, customers might be used to paying $100 a month for SaaS sales software but $4,000 a month for a junior SDR, so repositioning your product as an "automated SDR" might allow you to significantly raise your pricing.

How to Research Pricing

While lots of founders figure out what their customers might be willing to pay (or what they think is overpriced) in early sales calls, going into these calls with more confidence will help you get the answers you need, faster. Early pricing research can help you build confidence in your pricing hypothesis.

A super easy place to start—and, to be honest where most founders stop—is by researching their competition. Company X, Y, and Z charge this, so in order to be competitive, we must charge the same (or less). This logic holds true if you've created an undifferentiated me-too product in a crowded marketplace. However, we've seen from early chapters how important it is to differentiate yourself from the competition, have a strong position, and solve one or two big problems for a certain market really well. When you do this successfully, you can usually charge a premium. So though competitive analysis on pricing is a great first step, it's really there to inform your strategy, rather than be your strategy. As such, the next step is to engage in a spot of customer discovery (aka research).

Most founders already do at least some customer discovery. This typically involves hopping on calls with people who match your Ideal Customer Profile (ICP) to understand what problems they are trying to solve in order to create a product that better matches their needs. Good customer discovery calls are therefore about generating understanding and insight, while bad customer discovery calls are generally about creating a shopping list of features. While most founders focus solely on what the product does, I think it's important to have some early calls focused on what the product is worth. Here are some common pricing questions founders might ask on these calls:

1. What pricing would you worry was too cheap for a product like this and might make you think it's of low quality or doesn't really solve your problem?
2. What price would you happily pay for a product like this without a second thought?
3. What would you feel was an expensive price to pay for a product like this but that you'd still be willing to pay?
4. And lastly what price would disqualify us from your consideration?

This approach is known as The Van Westendorp Pricing Model, and it has become very popular among startups. These questions won't tell you what to charge, but they should help you hone in on specific cost ranges.

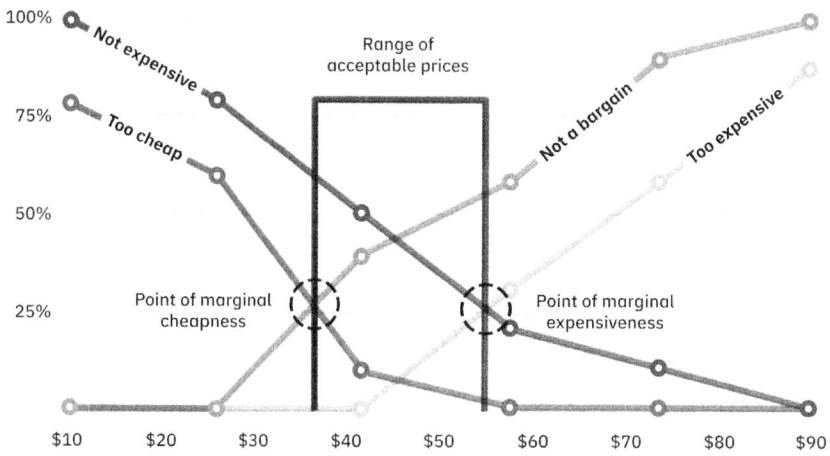

Figure 10.2: The Van Westendorp Pricing Model.

Bear in mind that different people and organizations will have a different propensity to pay, so it's worth segmenting your customers into different personas and then offering different features or levels of service accordingly (more on this later).

Another way to research pricing is to break your product down into its individual features, and then see which features your users think are most important and least important—and which they're willing to pay extra for. This can help you figure out which features should go in your basic package, which should go in your pro accounts, and which you might be able to sell as add-ons. For instance, in the example below, the features listed as being used by most or all users most or all of the time should be part of your core package, while features listed as being used regularly by a small fraction of your users might be better as add-ons or part of your pro account.

I recently came across a novel approach called the "door-in-the-face" pricing test. The idea is to suggest an outrageously high price by saying something like, "What if I told you our product cost $10K a month?" The person you're talking to will likely spit out their tea at this suggestion. But then you come in and say, "Yes, I agree that's a lot, but what would this product need to do to be worth that to you?" The prospective customer will then list off a bunch of requirements your product would need to have, in order to be worth such a premium price. If the product already does some of those things, you'll definitely want to do a better job foregrounding them. If not, they might be things you want to add to your roadmap in order to unlock premium pricing. Either way, you'll learn a lot from a "door-in-the-face" pricing conversation.

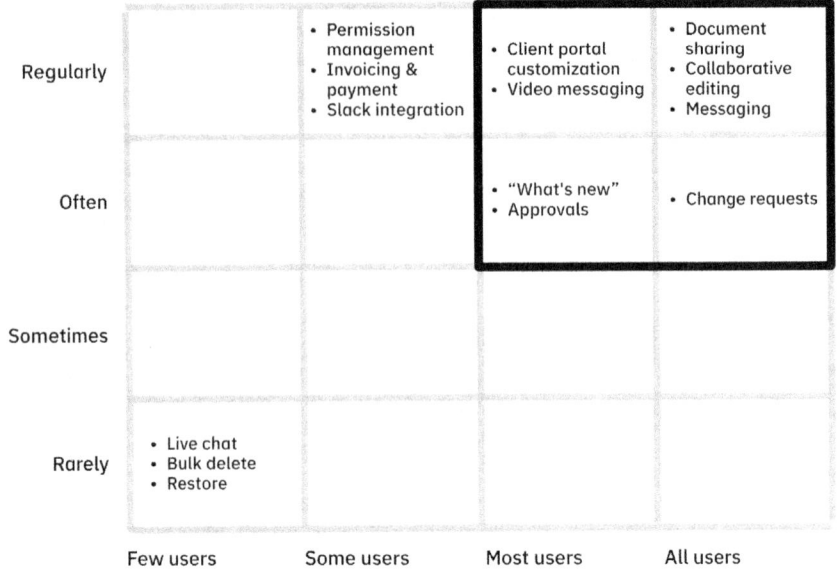

Figure 10.3: 4x4 Feature-Value Matrix.

How the Delta Between Value and Price Affects Goodwill

It's worth remembering that your pricing is strongly related to your product's perceived value: both the value you deliver to your customer and the importance they place on that value.

Some startups are able to price their products at exactly the value they deliver. Their customers might feel like the product is expensive and might constantly look around for an alternative that delivers the same value for less. However, they are generally happy to keep paying a premium—if the company continues to deliver the stated value, and if no clear alternatives are found (The V and C arguments in The Growth Equation). This is a great situation for those startups, as they are effectively able to maximize the value they can extract from each customer. However, it does mean they must stay one step ahead of their competition, lest these customers succeed in their search for better.

$$Growth = f[(A, M, \Delta V/t, S, K) / (\mu, C)]$$

Figure 10.4: The effects of value vs. competition.

For most companies, it makes sense to keep a positive gap between what you charge and the value your customers derive. This gap creates a sense of goodwill between you and your customers. They know they are getting more value than they're paying for, and they feel somewhat indebted to you for that. As a result, they are much more likely to cut you some slack when something goes wrong (and much less likely to shop around for cheaper alternatives and churn). I generally find that early stage companies are happy to make a little less money in return for goodwill—especially if they are hoping that goodwill will turn into referrals. However, as companies capture more and more of their Serviceable Addressable Market, there's a tendency to keep growing revenue through price optimization, which eats into this delta more and more. This has the tendency to reduce goodwill, and, without the goodwill, customers are more likely to churn when the next hot new startup emerges.

Pricing for Different Types of Customers

So far we've talked primarily around Flat-Rate Pricing, as this is how many SaaS companies choose to operate. Having a single price can make purchase decisions easier. However, with a single price band, one customer type may be priced out of your offering, while another would be willing to pay slightly more. As such, Flat-Rate Pricing is one of the least efficient models and generally leaves money on the table.

Most SaaS companies will offer several pricing tiers, with a customized enterprise package at the top end. Having too many tiers can complicate the decision-making process—a concept known as

Analysis Paralysis or The Paradox of Choice. To minimize complexity, it's common to see three main tiers, something that has become known as "good, better, best" or Goldilocks Pricing.

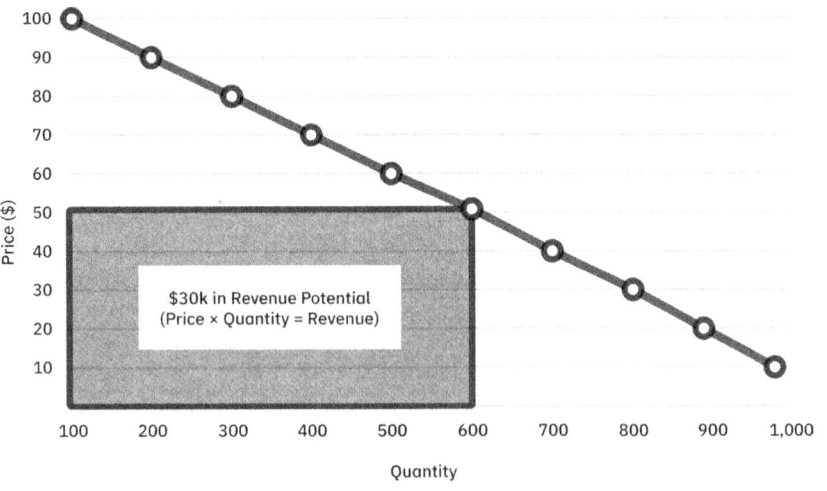

Figure 10.5: Graph showing how Flat-Rate Pricing leaves money on the table.

Airline pricing is a bit like this. The core offering—getting a customer from one place to another—is the same. However, airlines very shrewdly segment customers into different bands. They know that some customers want the cheapest possible experience, so will sell them a seat and nothing else. However, they also know that there are people who are willing to pay more for a bit more room, a slightly better meal, the ability to jump the queue at security, and a private space to wait away from the hustle and bustle of the airport. This is why airlines often have a number of tiers, ranging from super economy (where you don't even get a meal or checked baggage) through regular economy and premium economy (a bit more room and a slightly nicer seat) up to business class and first class (with lie-flat beds or even private cabins, china plates, complimentary champagne, and exclusive lounge access). Airlines also have secret rules like charging customers more if they don't have a Saturday night stay, assuming those people are traveling for business rather than pleasure. Some airlines also have their version of the custom enterprise package, which includes dedicated security and check-in, a VIP room just for you, a personal shopper, and black car transfer direct to the plane so nobody sees you board. Oh, the life of the super wealthy.

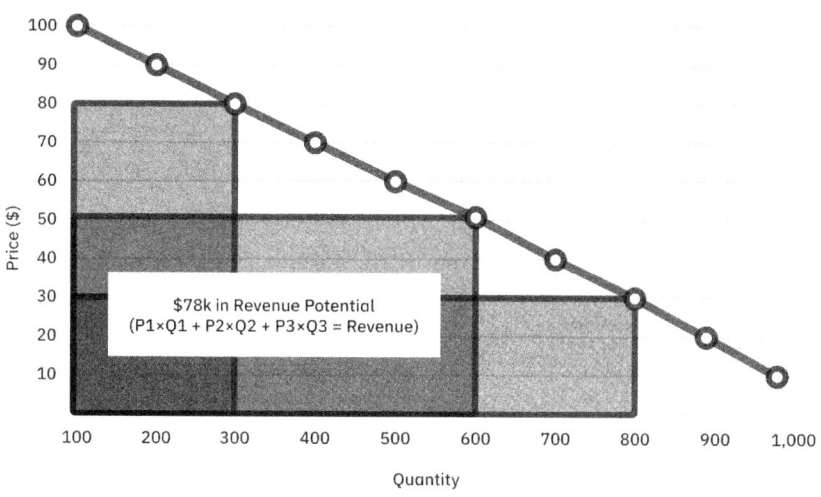

Figure 10.6: How offering different price points can help you capture more value.

Having the ability to segment your customers based on their needs and willingness to pay is one of the first techniques founders can use to grow per-customer revenue. And in larger startups, there are often whole teams dedicated to identifying customers on the edge of these segments and either moving them up—or moving the boundaries that trigger that higher rate down.

Changing Your Pricing Over Time

As I mentioned earlier, it's fairly normal for companies to start with one pricing strategy and then change it over time. Your strategy may be to take a big chunk out of a competitor, so you'll start with much lower pricing in order to grab market share (sometimes called Penetration Pricing). To be able to charge this competitive rate, maybe you have reduced your customer acquisition cost, or cost to serve. You might be serving less-demanding customers, offering a reduced feature set, or simply building from a new tech stack, which is much cheaper to maintain. Or it might be that you've raised a huge investment round, which is allowing you to subsidize customers and operate at or below cost. This approach doesn't last forever. However, if you do this for a few years, you might be able to secure enough market share that your competitor goes out of business or is forced to buy you.

Your pricing also might change once you've acquired enough users, as you may find ways to expand your revenue and charge more. You could argue that Figma deployed a version of this strategy, offering the product at a much more attractive price point than the Adobe Suite, encouraging people to switch over, and then making Expansion Revenue from all the additional stakeholders wanting to access their collaboration tools. This approach started cutting into Adobe's business model so much they tried to buy Figma.

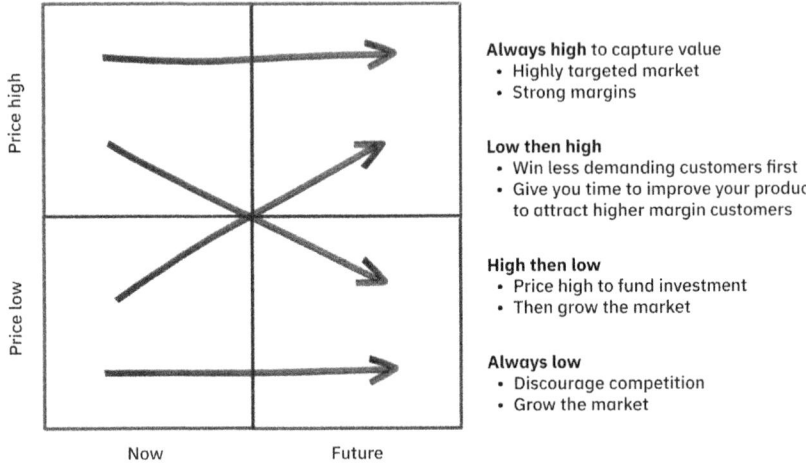

Figure 10.7: How to think about the way price changes over time.

Some companies choose to go the other way: starting with a high-end offer in order to hoover up as many premium clients as possible before offering cut-down or self-serve products for more price-conscious users. You could argue that Apple adopted this approach in the post-Jobs years, by offering up cheaper, pared-down versions of their iPhones and iPads in order to expand their market further. Sometimes you need to start with high pricing in order to fund your efforts, and to stimulate demand. This is the approach Tesla took, starting with high performance sports cars like the Roadster, before moving to the Model S and even more affordable Model 3.

Choosing which approach to take depends somewhat on your market's Price Elasticity—how changing price affects demand. The below graph shows an example of how conversion rates might change for a SaaS product based on pricing.

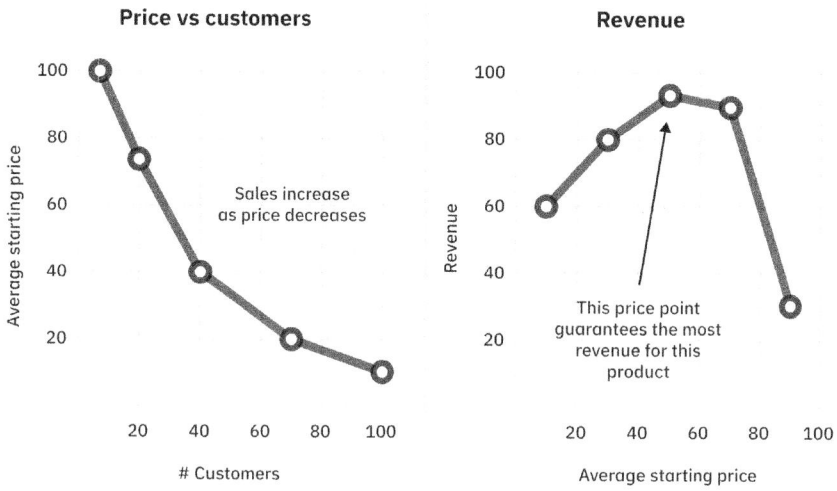

Figure 10.8: Chart showing Price Elasticity—essentially how conversion rates change with pricing.

Much of this comes from a founder's willingness to regularly experiment with pricing, in order to understand the shape of their demand curve. Hotjar CEO Mohannad Ali explains how this was one of the big mistakes they made in the early days: "We weren't doing active pricing work for a very long time. Now our packaging is changing in a meaningful way every six to 12 months." Thanks to this new focus on experimentation, Hotjar was able to raise its Average Contract Value (ACV) by 30% in 2019, without negatively impacting its NPS.

Mohannad goes on to explain how founders are scared of changing their pricing:

"My advice: Do not undervalue your own product. Most of the companies I see leave money on the table because they feel that they need to be worth more in order to charge more. But if you understand the willingness to pay from your customers and understand the value you provide to them, that gives you big indicators into how much you should charge."

A Quick Word About the Freemium Model

Many founders consider Freemium to be a pricing model. However, I believe Freemium is actually an acquisition model. There's a reasonable argument that monetization forms a barrier to use, adoption, and recommendations, so the later in the process you monetize, the better. The goal of this is not only to get users to that eureka moment as quickly as possible, but also to start embedding usage behaviors, which means users quickly rely on your product to get their work done.

Free accounts need to deliver enough value to turn visitors into paying users. They also need to include clear boundaries that users bump up against regularly enough to encourage them to switch over from a free to a paid account. Otherwise, you end up with too many freeloaders. To find these boundaries, it's important to constantly experiment to see what you can do to nudge more people from the free version of your product to the paid version. As such, when people talk about updating their pricing model every six months, they don't necessarily mean changing their price. More often than not, it's about reshaping those boundaries.

Some product people feel slightly awkward about this, as it feels like you are artificially limiting the usability of the product. However, it's worth remembering that free account users aren't free to support, and arguably their cost to service should be added to your Customer Acquisition Cost (CAC). This money needs to come from somewhere, and that usually means your paid customers have to pay more than they need to in order to support your free tier. It's reasonable to experiment with different ways to move Freemium customers to paid customers, just be aware that if you're too aggressive, this might negatively affect their goodwill and the overall sentiment people have for your product. A Freemium approach can be highly effective, but it doesn't come without challenges.

An emerging trend these days is the Reverse Freemium model. In this model, you start by giving users a free trial of your premium product, so they get to experience the full value you have to offer. Then, once the trial has expired, you move people onto the reduced functionality free package. The idea here is to give users a taste of what they are missing and, if I'm being cynical, trigger the psychological sense of Loss Aversion.

This is the approach used by Airtable, as Lauryn Isford, its head of growth, explains:

> "We offer a reverse trial: a 14-day free trial of our Pro Plan (top-tier self-serve offering), and then default users to our Free Plan if the user chooses not to upgrade. This reverse trial is more generous than a free trial, and more nuanced than Freemium alone. We feel this strikes the best balance of giving value away freely, while helping users understand what's possible with our premium offerings."

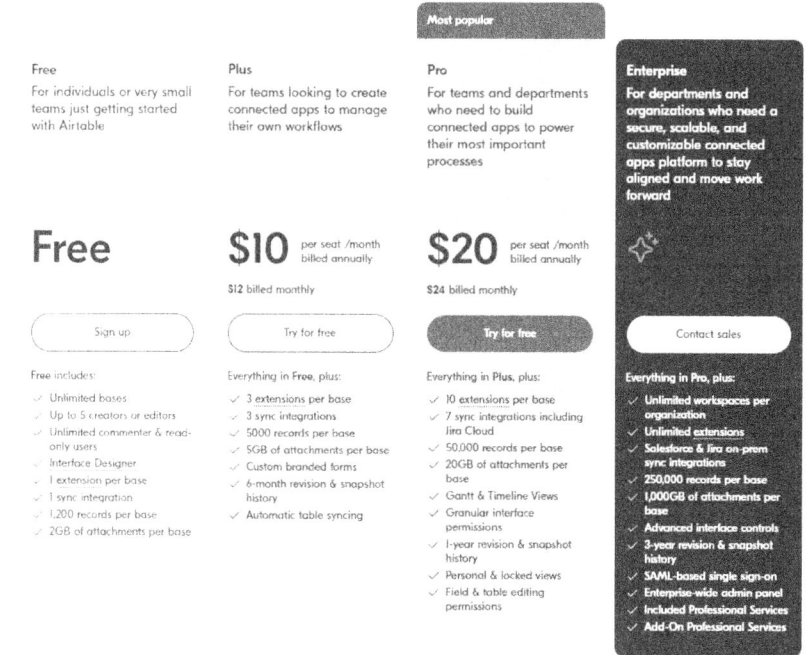

Figure 10.9: A common multi-tier pricing page.

How Usage-Based Pricing Helps Revenue Optimization

While many users and founders alike are happy with a Seat-Based Pricing model, the gaps between packages still mean leaving some money on the table. Because of this, we're starting to see more and more companies move to a Usage-Based Pricing model. A recent survey from Openview Partners[28] suggested that while Seat-Based Pricing was still the most popular approach for 41% of SaaS businesses, Usage- or Transaction-Based Pricing was hot on its heels, with 39% of respondents favoring this approach. By the time you're reading this book, it's likely that Usage-Based Pricing has taken over as the dominant model.

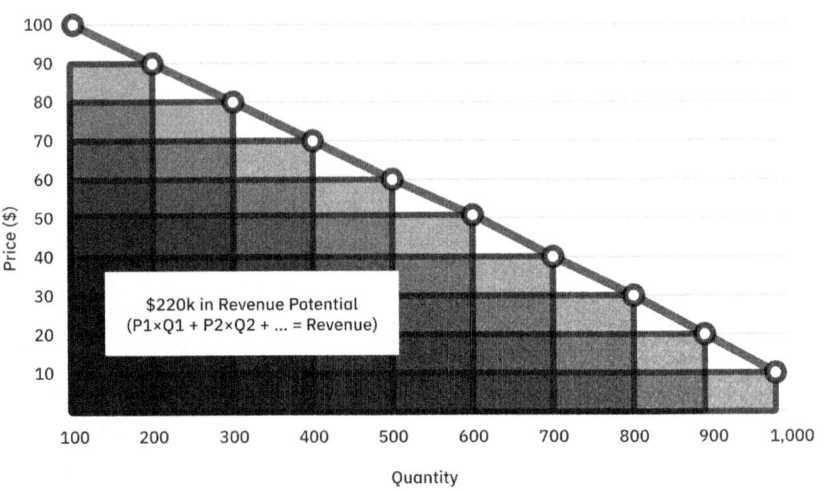

Figure 10.10: How Usage-Based Pricing can help maximize yield.

Usage-Based models generally work by picking some quantifiable unit of measurement that ties into the value customers receive and then charging for that. Usage examples could be the number of API calls you can make to a credit checking app or the number of people you can email in your mailing list app; the idea being that the more the customer uses your service, the more value they'll get, and consequently the more they'll be willing to pay. This works especially well if your product

[28] https://openviewpartners.com/blog/saas-pricing-insights/

directly makes the customer money, like an ecommerce platform charging a small percentage transaction fee whenever someone makes a purchase.

Usage-Based Pricing can work well for customers whose usage fluctuates fairly regularly: for instance, a hiring app where usage changes throughout the year based on fluctuating staffing needs. In this example, you might choose to charge based on the number of live roles you have rather than the size of the company or the number of seats being used. That way, customers don't need to upgrade to a higher tier when they need more features and then remember to downgrade (if they're even allowed to downgrade) when they know they won't be using the service.

Many companies like the gym membership-inspired element of Per-Seat Pricing for its simplicity. Much like a gym membership, it also means that people will often keep paying for your product, even if it's not something they use on a regular basis because they don't want to lose the option to use it in the future. If you've ever had a high-cost gym membership that you found yourself not using, you may recall feeling frustrated and even angry at the gym (rather than at yourself for not going). Once you finally canceled that account, there's a good chance you never returned to that gym again.

The same is true of Per-Seat Pricing. Often, companies will find they are paying for more seats than they need and cancel several accounts—often out of annoyance—then start shopping around for a better alternative. Per-Seat Pricing might also encourage people to share accounts, something Netflix has tried to crack down on. Charging based on usage avoids this problem, retaining goodwill and keeping accounts active for longer.

One of the main benefits of Usage-Based Pricing is that you don't need a sales team to identify customers hitting the limits of their current accounts and help move them to the next tier. It also does not require someone at the user's company to identify the need and choose to upgrade. Instead, Expansion Revenue comes from customers naturally finding more utility in the product. It also means that you don't risk losing a customer entirely if their usage drops.

One common argument against Usage-Based Pricing is that it's much harder for companies to budget against. Some companies prefer to know exactly what they will be paying each month and don't want to receive a huge bill if usage massively spikes. One way around this is to provide a price cap, so customers know that they won't receive a surprise bill. For instance, AppSmith charges $0.40 per hour to use its tool, but caps this to a maximum of $20 per user per month.

Growing Accounts and Upselling

It's often easier to sell more things to existing customers than it is to find new ones. Slack achieved a Net Revenue Retention (NRR) of 143% in 2019. This means that Slack grew its revenue from existing customers by 43%. As such, large tech companies will have whole teams dedicated to upselling and growing accounts. A simple way to upsell is to find things users are happy to buy on a per-item basis. This is how many free-to-play computer games work. As the name suggests, the games operate on a Freemium model in order to acquire large numbers of users. They monetize those users by selling them character skins, weapons, property, and sometimes even dance moves. Social media sites can work on similar lines, charging users for cool avatars, extended emojis, or reactions. Professional design tools might charge for access to fonts or image packs. One easy add-on is priority support. For some companies, this might mean getting a named account manager to help with all their queries. However, in most instances it's just a case of bumping their queries to the front of the queue (at no extra cost to you).

One-off charging might also be a clever way to graduate free users to subscribed users. I was recently chatting with the founders of a mood-board tool, which allowed users to embed 100 images for free before needing a monthly subscription. This model made sense for their ICP: professional interior designers who would use the tool regularly. But what about casual users who wanted to create a few boards for their one-off home renovation project? They wouldn't want or need a monthly subscription but might be happy paying a one-time fee for another block of 100 images. This would be easy to implement and allow the startup to monetize an extra 5% of their audience. Not a huge bump, but still a respectable revenue stream. If folks came back to add a second or third block of 100 images (pushing into Usage-Based Pricing), it might make the paid package with unlimited boards and images feel a lot more attractive. It's these sorts of optimization experiments that smart founders and product managers should be experimenting with on a regular basis.

Another popular way to grow an account is to look at which customers are constantly bumping up against the edges of their current package, and either contact them directly, or add in-app notifications that make it both easy and beneficial for people to upgrade. This process is often described as Product-Led Sales and has led to the relatively new role of Sales Assist.

Intercom does a great job here. While you might assume that Intercom is a single product, it actually offers a whole suite of products. By using in-app messaging, Intercom succeeds at helping users get more value out of the existing products as well as discover new ones.

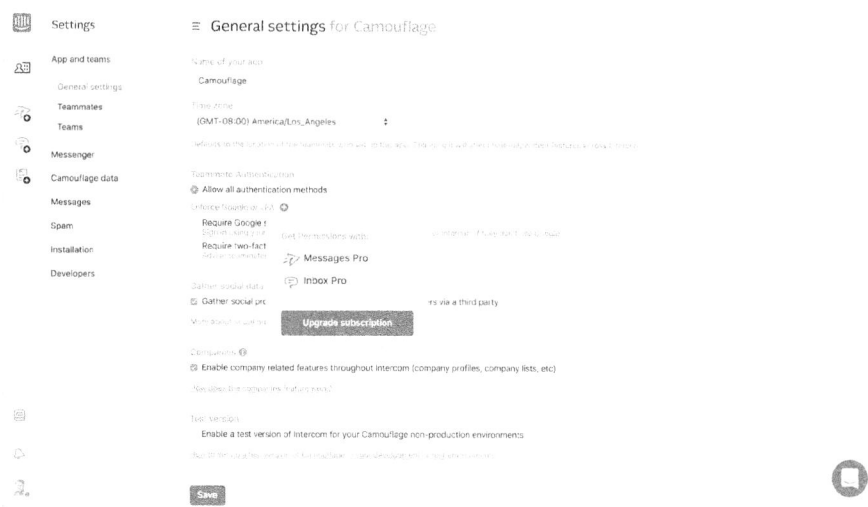

Figure 10.11: How Intercom uses in-product messaging to upsell.

As companies grow, they might find themselves with a number of different product lines, some of which are more popular than others. This is where the concept of bundling comes in. Let's say you're a company like Adobe, and the bulk of your revenue comes from designers using Photoshop. However, you have an entire suite of other products like Illustrator, InDesign, and Acrobat Pro that aren't getting as much use from this customer type. If you bundle them together in a single package, it suddenly feels like they're getting so much more value. As such, it's increasingly common to see companies bundle lesser-used products in with a few of their bigger brands as a way of extracting a bit more money out of their customers, while giving the perception of greater value.

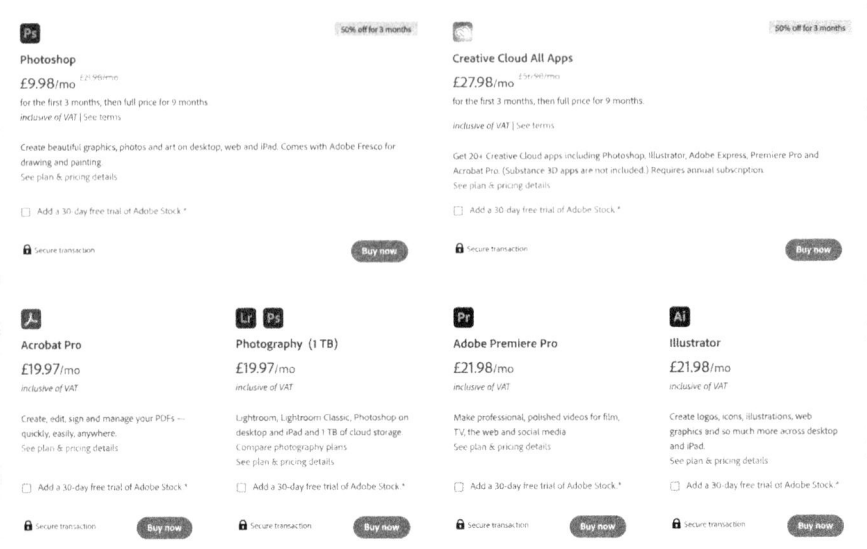

Figure 10.12: How Adobe uses bundling to upsell.

New Products and New Markets

As we mentioned earlier in the book, successful startups typically identify a less-demanding Beachhead Customer: someone who is happy to use a brand-new product with a few rough edges, simply because it solves one or two specific problems better than anything else available. This gives you time to build your team, your product, and your GTM strategy in order to acquire more-demanding customers. As a result of this approach, rather than a single target customer, you're likely to expand into a series of adjacent customer segments.

Figma's early customers were often students and freelance designers attracted by an affordable alternative to Adobe Photoshop. From that beachhead, Figma was able to work its way into larger design teams, and from there to grow its user base to include product managers, engineers, and executives.

As you learn more about your customers and expand into more markets, you're likely to discover additional problems or product categories you could move into. Think about Amazon, which started with books before moving into other product categories like music, electronics, homeware, movie streaming and even fresh food (not to mention cloud services). Or Figma, which started with their design tool before adding their collaborative whiteboard product Figjam.

When pitching to investors, startup founders often limit their vision to the immediate horizon: Who are we solving for today? In business strategy terms, this is typically described as Horizon One. Investors, however, are often looking at companies to understand what will happen once they solve these immediate problems and growth begins to slow, so it's useful to have a rough hypothesis of what complimentary customer segments, markets, or products you might move into, in order to maintain growth.

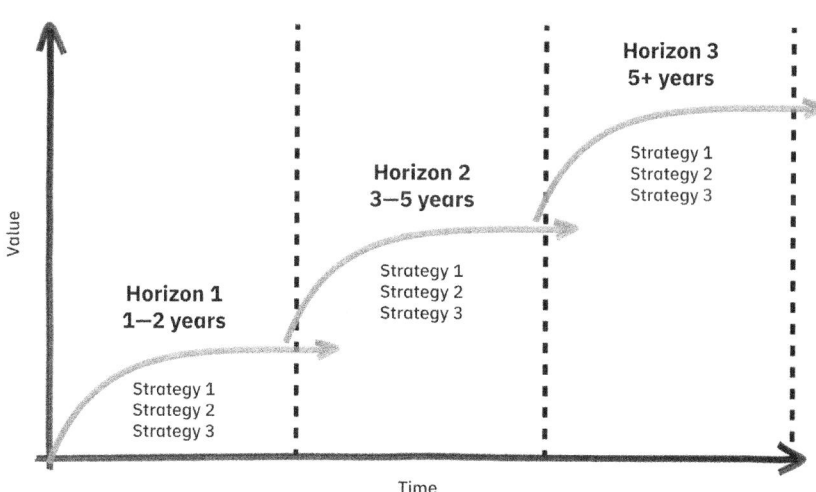

Figure 10.13: Three horizons of Growth.

Summary

Founders often come up with an initial pricing scheme based on what they would be willing to pay for a product, and then they stick with this scheme for far too long. Your initial pricing model should be seen as a hypothesis that you're constantly iterating and testing. Understanding the Price Sensitivity of your customers is key; otherwise you might end up significantly undercharging. You can test your hypothesis by watching user behavior on your live product, as well as asking smart questions during customer discovery sessions.

While Per-Seat Pricing is super common among SaaS businesses, Usage-Based Pricing is becoming increasingly popular. Putting different users into different bands and tweaking the boundaries between those bands can lead to higher per-customer yield—a practice known as Yield Management. Many people consider the Freemium model as a pricing model, while in truth it's really an acquisition model. As such, a big part of the Freemium model is about figuring out how to monetize as many of your free customers as possible. You can do this by moving them into paid tiers or by selling them individual purchases like extra storage, font packs, or reaction gifs and emojis.

Next Steps

To figure out your pricing model, it often makes sense to start by looking at your competitors. That can mean direct competitors, but it can also mean the processes and tools people are currently using to solve the same problem. Make a note of what charging models they're using. I like to print out competitors' pricing pages and paste them on a wall as if you were trying to solve a murder mystery (red yarn is of course optional). Are they using Flat-Rate Pricing, Per-Seat Pricing, Tiered Pricing, Feature-Based Pricing, Usage-Based Pricing, or some other mechanism? Group similar companies together and write a sticky note describing their pricing model.

If everyone is using the same pricing model, you might meet less resistance by following the pack. However, you might actually be able to differentiate yourself by choosing a different pricing model— especially if by doing so you can hoover up customers on the fringes of that model who might not feel they are getting value. Maybe you notice that there are several different business models being used, but no one in the market is yet experimenting with Usage-Based Pricing or Feature-Based Pricing. If that's the case, could you use a different pricing model as part of your competitive advantage? Potentially even as a company value: "Unlike our competitors, we'll never charge you for features you don't use."

Examine how these companies are bundling features together. Are there common patterns in existence or are things all over the place? If there are common patterns, do the bundles make sense to you? Do they map to different customer segments? If so, how would you describe those segments? Consider mapping the different segments and determining which bundles from which companies are doing a good job of serving them. Are there any obvious gaps in the market? Segments that are being poorly served by the current bundling strategy? Could you bundle things differently to better attack certain segments? Are there features that most companies put a premium on, which you could offer as standard? Or offer them on a Usage-Based Pricing model?

If your competitors are doing the usual economy, business, and first class packaging, could you be the first to create a premium economy offering? Offer super economy pricing, or go the other direction and do away with the distinction between business and first? Try redrawing the boundaries so you have a distinct offering that sets you apart from the competition. Consider testing the different packages on prospective users with the Van Westendorp Technique. Also, try testing your packaging on your competitors' customers. If something like this appeared in the market, could it tempt them to switch allegiances?

It's worth being clear around what your pricing goals are at this stage. For instance, is your goal to steal customers from the competition or to optimize your yield? Know what you're trying to do and price accordingly. Your initial pricing model will almost certainly be wrong, but it provides you with a useful starting point. Consider experimenting with your pricing model every six months or so, tweaking the levels of model, price, and packaging to optimize your desired outcomes. Remember to consider how these changes will affect net revenue retention, LCV (Lifetime Customer Value) and churn. At some stage, you'll want to hire a RevOps person to manage all of this, but for the time being getting this right is on the founder and their head of product.

CHAPTER 11

Using Existing Customers to Get New Customers

So far in this book, we've talked about tactics founders commonly use to land their early customers, by using either a Founder-Led Sales or Marketing approach. We then looked at the typical acquisition funnel through individual chapters on Acquisition, Activation, Retention, and Revenue, in order to explain the key levers founders can pull to grow their business. The final step in the acquisition funnel is Recommendations and Referrals: how you can use existing customers to get new customers.

Sam Altman, the CEO of OpenAI, spells out the importance of user-generated growth perfectly:

> "All companies that grow really big do so in only one way: People recommend the product or service to other people. What this means is that if you want to be a great company someday, you have to eventually build something so good that people will recommend it to their friends—in fact, so good that they want to be the first one to recommend it to their friends for the implied good taste."

My friend and author of The Mom Test, Rob Fitzpatrick, puts it even more succinctly: "Nobody recommends the second best solution," and he's not wrong. We talked in depth about the importance of having a remarkable product in Chapter 2. If you're not there yet, there's little use in investing in a recommendation and referral program. However, if you do have a remarkable product—literally, a product your users are happy to remark positively on—this chapter is all about harnessing that power to accelerate growth. But first, a quick editorial sidestep.

A Quick Note About Models

The nerdier among you might recognize that the classic Pirate Metrics Funnel—so called because the initials spell out AARRR (which as we all know is the sound a pirate makes, me hearties)—is generally written as Acquisition, Activation, Retention, Recommendations, and *then* Revenue. So why have I swapped these last two around? I've done this for two reasons. Firstly, I think it flows better this way. You acquire some users, you deliver value to them, they start paying for the product, and if they like it enough they bring more people into the top of the funnel.

Happy users might recommend your product at any stage (and people who aren't even users may be sending referrals your way), which brings me to my second, slightly meta reason for putting recommendations and referrals last. So far we've talked about growth as a linear process; however, much like light behaving both as a wave and a particle depending on the circumstance, growth also takes different forms depending on the context. Sometimes it is described as a funnel, and sometimes as a loop or flywheel. Where these models most notably overlap is in the area of user-generated growth, so positioning recommendations and referrals at the bottom of the funnel model makes it easier to transition from talking about funnels to talking about loops and flywheels.

We need this section on referrals to set the stage for a deeper dive on those growth models later. As such, we will refer to many concepts here that will receive much more detail in the next few chapters. With that in mind, let's dive in.

Viral Growth and the Viral Coefficient

Virality (the K in our equation) is simply how sharable your product is. The higher your Viral Coefficient, the more your existing customers will help you find new customers by spreading the good word. A Viral Coefficient of 0.2 means that for every 100 customers you invite, they'll bring in 20 additional customers, while a Viral Coefficient of 0.8 means that every 100 new customers will bring in a whopping 80 new customers.

$$\text{Growth} = f[(A, M, \Delta V/t, S, K) / (\mu, C)]$$

Figure 11.1: Virality and The Growth Equation.

One of the exciting things about virality is that it compounds, so a Viral Coefficient of 0.5 means that your 100 users will bring in 50 new users. But it doesn't stop there: Those 50 users will bring in 25 of their own, and those 25 will bring in 12, and so on. As a result, a Viral Coefficient of 0.5 means you'll almost double the number of customers to 200.

As you can see, companies with a low Viral Coefficient have to earn (or buy) every new customer. Companies with a moderate Viral Coefficient end up acquiring additional customers for free, while those who temporarily find themselves with a Viral Coefficient greater than 1, end up in that hallowed realm of Viral Growth.

One other benefit of having a high Viral Coefficient is that it brings your customer acquisition cost way down. These cost savings can be spent on acquiring even more customers, who will bring even more people with them. More customers means more revenue (and hopefully profit), which you can use to acquire even more customers. As you can see, creating Virality is an important aspect of growth.

Make Fans Rather Than Followers

The standard advice on how to create a viral growth loop is to create a product that's easy to recommend: a product that solves a meaningful problem, is a delight to use, creates goodwill by over-serving the customer and leaving enough value on the table, and is aligned with the customer's values. All of these increase the likelihood that a user has a great experience with your product and will share that experience with their friends—or at least, friends who share the set of problems that you've so elegantly solved.

Most founders believe their product is so great that this just happens naturally. However, this word-of-mouth style of marketing is actually rare. How often do you discover a new piece of software, realize how amazing it was, and tell all your friends? It does happen (think generative AI tools like ChatGPT and Midjourney), but those are the exception rather than the rule. If you really care about word-of-mouth marketing, you need to turn your users into fans, and you need to make it easy for those fans to spread the word.

People become fans as much for what your product stands for (and how it makes them feel) as for the product itself. Mission-driven brands like Patagonia are more than happy to upset prospective customers by taking stands on hot topic political and environmental issues, knowing that it will make their followers love them even more. In software, Linear appears as just another product management tool. However, the quality of their delivery speaks to engineers who value quality software, while their messaging speaks to the reason many developers started their careers in the first place. As such, switching from Trello to Linear is as much a statement about who you are and what you value as it is about the product itself. I'd argue Figma created the same sentiment—we're not your parents' design tool—and is one of the big reasons why Adobe tried to buy them.

In short, having a strong brand that resonates with your users' values and identities will make recommendations more likely, as doing so shares something about themselves in the process.

Driving (and Tracking) Customer Sentiment

If you're a Product-Led company (more on this later in the book), serving and delivering value to your customers though the product will play a major part in driving customer engagement. Your marketing team will articulate a credible and achievable vision for the product, which your product team will deliver. Your product managers will focus on delivering features that not only drive traffic and revenue, but also incorporate user needs. Your engineers will ship new features quickly, as well as ensuring that those features are fast and bug-free. However, of all the people on your product team, your designers are the ones who could have the largest impact on your customers' sentiment: delivering experiences that meet user needs, are easy and delightful to use, and serve outsize value. As such, designers are a crucial part of delivering delight.

As your startup grows, you're likely to build other teams that affect customer sentiment. One of the first is likely to be a customer success team. If you've not come across a customer success manager before, they do a little bit of sales (especially growing the value of existing accounts), a little bit of discovery (understanding what customers need), and a little bit of support (offering training and helping to navigate problems). A good customer success manager should be focused on turning your satisfied customers into happy customers, your happy customers into fans, and your fans into superfans. As such, it's important for your product team and customer success team to work closely together if you wish to drive this sort of engagement.

One way of tracking sentiment is Net Promoter Score (NPS). As we've mentioned before, it's a slightly odd metric that measures sentiment on a zero to 10 scale (rather than the more usual 1 to 10). The core idea is that you ask people if they would recommend your product to a friend, and you classify anybody who says 9 or 10 as a promoter (i.e., super fan). Anyone who votes zero to 6 is classified as a detractor, while anybody in between is ignored. By subtracting the percentage of people you classed as detractors from the percentage of people you classed as fans, you end up with a score that acts as a proxy for sentiment. For instance, if 50% of those surveyed are fans and 10% are detractors, your NPS is 40 (50-10). An NPS score of 70–100 is considered outstanding, 30-70 is good, while anything below that needs work. NPS is measured from -100 to +100, where -100 means that everyone is a detractor and +100 means everyone loves you.

It's worth noting that while many companies use NPS, I meet a lot of people—especially designers—who have a strong dislike for this measure. I think this partly stems from how frequently people (and by that I mean marketing and customer experience teams) try to game the metric, either nudging people to vote higher than they would normally or by discouraging detractors from voting at all. So as with any metric, if you plan to leverage NPS as a means of tracking and improving sentiment, make sure that the teams are actually treating the cause (i.e., making the product better) rather than just massaging the data.

Make It Easy for People to Recommend You

Sometimes the best way to get a recommendation is to ask for one. In a sales context, you want to ask customers to recommend other people to you when the relationship still feels new and exciting. The same is true for soliciting recommendations and referrals from users.

When asking for referrals, timing is everything. We've all visited desperate-looking sites that ask you to sign up to their newsletter, follow them on social media, and send a friend a discount code before you've even had a chance to look around. As such, the first thing to do is to identify the point or points where your early users find the most delight: that first aha moment, the first hint of value, or completing that first major milestone.

At that moment, consider sending them an automated email or in-app message asking a simple yes or no question about whether they'd be happy to recommend your product to a friend. If they say no, this can be an opportunity to find out why and what you can do better. If they say yes, you can take them to a page that thanks them for their feedback and offers a small reward for both parties if they make a recommendation now, either through a link or social media post. Consider that they may not use the recommendation straight away, so it's worth sending an email containing a referral link as well. It sounds obvious, but the easier you make it for people to recommend your product, the more likely people will.

While some folks might love your product enough to share a cold recommendation, marketing teams can encourage more recommendations by creating highly shareable content. Content that somehow taps into the sharer's values or identity is especially effective, like when Linear (a ticketing and backlog management tool) was looking to hire. The company created a job microsite that tapped into the reason why many developers started coding in the first place. This was a great way to advertise a few open roles, however the job site was shared so many times by so many developers who could relate that it drove tons of traffic to the company's main site. Apparently people wanted to know who was behind such an aspirational piece of content (myself included).

While the idea of a heartfelt, genuine, and organic recommendation is the goal, there are ways you can give people a gentle nudge in that direction. One such a way is by creating a referral program.

Setting Up a Referral Program

A referral program is a way to provide value to existing customers in exchange for bringing in new customers. One of the first documented referral programs was arguably created by Julius Caesar, who offered his soldiers 300 sestertii (around a third of their salary) for every person they referred to join the Roman army. Traditional brands have been doing this for years, offering customers cash, discounts, gifts, or points for signing up their friends. For instance, if you wanted a British Airways Amex card, we'd both get air miles if you used my referral link.[29] ;)

These programs are run by marketing teams who have a good understanding of their Customer Acquisition Cost (CAC). If you know it costs you $200 to acquire each customer through advertising, why not allow your customers to be advocates and give them something of equivalent value instead? Much better to give that money to your users than to Google or Meta—especially if they end up spending it on your website as a result. Not only have you found a great new acquisition source, but you've also generated goodwill with existing users at the same time.

In the early days of the web, online storage was seen as a rare and pricey commodity. If you used services like Hotmail on the free tier, you'd get a fairly miserly data allowance. Gmail realized this and rewarded each referral with an increase in your data allowance, leading

---

[29] https://tinyurl.com/32dvnjkt

to quite phenomenal growth. Five years later, Dropbox used a similar tactic with equally impressive results, scoping up 2 million new customers in a single month.

Dropbox achieved this growth by integrating its referral program into the final step of a six-stage onboarding flow. Under normal circumstances, most users wouldn't recommend a product to a friend before trying it themselves. However, Dropbox framed this step in terms of self-interest, suggesting it as a way users could get more space for free. The company even included a dashboard so users could track their referrals and resulting free storage, effectively gamifying their referrals and making it a competition to accrue as much free storage as possible.

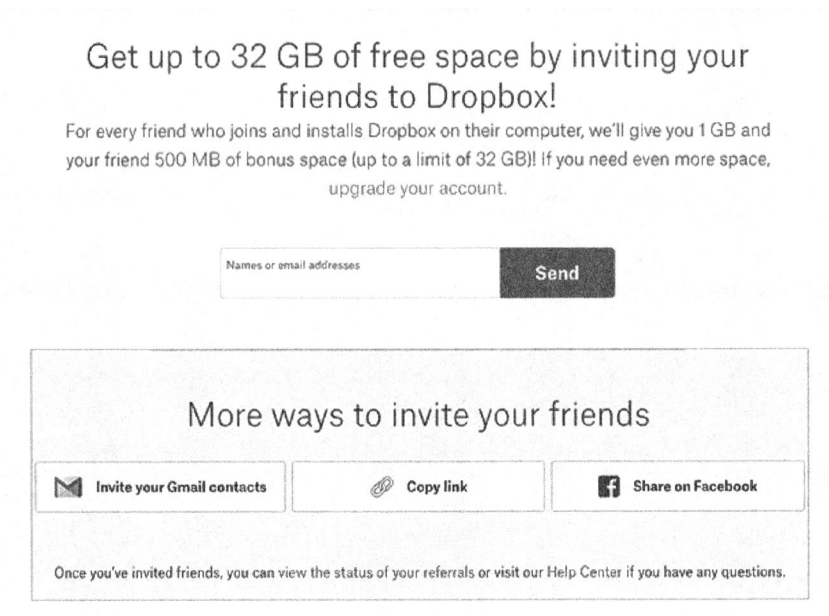

Figure 11.2: How Dropbox used to encourage referrals as part of the sign-up process.

While additional storage is less exciting than it was back in the aughts, there are still plenty of other ways to encourage referrals. Airtable offers a $10 credit for every user you refer, DocSend offers a $15 credit, and Fiverr offers up to $100 for every user who signs up and makes their first purchase. Fiverr also offers the recipient an incentive: 10% off their first purchase.

A cash incentive is easy, but a recent study found that non-cash incentives were 24% more effective.[30] For instance, Duolingo will give you a free week's use of their service for every person you invite; Harry's allows you to earn referral points to spend on goods like razors and shaving gel; while Tesla experimented with giving people "loot box credits," which can be redeemed for software upgrades.

While it's most common to offer incentives based on acquiring new users, you might be able to offer an even bigger—and therefore more attractive—incentive based on future usage. For instance, "You get $100 free credits when you sign up and spend your first $500" rather than getting "$20 credit for signing up." The best referral programs will often include some kind of ratchet, where casual referrers will get a small but meaningful reward, while active referrers can actually make serious money. As a side effect, having lots of people share referral links to your site can also help improve your SEO.

Planning a referral scheme is important, but it should also be scalable. Moodboard company Milanote offers Freemium users the ability to upload 100 free images to their mood boards before it requires payment. Millanote's referral scheme, however, grants an additional 20 images for each referral who signs up. The challenge with this scheme is that it's capped at an additional 100 images—meaning there is no incentive to invite more than five people. I'm sure the team has tested this, but I do wonder how many more users they could acquire, and how much bigger their Viral Coefficient would be if they capped this at 500 instead?

Making Your Offer

Once you've decided to set up a referral program, you need to figure out when and where you are going to place the offer. It's tempting to throw up a banner on your site, but we've trained users to ignore anything that looks like an ad. Much better to show the offer at some logical point in the flow when the user has just hit some important milestone. If you were Airbnb, you might consider asking hosts to refer other potential hosts after they've gotten their first booking, first positive

---

[30] https://www.saasquatch.com/blog/rs-17-referral-marketing-statistics/

review, or first payout. Similarly, you might want to ask renters to recommend Airbnb to other renters after they've successfully made a booking or completed a stay—especially if doing so might save some money on the booking or earn some money back. One clever way of doing this could be to allow renters to share a link to the place they've just stayed (who doesn't like bragging about the cool house they just rented?) and earn commission from anybody who signs up and rents a property as a result.

It's tempting to pick just one point to make a referral offer. I generally think referrals work best, however, if you embed them across several major touchpoints. It also makes sense to think about timing, especially if you find people are starting to see your referral campaign as part of the furniture. For instance, Uber would often tell drivers that they could earn extra money in the runup to Christmas by recommending new drivers. Tempting if you're feeling the pinch for all those Christmas presents you need to buy. They'd also run localized campaigns in advance of big concerts and sporting events, knowing that they'd need more driver capacity in the system. These referral campaigns would all come with new offers, new copy, and new "creative," effectively refreshing the campaign and making them more noticeable: a process Uber describes as "holidizing referrals."

Summary

As you've hopefully seen, recommendations and referrals are a powerful driver of growth. There are multiple ways to generate and scale recommendations. One way is by simply having a product so good it inspires organic recommendations (easier said than done, I know). Another approach is to build a mission and brand that connects with people on an emotional level and where choosing your product says something about their values and identity.

You can nudge people into making recommendations though targeted calls to action, or you can incentivize people into giving recommendations in return for some sort of reward. Just be conscious that your paid referral scheme might end up capturing people who might have been referred for free anyway. As such, it makes sense to understand your natural virality to ensure that your paid referral program is genuinely adding new referrals (rather than cannibalizing existing ones).

In the upcoming chapter on Product-Led Growth, you'll see that it's also possible to build products that naturally generate recommendations and referrals through their very use. Before we get stuck into that, though, we'll be looking at how an understanding of human behavior can help us further optimize products for growth.

Next Steps

The next steps for this chapter are absurdly simple. Once you have a good number of people who like using your product (e.g., NPS +30), set up a simple referral scheme. The first step is to consider what the incentive might be. Is it just goodwill (essentially asking people to recommend you simply because they like you)? Is it in return for a status boost among the community—giving people a badge once they've referred a certain number of people? Or is it something more tangible like more storage, more credits, discounts, entry into a lottery, or cold hard cash?

When and where you offer this incentive will have a big effect on uptake. So should you do it at the point of registration? The point of activation? Or when people meet some usage or satisfaction threshold? Building your own referral platform can be time-consuming, so it makes sense to start with pre-existing software. I don't have any strong opinions on vendors, but products like Cello, Referral Factory, ReferralCandy, and Friendbuy are commonly cited.

It's worth tracking your Viral Coefficient to see how well your product and referral scheme are working. Having a target Viral Coefficient as one of your KPIs might help focus both your marketing and product efforts, as it begs the question: "Will this feature make it more likely for people to recommend our product—or less?"

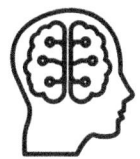

CHAPTER 12

The Role of Behavioral Science in Growth

While the first hurdle in any startup journey is shipping the product, driving growth is an almost constant activity. Sales teams are constantly prospecting for new customers and honing their pitch; marketing teams are constantly exploring new channels and fresh ways to attract customers; and product teams are constantly looking for ways to improve Acquisition, Activation, Retention, Revenue, and Referrals. These activities—and much of modern growth as we know it—are driven by a few core psychological concepts. It's important for founders to understand exactly how these concepts work in order to deploy them as part of a solid growth strategy. One such concept is Behavioral Economics.

As the name suggests, Behavioral Economics is the science of looking at the financial and economic decisions we make through the lens of Behavioral Psychology. Prior to the emergence of this field, most economic models assumed that we were all rational actors who made decisions based on logical self-interest. For instance, if you were offered $10 now or $20 in a month, the rational decision would be to wait for the $20. However, countless psychological studies have shown that we're anything but rational and are more than likely to take the $10 now than the bigger payout later.

This sort of behavior shows up in many areas of our lives, from the health choices we make to the way we plan for retirement. As such, it's important for a wide range of institutions—from governments and healthcare providers to banks and insurance companies—to have a better understanding of how people actually behave in order to work these behaviors into their Financial Models. In fact, having a good understanding of how your customers think, behave, and make decisions is vital to a whole range of commercial activities.

Behavioral psychologists have identified literally hundreds of examples of Cognitive Biases: the weird and sometimes irrational decisions we make without thinking. For instance, research has shown that we believe the things we own are three times more valuable than the equivalent item owned by someone else. We value things we've had a hand in creating more than things we haven't. We also have a tendency to underestimate how long things will take because we're bad at predicting inevitable speedbumps. These concepts are known as the Endowment Effect, the Ikea Effect, and the Planning Fallacy, and are three of the most common Cognitive Biases I see founders falling for.

Founders are also especially prone to Survivor Bias, where we listen to other founders (usually in books or podcasts) who have had success following a particular strategy, while discounting all the other companies who followed the same strategy but failed. Interestingly, knowing and understanding these biases doesn't protect us from their effects.

When it comes to designing more effective products, here are a few other biases that regularly come into play:

Anchoring Bias: We often don't know how much something should cost, so we use an "anchor price" to help set expectations. This might be by looking at the cheapest bottle of wine on the menu or by comparing one SaaS product to another. As such, you can affect people's Price Sensitivity by controlling the price on which they anchor; for instance, by increasing the price of your cheapest bottle of wine or comparing yourself to a much more expensive class of product.

The Bandwagon Effect: We have a tendency to follow the herd, so a busy restaurant or a long queue for a nightclub indicates it must be good. By doing this, we're essentially outsourcing our critical thinking facilities to other people, saving us time and energy. A high follower count or a long waitlist might be a digital equivalent. This is one of the reasons why early momentum and buzz can be so powerful.

Charm Pricing: For some reason, people seem drawn to prices that end in the number nine. The general thinking is that $39 feels a lot cheaper than $40 because our brains anchor on the 3 rather than the 4. However, this doesn't explain why a product marked at $39 outsold identical products at $34 and $44 in a study from MIT. As such, it seems that there's just something innately attractive about prices ending in this number.

The Decoy Effect: This occurs when our preference for option A or B changes when given a new option C. For instance if you had to choose between a porterhouse and a tenderloin steak on a menu, you might go for the cheaper cut. However, if the restaurant introduces a third even-pricier Wagyu option, studies have shown that more people will go for the pricier tenderloin instead. You often see this on pricing pages, where the introduction of an enterprise package makes the pro package look more attractive.

The Default Effect: This is our tendency to pick the default option when given multiple choices. Back in the bad old days, it was common to pre-check the box saying people consented to receiving marketing messages and many people just accepted the default. Thankfully this sort of behavior has been outlawed in most jurisdictions now. These days you often see the Default Effect on pricing pages, where companies like to claim that the mid-level package is also the most popular and serve that up as the default.

Effort Justification: This is our tendency to put more value onto things that were harder to achieve, like products with a steeper learning curve or more exclusivity. Effort Justification is related to the Ikea Effect mentioned previously (the tendency to place higher value on things we've built). I think this is one reason why things like Superhuman's waitlist can work: The effort of getting to the front of the queue makes it more likely that you'll sign up when given a chance.

Loss Aversion: This is our tendency to be less willing to give up something we already have. It's one of the reasons why companies might provide a reverse trial, for example. They let you experience all the pro features up front and then threaten to remove them at the end of the trial, causing people to choose to keep the higher cost package.

Peak-End Rule: This is our tendency to judge an experience (like signing up) as the average between the peak experience (good or bad) and the way it ended. Often people become bigger fans of a product when something went wrong but the company went out of their way to fix it. This is one reason why I recommended creating a positive offboarding experience in the chapter on retention and churn.

These are just a few of the Cognitive Biases designers and product managers come across in their daily work. If you're interested in learning more, my friends at Coglode have created beautiful card decks to explain all the Cognitive Biases (and the science behind them).[31]

Figure 12.1: Each Cogload "nugget" features a different Cognitive Bias.

---

[31] https://www.coglode.com/nuggets

Nudge Theory

Nudge Theory is a concept that emerged from the field of Behavioral Economics and examines how decision-making can be influenced through small, subtle tweaks (or nudges). The concept was first popularized in the book *Nudge*, which helped earn the authors a Nobel Prize for Economics for their pioneering work on the subject, so it's well worth the read.

The classic example of Nudge Theory is that of health authorities changing organ donor cards from being opt-in (which had historically low uptake) to opt-out (which few people could be bothered to do). This simple change—which you'll notice from the previous section leverages the Default Effect Bias (gold star to anyone who spotted that)—saw donor card usage jump from low single-digit figures to 80–90% in some countries.

A more recent example of Nudge Theory was the city of Stockholm using speed cameras to opt careful drivers into a lottery. You'd still get a fine if you drove too fast, but now you might potentially be rewarded for driving at or under the speed limit. This approach relied on the Reward and Punishment Super-Response Tendency, which highlights the power of incentives as well as punishments. While the trial in question was small, the average speed dropped from 32 kilometers per hour to 25 as a result of this approach.

Other examples of nudges include the U.K.'s National Health Service sending simple reminders to patients so they don't miss appointments (a literal nudge) or local councils reducing the size of waste bins to encourage people to recycle more. These approaches have proved so successful that many governments around the world have created their own dedicated "nudge units."

Not all nudges need to be so serious. For instance, one of my favorite nudge experiments was the subway station that installed "musical stairs" that would play a tune when you walked up them, in order to encourage users to avoid the crowded escalators and get a bit more exercise. There are also rumble strips that play a pleasing harmonic tune when you drive at the right speed—and an annoying sound if you don't. Both of these are fun proofs of concept but go to show how making small design decisions can affect the choices people make.

When it comes to digital products, small changes to headlines, body copy, images, calls to action, form layout, and more can create meaningful results. These sorts of changes are often advocated for by designers who understand user behavior. However, they rarely make it into a traditional backlog as they aren't the sort of large, meaningful feature additions teams like to debate, prioritize, and write user stories for. This is why I advocate for having dedicated growth teams with separate backlogs from more traditional feature teams, as it gives designers the freedom and flexibility to experiment with more subtle— but potentially more effective—approaches.

Choice Architecture

The idea of Nudge Theory is underpinned by the concept of Choice Architecture: the idea that the way we present choices has an impact on the actions people take. The organ donor card is an excellent example of Choice Architecture in action: Simply changing the default choice from opt-in to opt-out made a huge difference.

Choice Architecture shows up in the design of restaurant menus, where box-outs and specials drive customers to pick the higher margin items. Menus contain a number of other behavioral hacks, as in the earlier example of using high-priced items like Wagyu beef to anchor price expectations and make the slightly cheaper tenderloin feel more reasonable. Similarly, bracketing products involves putting products of different sizes next to each other in order to create the illusion of discounting or value. Charm Pricing and the Decoy Effect are also commonly used by menu designers. In fact, if you want a fun read about the persuasive art of menu design, check out the New York Times article "Using Menu Psychology to Entice Diners."[32] Just be aware that it might make you start second-guessing your orders. Did you really want that Wagyu beef or were you nudged in that direction by the restaurant owners?

---

[32] https://www.nytimes.com/2009/12/23/dining/23menus.html

In the below example, if the company presented only the $25 and $50 plans, I'd imagine the majority of customers would pick the cheapest option. However, introducing the $83 plan anchors people's Price Sensitivity higher and makes the $50 plan feel more reasonable.

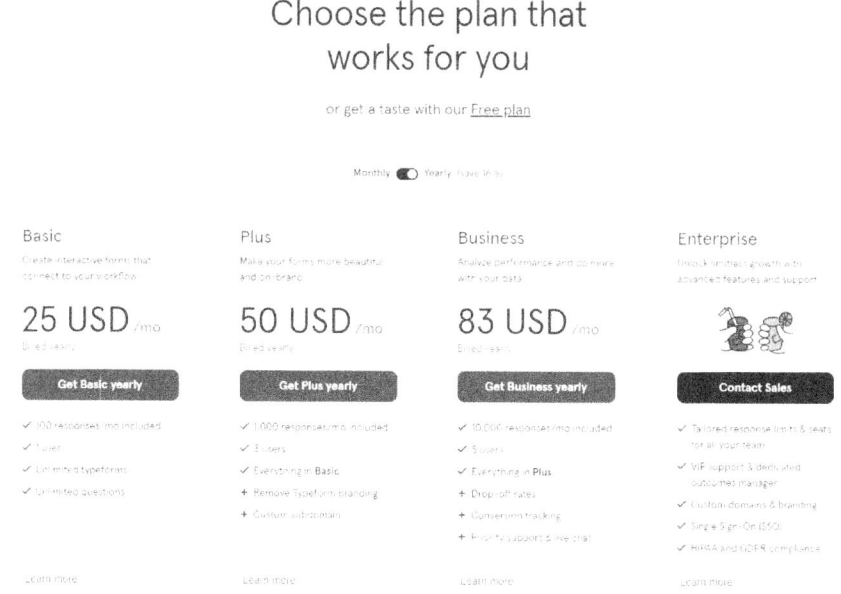

Figure 12.2: An example of "Goldilocks Pricing."

If you look close enough, you'll also see there's a free option available. However, this has been visually deprecated, nudging people toward the paid options. You're also given the ability to toggle between the yearly and monthly plans, allowing you to see how much you're saving if you commit to a yearlong contract. The yearly plan is set as the default, making it much more likely to be selected. All these subtle but deliberate design choices are nudging users toward the package the company wants you to choose. Even the names of the plans are meant to have a subtle influencing effect. So are you happy with just the "basic" plan or are you a more serious "business" user? Not sure? Then the middle plan is the way most folks will go. The effects of each of these design decisions are likely to be fairly small, maybe just a couple of percent. However, lots of small improvements have the tendency to add up.

Marginal Gains

This neatly brings us on to the subject of Marginal Gains: how multiple small improvements can compound over time to create a much larger competitive advantage.

The classic anecdote here is how the British track cycling team rode to Olympic success by making tons of tiny tweaks to their process. They did the obvious things, like redesigning their bike seats to make them more comfortable and redesigning their racing suits to make them more aerodynamic. However, they also did some unconventional things: shipping over the team's personal mattresses to ensure everybody got a good night's sleep before the race and putting blankets over their riders legs after warming up (so they wouldn't cool down again before the race and risk injury). On their own, each of these improvements might have had a marginal effect, but layering one on top of the other allowed the benefits to quickly mount up. Dave Brailsford, the team's coach, explains: "The whole principle came from the idea that if you broke down everything you could think of that goes into riding a bike, and then improve it by 1%, you will get a significant increase when you put them all together."

In general, we like to focus on the big wins: things that, if they work, will generate a 20% increase here or a 30% shift there. However, these bigger shifts are generally much harder to find, especially as products and markets reach maturity and become more likely to fail. It's estimated that over 60% of the features you add to your product will have no impact at all, and that only the top 10% will have any meaningful effect. So, rather than going after the big wins, why not go after a series of incremental improvements? A 1% improvement each day leads to an almost unbelievable 37 times improvement over the year: significantly more than you're likely to get from releasing a few big-bang features every few months.

This is why I encourage founders to set weekly—rather than monthly or quarterly—targets. Monthly and quarterly targets are so disconnected from the day-to-day work that it's almost impossible for one to drive the other. As a result they end up being noted for—to misquote author Douglas Adams—"the whooshing sound they make as they pass you by." It's far better to break your quarterly targets down into more manageable (and achievable) weekly goals: aiming to grow usage by 5% a week rather than 20% a month, for example.

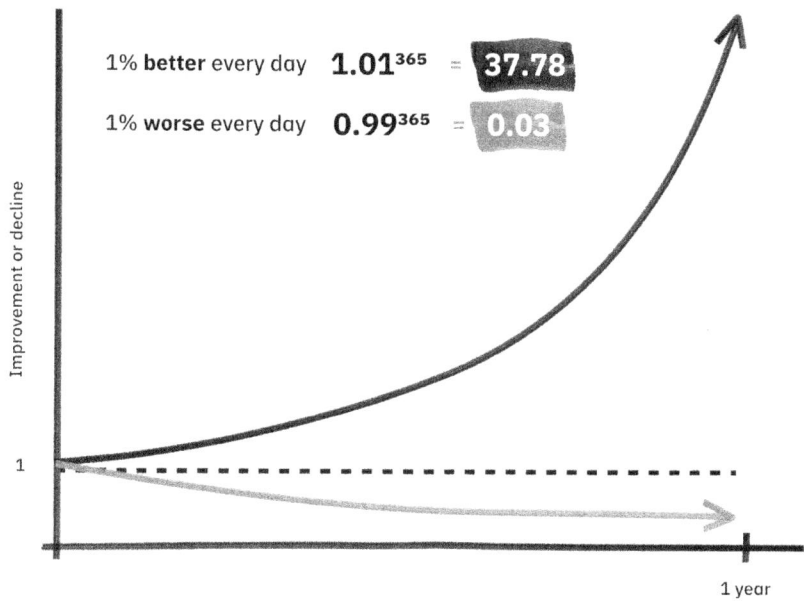

Figure 12.3: Graph illustrating the impact of a 1% improvement each day.

Gamification

While hugely popular a few years back, Gamification continues to influence many companies' digital strategy, especially among consumer products trying to foster daily usage patterns. Put simply, Gamification involves creating playful "game-like" interactions that tap into our competitive nature, are fun to use, and provide some sort of dopamine hit.

One common Gamification technique involves rewarding users with earned badges or animated congratulatory screens for completing tasks (like finishing the onboarding flow, making their first dozen posts, or hitting some sort of streak).

Duolingo is a great example of a heavily gamified product, leading to the company's impressive claim that "more people are learning a language through Duolingo than in the entire U.S. public school system." Users compete against each other and themselves, fighting to maintain a streak, come in at the top of the leaderboard each week, and earn the coveted "365 days" badge. In fact, the addition of the leaderboard feature contributed to a 17% increase of the amount of time users spent on the platform.

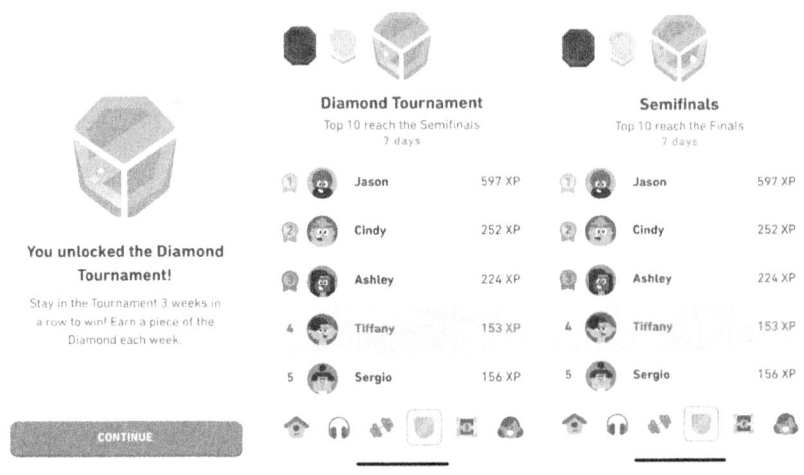

Figure 12.4: Duolingo's leaderboards help gamify learning.

Another gamified nudge within Duolingo is how the tool leverages notifications. The product team realized that users who maintained a 10-day usage streak were significantly less likely to stop using the app, so they implemented a late-night "streak saver" notification to help prevent users from losing their streak. I've been out at night more than once when a friend has pulled out their phone and said "Just a moment, I need to save my Duolingo streak"—and proceeded to complete a language lesson in front of me.

With streaks proving so powerful, the app began to add other features, including a streak freeze (it could be purchased quickly or earned slowly and would allow you to preserve your streak for up to four missed days).

People use tools like Duolingo because they actively want to learn a new language. However, the designers know that life gets in the way, and so they deploy game-like elements to trigger and cement positive new behaviors that ultimately help users meet their goals—and keep them using the app.

On social platforms, interactions including likes, follows, and shares are subtle examples of Gamification that drive user behavior. They contribute to a sense of status and competition, as well as incentivize the creation of further content and further engagement on the platform.

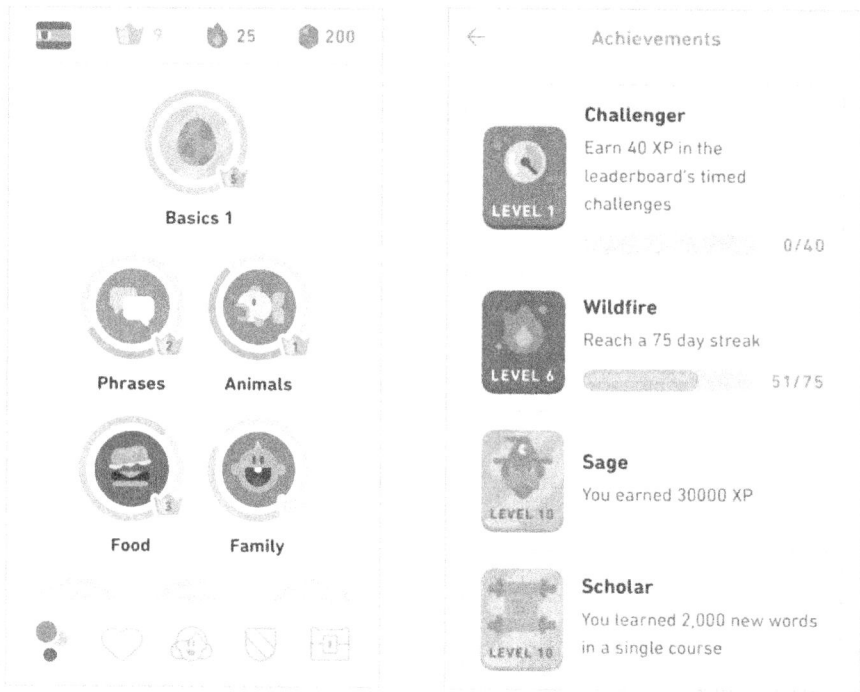

Figure 12.5: The Duolingo app is full of Gamification elements like badges, points, and streaks.

Behavior Change

Nudge Theory, Choice Architecture, and Gamification all fall under the banner of Behavioral Science: the science of understanding why people behave in certain ways and what we can do to influence that behavior. Interestingly, there's a fairly simple equation for Behavior Change: B = MAP, where B is the Behavior you want to influence, M is the level of Motivation the person has to change, A is the Ability that person has to change, and P is the Promotion or trigger for making the change. In fact it's this concept which inspired The Growth Equation.

Figure 12.6: BJ Fogg's model of Behavior Change.

If you think back to some of our previous chapters, the Motivation element comes from having a good understanding of user needs (especially a user's Jobs to Be Done) and clearly articulating how your product can help. The Ability element is partly down to product functionality and partly to good onboarding and user education. The Prompt element will depend on what's going on in the user's life and why they are looking for a product like this, but it will also depend on the messaging and feedback cycles you bake into your product.

The reason this is all so critical to founders is that encouraging users to adopt a new product requires them to let go of their default behaviors and to adopt new ones. This is one of the reasons why simply adding more features to your product isn't necessarily going to work. Instead, you need to understand how people build new behaviors and design your products in a way that supports this.

This model for Behavior Change was created by BJ Fogg, leader of the Behavior Design Lab at Stanford University in Silicon Valley. Many product managers, designers, and computer scientists have passed through BJ's courses over the years before taking roles at companies like Google, Facebook, and Twitter. As such, it's unsurprising that many growth techniques incubated in his course have found their way into companies across Silicon Valley.

Behavior Change was also the focus of Hooked by Nir Eyal, a highly influential book at the time. In it, the author explains how to help users get habituated with your product (something that aligns closely with the concept of Stickiness in The Growth Equation).

It's worth mentioning, however, that although these techniques can be used to help people make better life choices—like finishing that language course, completing their couch-to-5K program, or saving for retirement—they can also be used to create behaviors that are less personally beneficial. As such, these techniques must be used with care.

Growth Hacking and the Darker Side of Growth

Let's take a brief diversion into the world of Growth Hacking—an approach that dominated startup strategies back in the 2010s. As the name suggests, Growth Hacking focused on all the clever little tricks or "hacks" you could use to acquire users. Some of these were fairly benign, like experimenting with different headlines, layouts, or sign-up flows. As the pressure to grow became more and more aggressive, so did the techniques many of these hackers used.

You'll recall from earlier in this book (and perhaps from your personal experience, if you're on the other side of 30) that an early Growth Hacking technique involved asking new users to grant access to their address books—in order to help them connect with friends who were already on the platform. This sounds perfectly reasonable and of benefit to the user. However, what people didn't realize was that many of these platforms weren't just cross-checking details; they were also scraping the address data you had on your friends and spamming them in the background with invite messages that looked like they'd come from you. And it gets worse: If people didn't sign up, these apps created shadow accounts without your contact's permission.

These techniques worked for a while, but users quickly got wise and began to distrust the brands that used them. One of the biggest culprits was LinkedIn, who ended up paying a $13M settlement after relentlessly sending connection requests to users' contacts—on their behalf, without permission. You can bet the settlement would be a lot more in today's age of data privacy.

These sorts of techniques create a scorched earth approach to growth, making things harder for legitimate practitioners. For instance, imagine getting an angry email from a friend asking why you'd shared their email address with a third party without their permission. It is unlikely you would share your contacts list again with another app.

This approach set designers and engineers on a collision course with product managers and growth marketers, who would regularly push to use Growth Hacks (like automatically opting people in to receive email updates without a user's express permission). This was especially problematic for user-centered designers who viewed themselves as user champions and who would regularly push back against some of the more nefarious practices.

Of course designers weren't free of their own criticism, in fact far from it. Many designers (especially UX designers) came from a Behavioral Psychology background. Lots of the people who designed Uber, Airbnb, and Twitter studied Behavior Change techniques in Stanford under the tutelage of people like BJ Fogg or read books like Hooked and used this knowledge to create habit-forming products.

One popular Interaction Pattern that emerged at this time was the "pull to refresh" mechanism used by products like Twitter, Facebook, and Pinterest. This interaction mechanism would see users actively refreshing every couple of seconds to see what new information had been posted, sending engagement skyrocketing. These sorts of addictive behaviors were first documented in lab experiences on pigeons and rats who were taught to push a button to get a reward in a practice known as operant conditioning. The rats would soon get bored if a reward came on a predictable schedule—like on every first, second, or third push. However, those same rats would keep pushing the button almost indefinitely if the rewards came at random. Slot machines in a casino also use these same techniques of intermittent rewards.

Another common Interaction Pattern that's still prevalent today is the auto-playing video: a video that plays immediately when you land on a page, or the next video in a sequence playing as soon as the previous one is finished. While some product managers might claim that this is a great usability feature as it doesn't require users to hit play, this sets the effective default behavior to binge-watching. This makes sense in the context of Netflix CEO Reed Hoffman, who once claimed that sleep was the streamer's biggest competitor. However, you've got to question your moral compass if you're designing addictive behaviors into products to literally disrupt healthy sleep patterns. No wonder the issue of tech addiction has become an increasing concern.

Deceptive Patterns

Designers started describing the worst of these deceptive practices as "Dark" or Deceptive Patterns: Interaction Patterns that trick users into doing things they did not intend to do, consent to do, or are generally not in their best interest.

A great example of a Deceptive Pattern—and one I've experienced myself[33]—are subscription sites where (much like the Hotel California), "you can check in any time you want, but you can never leave." Sites operating like this begin with an easy and attractive sign-up offer: $1 per week for three months for a newspaper subscription, for example. It's much, much cheaper than the normal cost, and with such a cheap taste of a high-quality product, brands expect you'll want to stick around.

However, many take it a step further and make it deliberately hard for customers to cancel the subscription at the end of the trial period. For example, sign-up is done via a simple online form, but unsubscribing requires a phone call to a poorly staffed phone line operating during limited hours. Users might find it challenging to call during work hours, or to hold for 30 minutes (or more) while they wait for an agent. And if they finally do manage to get through, the obstacles continue: a long, scripted conversation designed to manipulate the customer into keeping their subscription. The script includes questions that force the caller to justify why they are leaving along with a list of all the things they'll be giving up. It might also contain emotional blackmail:

---

[33] https://andybudd.com/archives/2018/05/reoccuring_billing-_and_forgetfulness_as

questions like "Don't you want to know what's going on in the world?" and "Don't you care about current affairs?" Anything to prevent them from unsubscribing.

These barriers to unsubscribing may force people to try multiple times to cancel while continuing to pay the subscription. Some people will even give up trying because it's not worth the hassle. If you're a fan of the sitcom Friends, this might remind you of the episode where Chandler attempts to leave his gym several times. Eventually Ross goes with him for moral support, but rather than Chandler unsubscribing, Ross gets talked into joining as well.

Thankfully governments are aware of these deceptive practices and have actively started to legislate against them. Recently, the EU conducted a sweep of 399 retail websites and found 40% of them relied on Deceptive Patterns. As such, the EU has committed to regulating these deceptive practices moving forward. We're also starting to see people bring class action lawsuits against some of these brands, like the 2020 lawsuit against The New York Times for allegedly violating California law by automatically renewing consumers' subscriptions without proper authorization and making it "exceedingly difficult" to cancel existing subscriptions.

Social media companies have also started stepping away from some of these more egregious attempts to hack users' attention spans of late; thanks in part to documentaries like The Social Dilemma, which exposed some of these practices. In fact, the inventor of the "pull to refresh" action on Twitter is one of the main critiques of this approach now, while experts like BJ Fogg and Nir Eyal—fearing their work had been misused—have gone on to write books on how we can regain our attention and break the cycle of tech addiction.[34]

Summary

If you want to create sticky products that drive recommendations, usage, and growth, it's important to understand how people make decisions and cement new behaviors. Games have done an especially good job of this over the years, so it's understandable why ambitious

---

[34] https://amzn.to/3yGMxqR

designers and product managers might be inspired by board games, computer games, and slot machines. However, you need to use these powers wisely—and more importantly, ethically—so they help users cement positive behaviors rather than trick, trap, or disempower them. As such, it's important to be aware of Deceptive Patterns and avoid them where possible, especially as more and more countries are starting to legislate against this behavior. The last thing your new startup needs is to find itself on the business end of a class action lawsuit.

Next Steps

If you're interested in learning more about Behavioral Psychology, Behavioral Economics, and Behavioral Design, books like *Predictably Irrational*, *Freakonomics*, *Influence*, and *Nudge* are good places to start. Books like *Hooked*, *Hacking Growth*, and *Growth Hacker Marketing* are also interesting and provide important cultural reference points. Just remember that with great power comes great responsibility, so make sure you don't fall down the rabbit hole and end up on the sequel to *The Social Dilemma*.

One way to avoid this would be to grab a copy of *Deceptive Patterns*, by Harry Brignull. Not only is he an expert on this subject, but he's regularly consulted by governments looking to legislate against Deceptive Patterns. It's well worth reading his book and then doing a quick check of your product to make sure you're not falling foul of any obvious gotchas.

CHAPTER 13

Product-Led Growth

I n more traditional organizations, sales and marketing are the primary drivers of growth. As we saw in Chapter 4 on Founder-Led Sales, this typically involves prospecting for new customers, figuring out how to contact them, setting up new domains, and warming them up in order to avoid spam filters; then writing engaging outreach messages, setting up demo calls, dealing with sales objections, and helping get contracts over the line. While this approach works for a variety of customers, it works especially well for enterprise customers with big budgets and longer buying cycles.

If sales is spearfishing for customers, then marketing is trawling. The marketing team's job is to find where customers already are, connect them with the value your product purports to deliver, then drive that interest into the top of your funnel. If the product has a relatively low Lifetime Customer Value (LCV), marketers might be involved in driving customers to sign up themselves. For larger contract values, marketers might drive leads directly to the sales team. Either way, marketing teams will use a range of activities including Traditional Advertising, Digital Advertising, Paid Search, Social Media Marketing, Content Marketing, Influencer Marketing, Event Marketing, and Email Marketing to name just a few.

These approaches require founders to build and manage separate sales and marketing teams. Unless you know what you're doing, executing an effective sales and marketing strategy consistently can take a surprising amount of time. However, there is another way. As you've seen in previous chapters, there are several things that you as the founder can do to the product itself in order to impact growth—and you already have an existing product team who can help you. This is where the concept of Product-Led Growth comes in.

So, What Is Product-Led Growth?

As the name suggests, Product-Led Growth (or PLG as it's often called) is the act of using your product to drive growth. While it's fairly common for companies to do a mix of sales-, marketing-, and product-related activities, an increasing number of companies are leaning into PLG as their main driver for growth (with considerable success).

A lot of people wrongly assume that Product-Led Growth is about making the best product possible in the hope that people will use it. While having a great product definitely helps with a PLG motion, this attitude regularly leads to the Field of Dreams fallacy we mentioned earlier in the book—believing that if you build it, people will come. This can result in founders abdicating responsibility for growth, only to be surprised when it doesn't happen on its own accord.

Instead, PLG is a specific strategy that involves making direct and considered product changes with the intention of improving growth. This usually involves adding growth loops (more on this shortly) into the product in order to stimulate acquisition, and then optimizing how the product works to improve activation, engagement, and attention. Because this is a deliberate strategy rather than just the natural result of a good product, PLG requires companies to make decisions around company culture, team structure, product management processes, feature prioritization, and investment. For instance, one report suggested that Product-Led companies spend 44% more on product and engineering than their sales- or marketing-driven peers do, which obviously makes sense.

PLG activities might be simple optimization efforts that we've seen in previous chapters: increasing activation through better onboarding; improving retention through better messaging; making recommendations easier. You could argue that we've already spent a considerable amount of time in this book looking at PLG by stealth.

Each chapter has introduced concepts that, building upon one another, create a foundation for PLG. Before we start looking at how to use these techniques, let's look at why PLG has taken off so quickly.

What's Driving the Move to Product-Led Growth?

Traditional marketing channels become more expensive, more overcrowded, and less effective by the day. When YouTube, Facebook, Instagram, and Twitter were new, it was relatively easy to get noticed. Good content, like cream, rose right to the top. Organic reach was achievable, even with a low follower count. However, with changing algorithms and an oversaturated marketplace filled with noise from every brand, it's much more difficult to stand out. Additionally, users have a reduced tolerance for promotional content—many people go so far as to use ad blocking software that filters out this type of content completely. As prices for paid placement rise and effectiveness falls, companies now must spend even more money on ads just to have them seen (and invest much more time and energy creating dynamic creative that inspires engagement).

Looking at advertising budgets another way, every dollar spent driving traffic to your website is a dollar less to spend on making the product better. Rising acquisition costs, therefore, can lead to diminished product quality. And, when prospective customers are driven to a substandard product, they are much less likely to sign up, much less likely to recommend your product, and much more likely to churn as a result. Then, rather than investing time and money in improving the product, many sales and marketing teams try to compensate for falling acquisition, activation, and retention rates by diverting even more money to sales and marketing, creating a vicious cycle.

By contrast, Product-Led Growth is often a much more efficient process to help bring down your Customer Acquisition Cost (CAC), largely because you're not spending as much money buying ads, paying influencers, or generating a ton of expensive-to-produce content, but are instead using what you already have: your product.

PLG can also create leverage as it effectively multiplies your sales and marketing spend. A lower CAC means you can spend the same amount of money acquiring more users. Those additional users will earn you more money, giving you additional funds to acquire even more users. Ironically, this additional revenue can also allow you to outbid your competitor's ad spend, making it easier for you to acquire those hard-to-reach customers.

Because of this, many successful companies position themselves as Product-Led, and this trend is showing no signs of abating.

Figure 13.1: The rise of PLG over the years.

It is worth noting that companies that take a Product-Led approach from the outset tend to grow much slower than those who start with a more traditional Founder-Led Sales or Founder-Led Marketing approach. This makes sense, as you need initial customers for the Product-Led Growth loops to kick in. You also need a product that is already beginning to deliver value. As such, PLG becomes a more effective strategy once you have reached Product-Market Fit.

Growth Loops

While sales funnels are still important, PLG teams prefer to think in terms of loops or flywheels. This cements the idea that if you can attract customers, and then engage and delight them with your product, you can use those customers to attract more customers through their natural use of the product. Those customers will then attract even more customers and the growth loop continues.

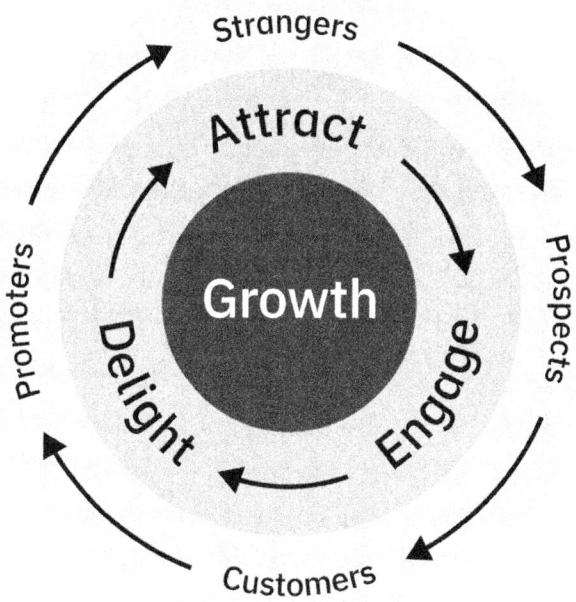

Figure 13.2: Illustration of a viral growth loop.

A classic example of a growth loop is Loom. If someone creates a Loom video and then shares it with someone else, that person discovers the value of the product through use and will likely sign up for a free account. This allows users to bring new users, not via a referral or recommendation, but through the core function of the product itself. Generative AI tools like Midjourney grow in a similar way. Every time someone creates an uncanny-looking image and posts it to social media, it helps new users discover the tool. As such, PLG experts are constantly looking for ways to engineer growth loops into their products. But how do PLG teams know their growth loops will work? Because they are constantly testing and iterating their approach through hypothesis and experimentation.

The Importance of Experimentation

As we've already seen, growth can be a bit of an arms race. Techniques that worked a few years ago become quickly saturated and lose their efficacy. Offering new Gmail users those few extra megabytes of storage encouraged sharing 10 years ago, but with storage now viewed as a given, that strategy is no longer effective. Growth designers, growth marketers, and growth engineers must constantly generate new ideas or hypotheses to test.

In traditional companies, it's not uncommon for executives to conceive an idea and then immediately put that idea into production. This is sometimes described as Feature-Driven Development or, less favorably, as a Feature Factory. It's rare for these companies to go back a few weeks later to see if these features did what they were intending to do. It's even rarer for these features to be stripped out later if they've proved unsuccessful.

To counter this, Product-Led companies tend to take a much more experimental approach, tracking outcomes and only implementing solutions that have been shown to work. This often requires having separate growth teams with a range of both design, content, analytics, and engineering skills. These growth teams can quickly come up with a hypothesis, put the experiment into production without needing the engineering team's help or permission, add the necessary tooling to track performance, and then remove it just as quickly if it doesn't work. Because of this, growth teams tend to sit outside traditional features teams (more on team structure in the next chapter) and work across many more touchpoints.

With this interactive and experimental approach, essentially what we are describing is applying the scientific method to product development. It seems so obvious, yet it's surprising how few companies actually work this way.

How Messaging and Notifications Encourages Use

The more frequently people use your product, the more likely it is that they'll experience value and end up becoming committed users. One technique PLG companies use to encourage users to return is to bake messaging into the system. People are innately curious, so when they get a notification that they've received a comment (in a collaboration tool for instance) or something important has changed (as in a data tool), folks will naturally want to check it out.

These messaging systems need to make contextual sense and actually provide real value to the product in order to be effective. For instance, receiving feedback on a design or an important status change are events that users will want to be informed of. Users will want to be notified of these events, will want to return to the product to view the feedback or status change, and will most probably want to respond. This is arguably one of the reasons Figma managed to gain popularity so quickly. Designers would solicit feedback from clients, product managers, and engineers and then manage feedback in the tool itself.

LinkedIn is another tool with many messaging features. It obviously makes sense to be able to message your contacts through the platform, so a rudimentary messaging system existed from the very beginning of the site. Back in the day, you would send a message to another user and it would be delivered as an email. Once instant messaging hit the platform in 2015, it created a super powerful growth loop. Rather than receive the message in its entirety off-app, in your email inbox, you now had to return to the app to view and respond. I often find myself using LinkedIn to contact people I haven't spoken to in a while over email, as I know their contact details will always be up-to-date.

Beyond instant messaging, LinkedIn has a range of other notification features, like telling you when you might know someone, when you've received a request to connect, when someone has tagged you as having a specific set of skills, or when you're mentioned in a comment or article. All of these notification options feel natural in the context of the product, but don't let that fool you. All have been deliberately engineered to create regular usage behaviors and drive growth.

LinkedIn also uses messaging and notifications to drive monetization: by telling you people or companies have been looking at your profile then driving you toward a pro account to get the full picture. This taps into people's natural sense of curiosity, as well as the desire to close an open information loop. As such, these techniques can affect monetization as well as activity growth.

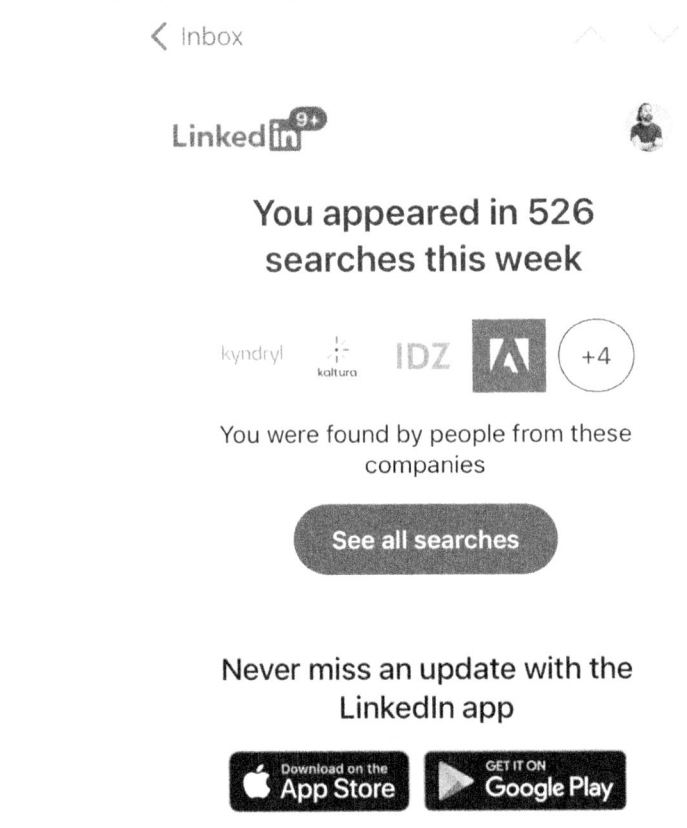

Figure 13.3: How LinkedIn uses growth loops.

The general term for this type of behavior is an engagement loop, and PLG practitioners are constantly experimenting with different loops to see which will encourage engagement (not all will). A strong engagement loop can allow new users to build usage habits quickly, and the more they use your product, the more value they should get.

As we saw previously, Duolingo uses engagement loops to great effect; messaging people when they are about to lose a usage streak, for instance. However, be careful not to overwhelm users with irrelevant notifications—especially marketing-driven ones—or people will start ignoring them or turn them off completely. As such, your goal with message-based loops is, as always, to provide user value.

How Your Product Can Acquire New Users

PLG also excels in helping existing users share your product's value with new users, simply through use of the product. This is sometimes referred to as Product-Led acquisition.

Before Figma came along, a lot of designers had started to switch from Photoshop to Sketch. However, Sketch was a typical standalone application that you would install on your machine and work from local files. This meant the product only had a single-player mode. If users wanted to collaborate on a design, they had to first export files then share them (or take screenshots, since in order to open a Sketch file, the recipient also needed to be on a desktop and have Sketch installed). Similarly, if they wanted to gather feedback, they'd need to export their work as images and then either email them around or load them onto a separate project management tool like Basecamp for feedback. This was slow going, but design work had always been like this, so people didn't bat an eye. That is, until Figma came along.

Because Figma worked in the browser, it was now possible to allow multiple people to collaborate on the same file in real time. As such, one designer could share a link to another designer through the app and work together in multiplayer mode. The file could be viewed without installing anything, on desktop and on mobile. This made it trivial for designers to expose Figma to their friends and colleagues, causing Figma's adoption to grow like wildfire. Companies realized that all of their designers were using their own personal Figma accounts and quickly sought to rationalize this by buying an enterprise package.

This acquisition loop didn't stop at designers. It was now easy for designers to share their work with all their stakeholders: founders, project managers, engineers, and anyone else who was interested. Figma offered a fairly generous free tier for these users in order to make sharing simple and valuable. However, they also did a good job of creating boundaries that encouraged companies to move those free users onto paid plans fairly quickly. As such, Figma turned a design tool, which had traditionally sat on a single designer's computer and led to a single license, into a collaboration and workflow platform that potentially had a dozen or more paid collaborators for every designer. The company shored up this position further by creating companion products like Figjam, which provided even more value to those additional users.

By baking a viral acquisition loop into the very heart of the product, Figma was able to capture a significant chunk of the digital design and collaboration market. This garnered the interest of Adobe—their largest competitor at the time—who made Figma a $20B acquisition offer, one of the biggest in tech history.

Product-Led Growth Examples

We've seen a steady rise in Product-Led companies over the past few years. One such company is Calendly, the meeting booking app. Rather than having to play a game of email tennis when trying to arrange a meeting, Calendly allows users to connect their calendars, set up some simple rules around availability, and then send people a booking link. This exposes your available slots to the other user, allowing them to pick a slot and set up the meeting.

This action contains an element of virality, as every time you organize a meeting you're exposing a new user to the product. However, Calendly makes this even easier by allowing the link recipients to create a free account and connect their own calendar. This then lets those people see where their availability overlaps, making booking even simpler. You probably won't sign up on the first or second try. But once you've received half a dozen such links, registering for a free account becomes a no-brainer. And once you have an account, you're probably more likely to want to share your Calendly link first, before someone else does, leading to a game of Calendly chicken.

Dropbox managed its growth in a fairly similar way by creating a file management tool that worked well in single-player mode. A user could connect a cloud storage folder with folders on different devices, making it easy to sync and backup all of one's data. Taking it a step further, Dropbox also made it easy for people to share their files right from their desktop. Dropbox wouldn't require you to sign up for an account to receive a file, but if you did, you'd get a nice chunk of storage for free. Very quickly you'd be linking up all your different devices and Dropbox would become a core part of your workflow.

This bottom-up approach to growth quickly led to systems administrators regaining control of company data, and therefore bringing all of those individual users and data onto a single platform. Users were generally happy with this as it meant they got to keep using Dropbox for their personal files, with even more storage, now on the company dime.

Both of these examples demonstrate how layering a multiplayer mode on top of an already useful single-player application and making sharing and collaborating with non-users as intuitive, helpful, and friction-free as possible, creates a powerful acquisition loop, allowing the product to propagate through people's personal and work networks quickly. You no longer need to ask people to make recommendations. PLG integrates them organically into the value of the product itself.

Product-Led Sales and Product-Led Marketing

While Product-Led companies generally view their product as the primary driver for growth, that doesn't mean they stop engaging in sales and marketing activities. In fact, whole fields of Product-Led Sales and Product-Led Marketing have emerged as a result. It's beyond the scope of this book to jump into these fields in detail, but it's worth pointing out a few of the obvious opportunities.

In the traditional sales world, we often talk about Sales Qualified Leads (SLQs) to describe prospects who have been researched and vetted by the sales team. In the PLG world, we similarly talk about Product Qualified Leads (PQLs) to describe leads who have signaled their buying potential through their usage patterns. This typically means users who are starting to bump up against certain product or package barriers and who might be able to be nudged into a higher package through a timely call to action or customer success call. Data suggests that PQLs convert at an extremely high rate (often 15–30%

or more) so it makes sense to track these leads and incorporate them into your process.

In the marketing world, we're seeing more and more marketing teams move away from pure acquisition and start looking at how they can also affect activation, retention, and recommendations. This isn't without its problems, however, and we'll touch on it in the next chapter.

Summary

While Sales- and Marketing-Led Growth is still dominant in traditional circles, many companies are starting to see their products as a significant—and sometimes even primary—driver of growth. In the early stages, this means creating a product that delivers significant value, connecting that value to prospective customers, and then optimizing their user journey. Design and product teams often start down the Product-Led path by looking for ways to plug their leaky acquisition funnel. This can be done by focusing on better onboarding, creating usage habits, and getting people to that aha moment as quickly as possible.

Advocates of Product-Led Growth regularly talk in terms of acquisition and engagement loops. By making products social and multiplayer and by baking in messaging systems, it's possible to create products that grow and propagate through their natural use—the holy grail of Product-Led companies. This approach is a specific growth strategy, which requires changes in culture, process, and hiring. So let's look at how companies might structure themselves for growth.

Next Steps

To truly adopt a Product-Led approach to growth, founders need to move away from the typical process of coming up with feature ideas (often requested by users) and handing them to the product team to implement. Instead, Product-Led Growth requires teams with a high level of agency, specific usage or adoption targets, and an experimental mindset.

My first recommendation would be to map out the user journey from acquisition to referral, along with some data to show how well each step in the process is doing. Target the poorest performing areas (often onboarding and activation), come up with a couple of hypotheses as to why you think those sections are underperforming, and run a series of experiments to see if you can move the dial. If your experiments work, ship those changes and see what other improvements you can make that align with that hypothesis. If those changes don't work, strip them out and try something else—revisiting the hypothesis if necessary.

Once you're able to adopt a more iterative, experimental, and hypothesis-driven approach by plugging the more obvious holes in your acquisition funnel, you can start looking for potential flywheels. Think about your core users. Are they using your product in single-player mode? If so, who are the other people they might wish to collaborate with, and how might you open your product up to those people? Does it make sense to allow for the creation of guest accounts with minimal sign-up to simplify sharing links and assets? How about real-time co-browsing or co-editing? What about adding in a messaging or notification layer?

On the subject of messaging, have a think about the different status changes your product might experience and how important, valuable, or interesting they might be to your users. Would it be useful to notify them when someone has visited or interacted with an object you created, or when some important data has changed? Would it be useful to give them a summary of what's been happening over the past week, or since their last login? Are there new features that would be useful to signpost?

List the potential areas where you see an opportunity to help users share what they're doing with other people and get more value out of the product by increasing their activity. Could you offer something useful to bring them back to the site? Pick the ideas you believe might have the highest impact, as well as the lowest effort of implementation, and test them out. If they have the desired effect, pay attention to what this tells you about your users. If the feature doesn't work, strip it out and try something else. Not every flywheel experiment will lead to a meaningful uplift. Your goal is to try as many high-confidence candidates as quickly as possible to learn which ones work, and then use this as a basis to iterate further.

Because PLG requires a slightly different mindset, process, and set of skills than the typical Feature Factory approach, this is going to have a big effect on who you hire and how you operate, which is the subject of our final chapter.

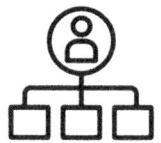

CHAPTER 14

Building Out Your Growth Team

L ike most things in life, there are multiple paths you can take that result in a successful startup. Some companies will try a Marketing- or Sales-Led approach to growth, while others will be more Product-Led. Some companies will put the bulk of their focus on acquisition, while others will focus on monetization and retention. Where should you focus your attention?

Because your (most likely) limited resources won't allow you to execute the multifaceted strategy of your dreams, you'll need to understand which of the growth levers (acquisition, activation, retention, monetization) to focus on. Once your company matures, it's likely you'll have individual teams who focus on each of these areas and work together like different sections of a symphony, but for now, it's important to focus on one.

Often your growth strategy will be decided by the type of business you are, the type of product you have, and the type of market you're serving. If you're selling a big-ticket item to a small number of corporate buyers, enterprise sales is probably where you'll get most of your early traction. By comparison, if you're selling to SMEs on a per-seat basis, you might find that a self-serve model supported through Product- or Marketing-Led Growth might be the way forward.

Product-led	Marketing-led	Sales-led
Awareness		
Users discover the product through other users	Users discover the product through content on other platforms	Sales teams reach out to specific users, usually through email or DM
Acquisition		
New users experience the product first-hand, and are encouraged to make a low-friction account	Marketing teams build demand and drive prospects to self-serve or connect with sales teams	Sales teams offer a demo and attempt to close the sale
Activation		
A well designed in-app onboarding process drives users to their first eureka moment	Email drip campaigns help drive new users through onboarding and towards activation	Customer success team manually onboards new users
Retention		
Product improvements help unlock value delivery	User education helps connect users with untapped product value	Account managers ensure customers are getting value
Referral		
Acquisition loops make it easy for existing users to share the product with new users	Marketing teams run recommendation and referral campaigns	Account managers ask for customer referrals
Revenue		
Increased usage plus obvious product barriers encourage expansion revenue	Marketing promotes and highlights additional paid features	Account managers upsell new features

Figure 14.1: Where growth lives in different teams.

As your company grows and matures, so does the chance that you'll need a blended approach. Even companies like Dropbox and Figma—arguably seen as spearheading the PLG movement—have strong sales teams to support their corporate clients. It's rarely an "either-or" situation; it's more of a "what and when."

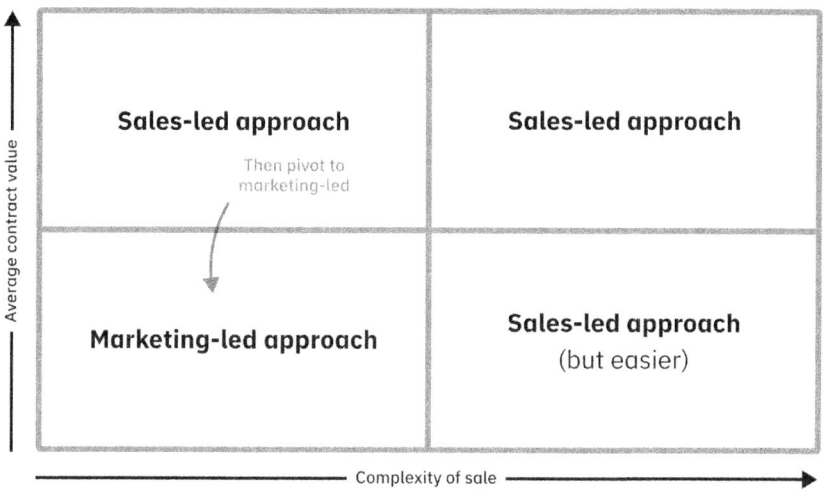

Figure 14.2: How average contract value affects growth strategy.

Cultivating a Growth Mindset

No matter your approach, I think it's important for companies to cultivate a strong growth mindset. This can mean a couple of things, but first and foremost I believe it means that you and your team can answer this simple question: "Where does our growth come from?" If they can answer this, they should also be able to answer this second question: "How do I contribute to our company's growth?"

This is important because I meet a worrying number of tech workers who never really think about growth. They're too busy writing the article they've been told to write or shipping the feature they've been told to ship. In most companies, growth is someone else's problem, and "I'm just here to do what I'm told." This often results in a lot of bikeshedding (the act of discussing trivial things like the color you're going to paint the bike shed at the nuclear power plant you're building) or deckchairing (the act of rearranging the deckchairs while the ship is sinking). Founders need to have a clear strategy around growth—and be able to connect that strategy in a meaningful way with those they've hired to deliver it.

It would be tempting to blame this malaise or lack of involvement on the people we hire. However, I see a lot of executive behavior that strips teams and workers of their agency and impact. It's common for the executive team to have conversations about growth, come up with features they think will move the dial, and then hand them over to others to build—often without measuring if they've been successful or not (that's the Feature Factory we discussed earlier). This behavior is the antithesis of a growth-oriented culture.

Growth-focused cultures empower teams to deliver outcomes rather than outputs, and then let those teams decide the best way to deliver the required results. This might seem like a radical departure from the usual top-down approach to leadership; however, interestingly this is how military units have been managed for the last 40 years. Gone are the days where generals tell their troops what to do and how to do it. The modern way to govern military units is through Command Intent: The commander explains what outcome they are looking for but looks to the team on the ground (the ones with the skills and most up-to-date intelligence) to determine the right approach. If we've been treating military units like this the past 40 years or more, you've got to wonder why more startups don't take the same approach with highly skilled knowledge workers.

Where Does Growth Fit Inside Your Org?

As we touched upon previously, Founder-Led Sales or Founder-Led Marketing is usually the first growth lever startups engage. When that begins to eat up too much time, founders will often hire a head of sales or marketing to lead that growth function.

Though marketers were traditionally focused on awareness and acquisition, digital product marketers quickly realized that it didn't matter how many eyeballs you threw at a product if they didn't turn into customers (and ultimately revenue). As such, it's not uncommon to see marketing teams expand further down the funnel. In fact, a whole new field of growth marketing has grown around this approach, with growth marketers designing onboarding flows, specifying interface copy, writing updates and notification emails, setting up referral programs, and pretty much anything else that will drive growth.

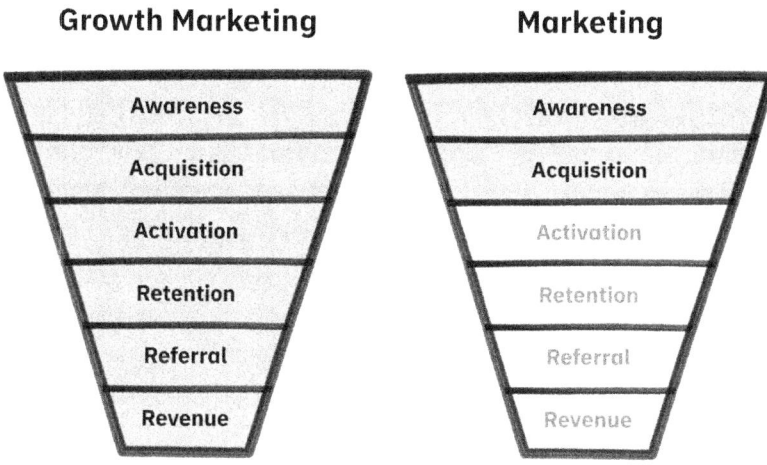

Figure 14.3: How marketers see the acquisition funnel.

Rising Tension

While it's fairly common for marketing teams in more traditional organizations to be responsible for the growth movement, the further marketers move down the acquisition funnel, the more likely they'll come into conflict with product, design, and engineering teams.

This conflict happens for several reasons. Marketing teams often don't have their own digital design or technical capabilities, and even if they did, someone else is likely to own that part of the product. As such, growth marketers typically need to negotiate with the product team to get their changes implemented. However, the product teams have their own goals, deadlines, and backlogs, so slotting in marketing team requests can be challenging.

I also find that product teams and marketing teams work on fundamentally different schedules. Product teams often plan their work in well-defined cycles, pull from a prioritized list of items, and work toward pre-defined deadlines, typically set many months in advance. By comparison, marketing teams are often a lot more reactive, spontaneous, and opportunistic, needing work done urgently to respond to a news story or external event. Even product teams working in a highly agile fashion can find it frustrating constantly having to push "urgent" but possibly not "important" tickets to the front of the queue.

This is especially true if each team is working toward a separate set of OKRs or targets. The product team may not see the value in marketing's copy change requests; conversely, the marketing team may not see the importance of fixing Technical Debt. But if everyone on both teams has a shared understanding of how their work individually—and holistically—contributes to overall company growth, this conflict can be mitigated. And how do you bring these two teams together, united by common goals? Product-Led Growth.

Who Owns Product-Led Growth?

Product teams often move toward taking ownership of the growth levers that sit within the product's boundaries. This is partly to make sprint planning and roadmapping easier for their team, and partly because good product managers want to drive outcomes (of which growth is arguably one of the most important) rather than work as a glorified project manager. And of course, there's a bit of empire building going on here as well.

Much of this comes down to where power sits inside the organization. A super powerful and influential CMO with a large marketing budget can easily reposition the marketing team as growth marketers. However, in large tech companies, it's common for the CPO to have more power and be closer aligned to the CEO than the marketing head, making it easier for that person to own the product elements of growth.

These battle lines are often drawn around the promotional website. Does the marketing team own the content, design, and customer experience of the website and act as the client to the product team? Or is the website owned by the product team and treated as an extension of the product itself? Does the responsibility of marketing stop when a user visits the site, when they sign up for an account, when they finish onboarding, or somewhere else entirely? What about in-app messages about promotions to existing customers or referral campaigns? Are those the responsibility of the marketing team or the product team? What about sending out emails to lapsed customers? You can see how this can get complicated quickly.

Early PLG teams are usually fairly small and emerge from a few people on the project showing an interest in growth. Maybe there's a product manager who's more interested in analytics and experimentation than their colleagues? Maybe there's a designer who is really into Behavioral Economics and Nudge Theory? Maybe there's a front-end engineer interested in experimentation and multivariate testing? Whatever the combination, early PLG teams are usually moved away from delivering the core product backlog and given a few growth targets and the freedom to experiment.

The Rise of Growth Design

As we've seen, growth is often viewed as the preserve of business or marketing teams. When applied to the product, it's often owned by a product manager—sometimes called a product growth manager. It's worth noting that a lot of the ideas covered in this book are essentially design decisions. This is unsurprising, as good designers—especially user-centered designers—have a strong understanding of human behavior and use their design skills to remove barriers, smooth journeys, and drive people to make one choice over another. One of the benefits of using designers in this role is they often see themselves as the champions of user needs. As such, they're generally pretty good at spotting and avoiding Deceptive Patterns.

Doing this well requires designers to take a more experimental approach to design, as it's often impossible to know from user interviews which tweaks will have the necessary impact. This is where growth designers excel: coming up with hypotheses on areas that will improve marginal gain, running a series of often quick and dirty experiments, seeing which version has the biggest effect, and then launching those successful candidates and starting again.

Growth designers tend to have a more analytics-based focus than regular product designers and often have some front-end dev skills (that is, at least enough to launch simple experiments without needing to push them to an ever-lengthening backlog). For a primer on the emerging field of growth design, Design Driven Growth, by Molly Norris Walker is a good place to start.

The Growth Team

As Product-Led Growth starts to take off inside organizations, team sizes naturally grow. Maybe you'll bring someone in from the content team to help write and test copy. Maybe you'll add someone from the analytics team to help tooling and reporting. You might want to add somebody to the marketing team to help optimize the website. Suddenly you end up with a multidisciplinary team that's neither a traditional marketing team nor a traditional product team but its own thing.

When trying to describe how the growth team differs from the product team, I usually explain that the product team is all about adding new value to the product, while the growth team is all about helping as many users as possible access that value. Growth teams tend to be super experimental, have much shorter horizons, and focus even more on KPI delivery than their pure product cousins.

Having a dedicated growth team is an important transition, especially for companies that have figured out Product-Market Fit, raised growth investment, and are chasing specific targets, possibly on route to IPO. Eventually, growth teams also start to become unwieldy and end up forming their own decentralized pod structures comprising growth product managers, growth engineers, growth designers, growth data scientists, and growth marketers. While this is going to be a long way off for most of the readers of this book, it's useful to have a vision of where you're heading, an understanding of how you're going to get there, and an awareness of the structural changes that are likely to occur along the way.

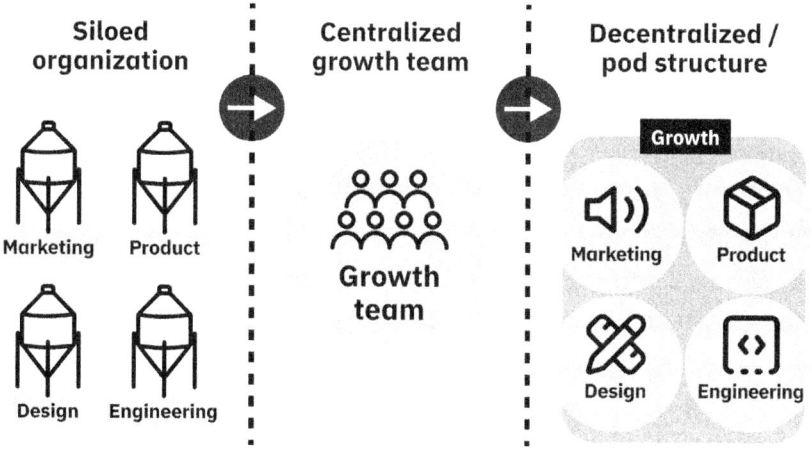

Figure 14.4: How growth teams emerge and scale.

Summary

Growth should be a deliberate strategy, rather than something you hope will happen as a result of launching your product. You'll need to make decisions on where to invest your time and energy. Should you follow a Sales-, Marketing-, or Product-Led approach? The answer will depend on a number of factors including the size of your clients, the size of the contracts, the nature of your customers, the nature of the market (and what your competitors are doing), and the natural skills you have on your team. The approach you select will have an inevitable effect on your company culture, team, and ultimately your growth trajectory.

Rather than spreading the responsibility of growth across too many different silos, it's increasingly common to see successful tech companies like Netflix, Pinterest, and Airbnb build dedicated growth teams. While this might not be something you need to consider at the moment, it's important for your team members to realize the role they play in growth and to make decisions that prioritize growth over shipping the next feature in the backlog.

Next Steps

Most startups begin with a single product team, typically composed of a designer and a half-dozen engineers. In the early days, you'll be laser-focused on delivering your product vision (the thing you raised money against), which for most founders means a specific set of features wrapped in a nice-looking user interface. While most founders secretly hope that "if we build it, they will come," early growth is often fairly lackluster. The natural response is to ask existing and prospective users what extra features they want and then build those in. This requires additional engineering capacity, and so they set about boosting out their engineering team.

More established companies tend to aim for one designer and one product manager for every five to eight engineers. However, founders obviously want to stay as capital-efficient as possible, so will often try to do a lot of the design and product work themselves. It's not uncommon to see early stage teams with one designer, 10 engineers, and no product managers at all. The downside of this approach is that the founder has to manage the software delivery process, as well as making tons of tiny design decisions—two things they might not have much experience with.

This situation isn't much fun for the founder. It's even less fun for the product team, as it can result in process inefficiencies: lots of chopping and changing and lots of disgruntled employees. Eventually, things get to the point where you'll bring in a product manager, a second designer, and consider splitting into multiple teams. At this point, it's tempting to split your teams across different product boundaries. While there's no hard and fast rule, I personally like to have one team focused on acquisition, onboarding, and activation—effectively, your top of funnel—and have the other team focused on core product functionality.

The core product team is all about creating long-term value for their users, so they should have a deep understanding of the problems your users are trying to solve, know the competitor products inside out, and be able to deliver new capabilities—all of which will increase the value of your product long term. You will most likely want to build this team with more traditional product managers who are good at customer discovery, designers who have a strong interest in delivering long-term user value, and engineers who want to create a solid, performant platform.

By comparison, the acquisition and activation team are all about understanding what motivates users, what makes them successful, and how to connect users with the value delivered by the product team. While the product team will be focused heavily on delivering a feature roadmap, the acquisition and activation team are much more focused on running experiments and improving metrics. They'll work closely with your customer success manager, as well as your marketing manager when you eventually hire one.

Organizing things this way allows you to have one team focusing on enhancing the capabilities of the product, and another team focusing on product optimization. It also makes things much easier later on when you decide to spin out growth into its own separate function.

In Conclusion

I created The Growth Equation as a handy lens through which to view your day-to-day activities as a founder—as well as a debugging tool for when things go wrong.

$$Growth = f[(A, M, \Delta V/t, S, K) / (\mu, C)]$$

Figure 15.1: One last look at The Growth Equation.

Growth is a function of many things, so you may end up with your own personal formulation. However, I believe that Audience Size and Motivation—along with the ability of your product to deliver ongoing value, share that value with others, and keep people coming back from more—play an outsize role in product growth. At the same time, the natural Friction that accumulates in your product frustrates users and blocks growth, providing ample opportunity for your Competition to tempt people away. While this won't necessarily guarantee success, addressing these seven arguments should leave you with a strong platform to build upon.

So how do you put this into practice?

First of all, it means that building a successful product is more than just building a good product that meets user needs. Product teams are making a thousand little decisions every day, and each of these decisions has the possibility to impact your company's growth. Rather than making these decisions blindly, product teams need to be thinking about the growth potential of every product improvement they make.

But simply considering the growth potential is not enough. Successful product teams need to constantly define hypotheses and find ways to validate (or invalidate) them quickly and without a ton of resources. They need to constantly evaluate what is working and scale it—and determine what isn't working and ditch it. And they need the agency and authority to make these decisions quickly. This approach helps build a learning team focused on growth, and it's also at the heart of the Lean Startup movement.

Finding the right channels to acquire customers cost-effectively is still vitally important, because you need a steady flow of new users to test many of these hypotheses. This requires experimentation, graft, and grit. Funnels are still a useful metaphor, so don't ditch them just yet (whatever the PLG people might say). Use the talents of your design, product, engineering, analytics, and marketing teams to find the holes in your funnel and plug the leaks. Speed of experimentation is key. The difference between releasing three or four improvements a week versus three or four a month will be huge—especially when considering the compound benefits.

The secret sauce behind PLG is to identify product features that create growth through the natural use of the product. This is done either through loops that draw people into your product through use or that encourage repeat use. All of this is designed to help people experience the value your product delivers faster and more frequently. It's worth brainstorming as many potential loops as possible that your product could leverage. Many won't work, but the ones that do are likely to have an outsize effect. Products that take this approach in order to create a large Viral Coefficient are inherently capital efficient, allowing you to outmaneuver competitors and re-invest the money you save into further growth.

It's also worth noting that this doesn't happen automatically. While it's fun to keep your head in product development, founders will often need to step into the role as company rainmaker and adopt a Founder-Led Sales or Founder-Led Marketing approach. As such, your ability to acquire early customers and early investors will have a lot to do with your ability to deliver this role successfully. I've seen many great products fail because founders were simply unable to position their product effectively, articulate why the product was better, get people signed up and experiencing value as quickly as possible, and then have those people introduce the product to their network.

There's a temptation to read a book like this, nod along in agreement to the advice, but then fail to put any of it into practice. As founders, sometimes we're just looking for a silver bullet: the one piece of arcane knowledge we can discover that will revolutionize what we're doing. However, startup success is rarely about finding a single silver bullet, and more about making tons of tiny (and often boring or obvious) changes, which compound over time. It's also about being comfortable getting things wrong. The more shots you take on goal, the higher the likelihood will become that you score—and score big.

Finally, I want to leave you with one last bit of level-setting. It would be unrealistic to believe that, were you to implement every single piece of advice within this book to the exact specifications I've outlined, you would see immediate and shocking growth. Nor would it be reasonable to expect that a bootstrapped solo founder could build a growth team like I've outlined on goodwill and the promise of equity alone. I've made sure throughout this book to include as many low- and no-budget ways to put some of these methods to use and to show you how, as your company and revenue grow, you can orient your strategy and team around growth.

My hope is that I've provided a realistic and practical guide that helps early stage founders figure out their Go-to-Market strategy, build an early growth engine, and iterate their way to Product-Market Fit. I wish you the best of luck in your journey to your first million or two in revenue, and hope when you're interviewed on the TechCrunch stage you mention this book!

About the Author

Andy Budd is a design leader turned investor, advisor, and executive coach. For many years he ran Clearleft, an award-winning design consultancy that pioneered the field of user experience design in the U.K. During this time he helped clients like Just Eat, Farfetch, Rapha, Funding Circle, Mozilla, Virgin Atlantic, Penguin Books, and Burberry make the most of their digital experience. Andy sold Clearleft in 2020 and joined Seedcamp—one of the most successful and best-known early stage venture funds in Europe—as a venture partner. As well as helping source and review new investments, Andy uses his knowledge of Sales-, Marketing-, and Product-Led Growth to help portfolio companies figure out their Go-to-Market Strategy, raise money and find Product-Market Fit. This book was born out of that experience: witnessing all the things startups get right (and occasionally get wrong) about early stage growth.

In addition to working for Seedcamp, Andy advises a small number of founders on the concepts found in this book. He also runs a syndicate of design and product angels who love nothing more than supporting Design- and Product-Led founders. In his spare time Andy—a former dive instructor and "shark wrangler"—loves exploring underground cave systems and tropical atolls. As a recently qualified pilot, when he's not under the water he can be found soaring over the Sussex countryside in a rented Cessna 172.

@andybudd
andybudd.com

Printed in Great Britain
by Amazon

63086908R00161